Praise for

PSYCHOLOGICAL SECRETS FOR EMOTIONAL SUCCESS

"I invite you to engage in the warm and wise conversation that I just had with Doctor Kelly while reading her wonderful new book. That I refer to this experience as a conversation speaks to the sense of connection that I felt in reading each kernel of insight that Doctor Kelly shared in these pages. This book will touch your heart and head; in doing so, it encourages us to become the best version of ourselves. As in the best therapy sessions, Doctor Kelly's thoughtful writing will enlighten you and nurture your soul. I heartily recommend this book!!!!"

—Dr. David L. Blustein, PhD, Professor and Golden Eagle Faculty Fellow, Boston College, Author of *The Psychology of Working* and *The Importance of Work in an Age of Uncertainty*

"Doctor Kelly is a dynamic and passionate psychologist and she has brought those gifts to a broader audience with her new book. Highly recommend!"

—Dr. Anthony J. Isacco III, Professor, Chatham University Graduate Psychology Programs and Director of Training, Doctoral Program

"Doctor Kelly gives us the tools to create better relationships in all the areas of our lives. She wants us to succeed and knows how to help us get there. We all know how essential corporate culture is to success. As a CEO and business owner of a fast-paced mid-size company, I will share Psychological Secrets for Emotional Success with my co-workers to build a shared language for better communication. I've already taken what I learned from the book and applied it at home as well--who doesn't want to improve your connections with the people you love?

One of the great things about the way Doctor Kelly writes is that you can read it cover-to-cover or pick it up and start anywhere, which I appreciate as a person who is juggling many responsibilities. Buy the book for you, your employees, your friends. You're welcome."

—Patrick Patterson, President and
Managing Partner, Level Agency

"It's just like having your favorite therapist in your pocket. Doctor Kelly fills the pages with love, compassion, and warmth as she gives everyone simple, effective steps to delve a little deeper and move towards Emotional Success. Whether you're just starting or have been doing self-development work for years, you will find something that supports your next step within this book."

—Emily Andrew, Founder of We Are MindBody UK

"Doctor Kelly deals in truths; not the kind of truth that hurts, the kind of truth that wraps you in a warm blanket. If you want to learn all manner of complex secrets of the mind while feeling completely safe, read this book. Give it to your colleagues, kids, parents, friends, and help them rethink health."

—Stephanie L. Trunzo, Global SVP &
General Manager, Oracle Health

"A transformative journey of self-discovery. Doctor Kelly gives us the tools to build lives of deep connection, intention, and authenticity. With warmth and brilliance, she will shift how you show up at work, in love, with your children, and to yourself."

—Jenna Abetz, PhD, Associate Professor, Department of
Communications, College of Charleston

"This book provides an uplifting and refreshing take on self-help books that is focused on fostering deeper connections. Doctor Kelly offers the opportunity for honest self-exploration and self- reflection that is grounded in psychological theory and research. *Psychological Secrets for Emotional Success* is a very timely, must-read book!!"

—Angela DeSilva Mousseau, PhD, Licensed Psychologist, Professor of Education and Counseling, Director of Training, Counseling and School Psychology, Rivier University

"I was delighted to read an advance copy of Doctor Kelly's Psychological Secrets for Emotional Success. One of the chapters that was most moving to me and a cornerstone of Doctor Kelly's work is her commitment to acknowledging the importance of empathy in our lives and the lives of those around us. Her focus of empathy as the Platinum Rule of "Do unto others as you'd have done to you…. IF WE WERE THEM", was moving to me as a clinician. It allows us as helpers and humans to see and assess empathy from the role of the person, instead of ourselves. An important rule for all of us to follow more openly in our lives. Her takeaway is to help us unlock empathy within our lives—which leads to transformational progress. The whole exploration of empathy and opening ourselves is one that embodies who Doctor Kelly is as a psychologist and her commitment to healing those she reaches."

—Meaghan F. Dupuis, MA, LMHC, Executive Director, Health and Criminal Justice, UMass Chan Medical School

"…A feast of enlightenment to contemplate and consume."

—Kelly Kinsey, MEd, LBS Behavioral Therapist, and author Table Magazine and MANI

"I was struck (although not surprised) by how accessible it is—it's like having a conversation. It strikes a fantastic balance between being direct, pragmatic, clear about intentions and instructions, with an infusion of empathy that includes infectious self-compassion without feeling sappy. Several times I thought "I'm glad I'm reading this". It seems appropriate for someone who's seeking a change in their life as well as someone who's been in the field for some time. I found myself being curious and impatient to read more."

—Dr. Kym Jordan-Simmons, PhD, Licensed Clinical Psychologist (with 20+ years of clinical experience), Therapy Group Facilitator, Clinical Supervisor, College Student Mental Health Transition Consultant

"This book reads like a conversation with a trusted and knowledgeable therapist who genuinely cares about your well-being and wants you to be the best version of yourself that you can be! Doctor Kelly provides readers with knowledge often known only to those who study psychology and psychotherapy, and she does so in an easy-to-understand, authentic, and reassuring voice. Equal parts information, encouragement, and a personalized pep talk, this book will provide you with the tools for emotional success and stability."

—Dr. Laurie Mintz, Psychologist, Professor, and author of *A Tired Woman's Guide to Passionate Sex* as well as *Becoming Cliterate: Why Orgasm Equality Matters—And How to Get It*

"With so many voices offering ways to think better and act differently, audiences need to listen and filter carefully to find those that ring authentic and trustworthy. Such is the voice I hear as I read Kelly Rabenstein's Psychological Secrets.... I trust her research, experience, and synthesis of very important concepts so much that I plan to use this book as part of assigned course work in the Fall in a course preparing teachers of secondary English, especially chapter 10! Doctor Kelly offers us hope for healing a society currently gashed by distrust and uncertainty."

—Dr. Collin Wansor, PhD, Professor, Seton Hill University, Secondary Teacher Educator

"Doctor Kelly's book is not only a masterpiece but a manifesto for emotional success. As humans we don't get a manual that guides us through our uniqueness, our lack of self-awareness or even our ability to have empathy. This book IS our manual. Our manual to unlocking our better selves. The common thread? Love."

—Gina Lombardi, Celebrity Fitness Trainer &
Host of the Health Interrupted Podcast

Psychological Secrets for Emotional Success

by Dr. Kelly Rabenstein

© Copyright 2022 Dr. Kelly Rabenstein

ISBN 978-1-64663-760-7

Published by

◄ köehlerbooks™

3705 Shore Drive
Virginia Beach, VA 23455
800-435-4811
www.koehlerbooks.com

DR. KELLY RABENSTEIN

PSYCHOLOGICAL SECRETS

FOR EMOTIONAL SUCCESS

(IT'S ALL ABOUT LOVE)

VIRGINIA BEACH
CAPE CHARLES

For Ella and Annie, for your light knows no bounds.

TABLE OF CONTENTS

There was a new voice which you slowly recognized as your own, that kept you company as you strode deeper and deeper into the world.

Mary Oliver

CHAPTER 1

Journey with Me

Would you like to understand yourself better?

Do you feel misunderstood?

Are you often angry? Sad? Frustrated? And you don't know why?

Do you want to grow as a person to connect better with others?

Do you desire deeper intimacy?

Would you like to know more about how to enjoy emotional success?

Why does the idea of emotional success speak to you?

Do you feel stuck?

These questions are some of the reasons I wrote this book. I've been thinking about you, and I know there are secrets I can share with you. I'm a licensed psychologist, and I love my work. My goal is to help patients thrive and to find the freedom to be authentic. When you are real with yourself, you can love deeply. Otherwise, you are too busy holding tight to your facade to become your best self. People feel whole when they are genuine. Whole people create connections. Connections lift us all up. This is my goal. It's nice to meet you.

I've spent two decades sitting with patients, hearing their stories, exploring their emotions—moving with them as they pass through the intensity of their lives. Desire for connection is at the center of everything. When you connect, it gives you purpose and meaning. But people have learned to hold back. For instance, you might wonder if you will be misunderstood if you engage in a sticky conversation. Digital interactions bring people closer, but sometimes in the freedom of anonymity, they can polarize. Sometimes it seems easier to erase your differences and pretend everyone is the same, rather than to dive in and get closer. It can be the same at home. Tired, you avoid conflict versus working toward resolution.

This is flawed thinking. Everyone is different. Instead of turning away from variation, what if you had tools and confidence to move closer? You will make mistakes. I've created psychological secrets to help you—as if your therapist, mentor, and best friend are in a room together, moving you toward your best self.

The book is meant as a balm. It will help you move from feeling alone to being connected. What I've learned—working with clients, in my academic training, as a woman, lover, parent, eater, human being—is wrapped up in these pages. I thought of you as I wrote, and I hope you can feel that.

AWARENESS+ EDUCATION + EMPATHY = EMOTIONAL SUCCESS

I suggest you start a diary. Write down a sentence or two about each day, placing yourself as the narrator in your own life. Add more when you feel like it, without the pressure to catalogue every detail. You can use the journal as a companion to this book. I take a messy approach to journaling—mixing recipes for dough with writing ideas. It is colorful, private, and has bits of chocolate smashed in. Writing a few words at a time doesn't feel momentous, but often, when you look back at your life from your own perspective, it can be quite moving.

The key to emotional success is knowing who you are and how that impacts others. One way to adapt to alternative ways of thinking is to move from passive reading toward action. With that in mind, I've included exercises after each major concept. These activities will help your mind transform information into action—all through the exercises I've laid out for you to do each step of this journey. I refer to these activities as "actions" because action equals movement *with intentionality*.

These actions will suggest you write things down. You can use the aforementioned journal for this. We have also provided several pages for notes at the end of the book. Please take the time to write your thoughts, though it will obviously take more time, we know that the behavior of writing deepens both our understanding and memory of new information. The very act of writing forces you to metabolize what you've read, and this is part of what I want for you.

Movement with Intentionality

When you set an intention, you prepare for the journey ahead with clarity and purpose—which brings greater success. Without purposeful time set aside to delve into the topics, you will have a surface-level experience. Your brain learns best with repeated exposure to novel ideas. Personal growth is no different. I'll give you an outline for how to approach the exercises to achieve the most meaningful outcomes.

Be yourself. Throughout this journey, I'll ask you to reflect on yourself. Don't try to answer in a way that shows you in a certain light. Let it be a raw, truthful, honest response. Answer as fast as you can, and let it be whatever it is. You can't move forward if you don't know the reality of where you stand.

Set your intention. What are your goals for this journey? Start big and then break things into smaller components until you're left with your plans for this book, this chapter, and the action you are about to complete. When you are clear about your intentions, you are more likely to reach them.

Process. In therapy we always say, "Beginnings and endings are important." Think about it—beginnings color how you frame the experience, and endings shape what you remember. Allowing space to narrate an experience gives you power to mold the ending. Therefore, processing is vital to growth. After each action, I'll ask you to give weight and space to process the actions you've taken.

I've created layers of exploration to move you toward more meaningful experiences and deeper connections. Start with honesty, set your goals for the experience (prep your mind), and then process what you've done. Each step creates depth and opportunities for growth. If you find yourself on autopilot as you work through the reading or the actions, notice this, and start again at step one. This three-step process can help you engage in more meaningful experiences in all parts of your life.

AWARENESS

Let's begin our journey. We start with an action that centers on uncovering more about who you are in this moment.

What About You?

Be yourself. Set your intentions. Please use your journal, notes pages at the end of the book, the margins, or anywhere you write to describe yourself in five words or less . . . GO!

What parts of your identity are you most proud of?

What comes from your family?

Are there aspects that are in conflict with one another?

Think about why you chose each of those five facets.
Why those five?

Now we know more about what gives you purpose/meaning in life. If I were you, I'd write those in enormous letters on a wall somewhere and take a good hard look at them.

Who Are You?

You know a little about who you are in the world and how others experience you. But there is so much you don't know. Unfortunately, much of this information is inaccessible.

What do others see when they look at you?

Would you like to know?

Imagine that you exist within layered systems. You start with the small micro system (your family) and move to ever larger systems, including your school, work, communities, country, and even the entire world. You impact the systems, and the systems impact you.[1]

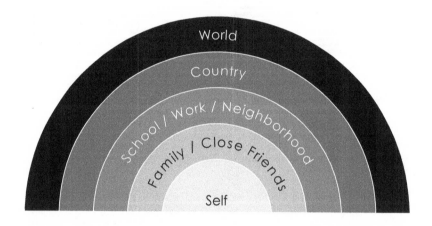

Let's look to the smallest part—yourself—and focus on identity. When I ask you to list five things about yourself, I am asking you to consider your identity.

Identity is made of attributes that cannot easily change in the moment. Some parts are considered fixed, while others may be more fluid. Is your identity mostly fixed or fluid?

Health Ancestry Skin-tone
Family status Educational attainment
Mental health IDENTITY Family **Heritage**
Physical appearance **Sex Gender** (dis)ability status
Personal history Race Ethnicity **Educational level**

Identity is a complex concept. It has physical, emotional, and mental components, and it changes with setting and time. Imagine all the aspects of yourself like a solar system, spinning while also pushing

---

1   This concept is based on the brilliant and ever important work of Urie Bronfenbrenner (1917–2005) and his ecological systems theory—which you will learn all about, I promise (see chapter 3 if you can't wait). Urie and I go way back. I mean, back to Psych 101 because, sadly, we never met in real life.

and pulling with various forces of the systems in your life. It won't ever be simple, but we will work together to increase your clarity through awareness. Every brain works differently, and everyone has individual ways of absorbing information. As a therapist, I work hard to find ways of "meeting my patients where they are," and I will do the same with you. Let's begin with a shared understanding and language about how the brain works. Let me tell you the science behind learning something new.

EDUCATION

Awareness helps you see yourself better. Education is the magic wand that lets you see another person's reality. Education can happen formally; any class you take enriches your understanding of what it is to be human. It can also be informal, built into your life. For example, reading can be a simple way to learn more about others. Traveling broadens the mind and helps you to grow. Education can happen anywhere, such as talking with people different from yourself in a nonjudgmental and open way.

How to Change Your Brain

Do you know how your brain works? How you think impacts your perception of others! You have a unique way of gathering, keeping, and processing information. Let's conceptualize the way *you* operate. Positive change can occur, but first you have to be aware of your patterns. For now, let's focus on processing and working with information. Psychologists call these *multiple intelligences* and *learning styles*.

Sometimes when talking about "intelligences" or "learning styles," you might assume it applies to formal education . . . but it is *so much more*! Gaining a clear picture of how your mind works has many benefits, including increased understanding of how you engage in the world, where your talents lie, and how you metabolize new information—the way you perceive the world around you. It doesn't get more fundamental than that.

Understanding your perceptions is important to your overall increased self-awareness. For example, it is essential for you to be aware of whether reading a book and working through exercises will get you to a new way of being—or if there may be other/additional ways for you to engage with the material to move toward improved connections with others. Knowing how you take in new information can help you let go of ways of learning that don't help you.

What kind of learning doesn't help you? Here's an example: I had a client who had high interpersonal intelligence combined with a passion for computer coding. She struggled with the type of instruction and assignments in her program. Frustrated, she decided to drop out of the program. Thankfully, during our sessions, she was able to define her learning styles and thereby seek new ways of getting the material. This shift in expectations from the traditional way of considering intelligence and education helped propel her into her chosen field.

Sometimes you mistake faulty information-gathering as limitations. It's time to stop doing that. Knowing how you perceive the world is key to connecting with others.

How do you process, gather, and keep information?

Multiple Intelligences and Learning Styles

What's the difference?

Multiple Intelligences = How you **process**

Learning Styles = How you **gather and remember**

Multiple Intelligences: Here's How It Works

"Everybody is a genius. But if you judge a fish by its ability to climb a tree, it will live its whole life believing that it is stupid."

—Albert Einstein

I'm not a huge fan of IQ. It was a brilliant construct created by two French geniuses with good intentions over a century ago. However, it is limiting. It has been proven to be directly linked to socioeconomic status. Assessments are also largely biased toward White males. In addition to these disturbing facts, it only grasps a certain type of thinking, what psychologists call *G*. G is made up of a group of skills that are thought to be correlated with the idea of intelligence. This is up for debate.

Thank goodness in 1983, Harvard professor Howard Gardner offered the theory of multiple intelligences (MI). He argues that limiting oneself to the classic notion of IQ ignores all the ways people are smart. I tell you this for two reasons:

1. **The theory of multiple intelligences is an important shift in the general notion of intelligence as we know it.**

2. **I keep multiple intelligences front of mind as I share information. I want to help you use your mixture of intelligences and learning styles to grow.**

First, let's explore how you work so you are prepared to engage with the text in the deepest way. Here is your second action—a chance to consider how your brain works and evaluate your people skills.

Multiple Intelligences: Which Mix Are You?

Review the chart below. Interact with it in any way you would like. Remember that no one has just one type of intelligence; everyone has a mixture. How do you process new information? By reading? Singing? Moving around? How you process fastest = what your intelligences are. Use crayons, markers, etc., and draw connections between them, jot down your thoughts, write a poem, or sing a song.

Remember to set your intention for the action, be yourself, and then process the experience. Please interact with the ideas and prepare your mind for greater self-understanding.

The information in this chart is based on the work of several researchers in the field of Multiple Intelligences in addition to Howard Gardner (mentioned above) including Cano and Whittington (2014), Lewis (2008), McClellan and Conti (2008), Brill (2001) and Sir Ken Robinson (2018).

Intrapersonal:

People with interpersonal intelligence have a grounded understanding of their direction in life with a positive self-concept and they are able to see and change things about themselves according to their own sense of inner reflection. The skill of self-management or perhaps emotional intelligence could be considered as intrapersonal intelligence.

Naturalistic:

Do you know someone who absolutely loves nature, who is perhaps an environmental scientist or a botanist, or someone who collects plants. Typically, people with naturalistic intelligence have a broad knowledge of plant species and or animal species and enjoy categorizing and classifying the neutral world. Perhaps even just avid gardens who love propagating, pruning, tending to and love their gardens could fit in to this category as well.

Logical:

Understanding numbers and the capacity to understand logic and reason at an advanced level are the hall marks of people with logical/mathematic intelligence. Think about the great scientists, mathematicians and physicists you know, apart from Sheldon from The Big Bang Theory, Albert Einstein, Pythragoras and Isaac Newton are just a few that come to mind.

Linguistic:

Do you know someone who never stops talking? Or writing? Perhaps they work in journalism or marketing, or they have an academic career as a linguist. Garden claims that verbal/linguistic intelligence is the ability to understand, use and manipulative words productively. (Gardner, 1983, pp. 77-98).

Interpersonal:

Highly social people often fall into the category of having interpersonal intelligence they are capable of sensing the motivations, moods and agendas of other people proficiently. Used for good or evil, people with this skill are often highly capable of manipulating social situations and people to serve their own end. Or perhaps they are just people who love people—the luckiest people in the world!

Kinesthetic:

Just like the song says, "We like to move it move it! MOVE IT! Kinesthetic intelligence is all about moving the body to express ideas, to think. Consider your favoirte sports team, they are all surely brilliant players to be at elite level, but some seem more gifted in their ability to think while they move. Sir Ken Robinson, in his TED talk, Multiple Intelligence, stated that, "kinesthetic people have to move to think."

more musical than others. Musical intelligence is the ability to partake in anything to do with music including but not limited to singin, composing songs, playing instruments and distinguishing instruments. It's easy to identify this kind of intelligence in people, you can often simply hear it in their voices or hear them singing or playing thier instruments.

Hands up all the artists in the room? If you consider yourself to be able to see spatially, perhaps you are an interior designer, graphic designer, artist illustrator, industrial designer, 3D designer, character modeler, animator, botanical artist, oil painter, fine artist, sculptor, jewelry designer, fashion designer . . . If you have a strong eye for design and aesthetics, chances are you have visual/spatial intelligence.

Now we have some deeper knowledge about where your processing strengths lie. Next, let's explore how you gather and keep information.

Learning Styles: Here's How It Works

Remember:

Multiple Intelligences = How you **process** information

Learning Styles = How you **gather and retain** information

"Each learner has a primary learning style and can be taught how to study and concentrate capitalizing on that style."

—Stephen Denig

In the early 2000s, a man named Stephen Denig realized that the way people learn is influenced by their intelligences. Where does your greatest aptitude lie? What comes easy to you? How do you interact with the world? These answers point to both your ways of being "smart" and how you assimilate new information—otherwise known as how you learn.

Your mind loves new information. How you gather and retain information impacts every unfamiliar thing you encounter! And again, this is how you learn. Now you have a clearer idea of your intelligences, which is the way you process information. Let's consider how those intelligences translate into learning.

Learning Styles: Which Mix Are You?

On the chart below you can see a description of some typical ways each type of intelligence learns. Find your type(s). Read through them; see if they fit for you. As always, draw, sing, paint, write—just absorb the material in your way, and get used to this practice as it will help you have the most effective journey.

 Linguistic learn best through reading, hearing, and seeing words and speaking, writing, discussing, and debating ideas.

 Logical learn best through working with patterns and relationships, classifying and categorizing, and working with the abstract.

Spatial learn best in working with pictures and colors, visualizing and using the mind's eye, and drawing.

 Kinesthetic learn best touching, moving, and processing knowledge through bodily sensation.

 Musical learn best with rhythm and melody, singing, and listening to music and melodies.

 Interpersonal learn best through sharing, comparing and relating with others, interviewing, and cooperating.

 Intrapersonal learn best through working alone, doing self-paced projects, and reflecting.

 Naturalists learn best when working in nature, exploring living things, and learning about plants and natural events.

Now we have a rough draft of five aspects of your identity and a basic understanding of how you process, retain, and gather information. You are developing a baseline to get you started. You can't move forward without an honest appraisal of where you are.

EMPATHY

What is empathy—and how is it compounded by awareness and education? You may have awareness and education. However, without empathy, you do not have attachment to others. Empathy leads to openness. Empathy comes from vulnerability and genuineness, and you can learn both ways of being.

In this first chapter, we are building your foundation for the rest of the book.

While we think about empathy, I want to introduce a framework for the language people use. How people refer to one another is a simple way to express empathy.

Person-First Language

How you speak matters. Have you heard of *person-first language*? This is a way of speaking that puts humanity central in the way you talk. Sometimes people bristle at the idea, calling it "political correctness," as though being kind is too much work. Just as you wouldn't let the door slam in someone's face, you can think of person-first language as holding open a door—an invitation to connect.

Person 1ˢᵗ Language

An Easy Way To Be Kind

People often tell us how they would like to be referred to—this is a simple step to make everyone feel more comfortable.

Ask If Unsure

If you aren't sure how to refer to someone—such as whether they prefer a particular pronoun, it is generally alright to ask in a supportive way. 'My pronouns are she/her, which do you prefer?'

Put The Person 1ˢᵗ

Rather than referring to a person as though the situation defines them 'schizophrenic'—put the person 1ˢᵗ—'a person who has a diagnosis of schizophrenia'. This is much more empowering.

Think Of Yourself

In your own life there have been times when you would have preferred to be discussed in a different way. Thinking of these experiences helps us to have empathy.

Try To Be A Good Human

Remember that we all make mistakes—so keep trying and learning, and if judgement comes up for you, try to figure out why you have resistance to taking this step to be kind and welcoming to your fellow humans.

What an uncomplicated way to show empathy. I'll ask you to please consider person-first language in your way of speaking, no matter where you are, as how you speak has the power to reverse engineer how you think. If you speak with empathy, your empathy will increase. Empathy is a pillar of emotional success; how wonderful you can begin so simply with your words.

LOOKING AHEAD

"The question is always blah, blah, blah and the answer is always love, love, love."

—Dr. Mary Beth Mannarino

The recent pandemic has given the world gifts. Though it has been and still is horrific, lonely, terrifying, and devastating, Covid-19 shines light on a two-sided coin. Endings make beginnings. Without destruction, new growth stalls. There is an ancient Hindu goddess named Kali. Many consider her a harbinger of death. But Kali also brings life. She embodies the idea that without loss, there is no new life. To start something new, you must be open to a change from the old ways.

You can decide to be a flexible reed and bend in the rain, or a stiff branch that may break.

In therapist training programs, we have a saying in response to almost any question . . .

It depends.

+

Ask your supervisor.

"It depends" refers to the notion that nearly everything in the universe is fluid. When I began grad school, I thought I would be given clear edicts. Instead, I was taught to see patterns and to accept that no two situations are the same. The second part—"Ask your supervisor"— refers to the idea that no matter what, we all need *support scaffolding*. I wasn't taught how to respond to each specific ethical situation but rather how to seek appropriate support and then attempt to work through the problem. Life is a lot like this—everything is gray, and it never hurts to have great support scaffolding.

Change can bring up pain. As we move deeper into our time together, I will ask you to consider your support scaffolding.

> **Support scaffolding is anyone who holds you up and propels you forward.**

Support scaffolding can include friends, family, colleagues, and professional help such as a therapist. Everyone needs support—and like scaffolding, it can hold you up while you rebuild into something new. When you need a break from psychological secrets, it is time to engage your support scaffolding. When you feel stress, you can't learn. To achieve emotional success, you need to know when you need support.

Life is about making the choice to lean into experiences, take what you can gather as tools, and move on as best you can. You've chosen this book because you want to be a reed bending in the wind, and that means letting go of the way you've always done things. It's time to connect.

CHAPTER 2

(Self) Aware

D o you know what your limitations are? When do your defenses rise to the surface, limiting your ability to connect with others? What do those emotional blocks do to help you? To hold you back? Chapter 2 is an exploratory chapter that will help you begin to experience your inner limits more clearly—not to remove them, but to know where your growth edges lie in a more objective way so you can connect more deeply with others.

"What's your name?" Coraline asked the cat. "Look, I'm Coraline. Okay?"
"Cats don't have names," it said.
"No?" said Coraline.
"No," said the cat. "Now you people have names. That's because you don't know who you are. We know who we are, so we don't need names."

—Neil Gaiman

Are you approaching this chapter feeling smug and prepared or uncertain and apprehensive? Maybe you are angry and feel like it's a pointless endeavor. There are as many reactions to inner work as there are people working through the book. Everyone has something to learn about themselves. Human beings are both curiously intelligent and unaware. You are also complex and simple at the same time. First, think about your own traits. Next, you will consider known and unknown aspects of yourself. And lastly (in this chapter) you will work through how you self-protect, sometimes to your detriment.

As we consider self-awareness, let's agree on these dichotomous theorems as a starting place.

Theorems

You know yourself & are unknown to yourself.
You are an expert & are a beginner.
You are seen & are never fully known.

As a therapist, I believe everyone can dig a little deeper. Get to know the corners of yourself and shine some light where you maybe haven't explored before. There is a universe inside of you, and if you can't dig, you are finished with growth—so let's close shop and call it a day. If you are ready to see some glorious magic inside of yourself that you may have been unaware of . . . let's go! I'm right here with you, believing you are a wonderful being, and only through knowing yourself better can you connect more deeply with others. I know you're on board. Woo-hoo!

We will discuss four *psychological secrets* in this chapter—aspects of identity, personality theory, ego development, and defense mechanisms. We start with the parts of yourself everyone can see or assume (identity) and move inward: first personality, the parts you are used to sharing with others; then deeper to your ego; and last, how you defend your weak spots.

I chose these four secrets as the starting point to greater self-awareness because they are the basic building blocks I use as a therapist to better understand each patient. When I meet someone for the first time, I have these four constructs in the front of my mind, and as I gather information about each new person, I am placing this new knowledge into these categories to help me better understand the person before me—from the outside all the way in. All these components work together to create the full experience of my patient, as well as how others perceive them.

Many times, the interpretations I offer during therapy are based on my conceptualization of the person based on these theories. I apply these ideas to my own life as well, to break down when I repeat a pattern or make a choice that doesn't fit with who I want to be. I share these with you because they aren't complicated and can quickly help you to see yourself more clearly.

Known and Unknown

Look at the circles below. Begin to jot down aspects of yourself that feel very well explored on the "known" side. Then pull up pieces of you that may have gotten less attention—for example, are you adventurous? Curious? Look or remember back to what kind of learner you may be, and where your intelligences lie—a good starting point when considering what you know about yourself and areas you may be less familiar with. People tend to stick to parts of themselves where they feel like experts; therefore, it's likely you will have much more to add in the *known* circle than *unknown*.

Once you warm up to the task and you're feeling centered, engaged, and *open*, look at the list you worked on above, and begin to place those aspects of yourself on the circles as well. If you'd like, add colors, shapes, stickers, drawings—whatever works for you to begin to suss out how you see your own self-awareness. This will give us a starting road map for the work ahead. Enjoy.

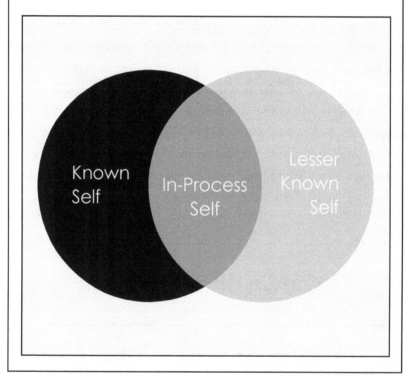

One of the things I loved about becoming a psychologist was the forced adventure into self-awareness land. In my doc program, we were constantly scrutinized—rightfully so, as we were about to become therapists. It is a normal part of the process to be evaluated not just for your formal education but also for your personality. You bring it all to the therapy room, after all, and it's essential that a therapist is open to evaluation, even of things we don't want to reconsider about ourselves.

There was a joke in my program that the faculty could hear us talking in our "lounge" down the hall (by lounge I mean a little room with donated, somewhat ruined furniture). When one of us said something the director didn't approve of, she would yell down the hall, "Hey, what are you thinking?" Thus, many things I thought were good or even marginally acceptable were suddenly up for consideration, from way down the hall. It was loving, deep, and constant feedback that was sometimes surprising but always enlightening. There's just so much we don't see about ourselves. We all experienced the hallway re-parenting, and it helped us grow into better therapists. We call this *supervision* in the therapy world, and everyone experiences it.

I dream of this constant evaluation for you too. Perhaps I can only yell down your metaphoric hall, but I'm here through this book to kindly ask you exactly what it is you are doing. Of course, my dream is for you to continue asking yourself that every day for the rest of your life.

What ARE you doing?
—Management

When you accept yourself "as is," you miss brilliant opportunities to grow. Do you know what a "growth mindset" is? It's a fancy way of saying you're open to improvement. If you imagine the front door to the shop that is you, does it say *Open* or *Please come in*? Are you willing to adapt with time, resources, new information? I hope so. No one is open all the time—but you can try to hold a welcoming stance as often as possible.

In graduate school, my reaction to endless feedback was varied. Sometimes, when I got yelled at from down the hall, my twelve-year-old self would show up—wanting to roll my eyes and ignore. Other times, I instantly saw the behavior wasn't useful, but I had not examined it. Throughout my training, I was expected to manage myself appropriately—to leave myself open to feedback and be self-reflective and able to consider how I impact the situation and others. Because of all that hallway management, these considerations are now largely reflexive (at least in my therapy work). My open stance to growth has enriched my life. It can do the same for you.

Comfort Zones

In this chapter I will ask you to unpeel layers of information about who you are and where you fit in the world. At times you may react by rolling your eyes. Getting angry. Feeling bored. That's all natural; we are exploring *you*. It can feel threatening or pointless to venture into self town. We are going to see how you react to the world around you, and to allow you to see what is—as it is. Shifts in awareness can happen on your own, with a group that makes you feel comfortable, or in therapy, among other places. Let's begin with as much openness as you can summon. The process of self-exploration is like any adventure—you're most likely to enjoy (and remember!) if you are slightly outside of your comfort zone but not so unhappy that you're shutting down.

Here's how many people conceptualize this idea . . .

> *"I like traffic lights.*
> *I like traffic lights.*
> *I like traffic lights,*
> *No matter where they've been."*
>
> —Monty Python

Red
No Way, Danger, Warning

In this zone you can't learn new things because your cortisol is too high, and your central nervous system will react in a flight-or-fight way. This is not an ideal place to try new things. This zone normally means stop. It's red for a reason.

Yellow
Uncomfortable But Manageable

In this zone you are unsure, and it feels new and different, but you feel safe enough to continue. Anxiety may arise but not so much that you can't focus on moving forward. This is the ideal zone in which to exist—trying new things, failing sometimes, but feeling alive and productive.

Sometimes I feel as though this zone grows or is the biggest zone as it comprises such a range of reactions for me—from what it feels like to walk into a room with unknown people all the way to being a guest on a nationally televised show.

Perhaps it is large for me because this is the zone I hang out in, where I feel the most alive. For you, it may look different. This is something to consider.

Green
Easy-Peasy Street

This zone is sleeping, eating, doing everyday tasks. You could easily live in this zone and never venture anywhere else. Perhaps you are doing this. Many patients come to me after feeling bored, and it is common to find them living in the green zone. The green zone is also restorative—and important. Some portion of our lives must be spent in rest and safety; only you know what the balance may be for you.

Traffic Lights

Take a minute to look at the traffic light image and consider where you live your life.

Draw what your traffic light looks like. Please take some time to think about how much risk you take, how alive you may feel, and then consider what you would like it to look like. Perhaps the two are identical. Or vastly different. This process can give you a starting point for understanding how you approach the world and how you would ideally like to live your life.

Lastly, I'd like you to please make a star somewhere on your current traffic light to show where this book—and growing your emotional success—rests. Does it seem natural, within your easy places, or perhaps a little higher up, into yellow? Is it red?

Wherever you are, consider why you are there. Perhaps you've challenged your ideas many times before, or this may all be new to you.

Where you are is great! You need to know where you are to move onward!

You can apply the traffic light idea to your life and even use it to create a shorthand with employees, loved ones, or children you are around to help quickly understand how each individual approaches a given situation. Many times, when you are in the green or red, someone on the opposite end of the spectrum just wants to drag you along; that rarely works. Just knowing where one another stands can help to bridge a gap. I hope this will help you as a comfort-zone shorthand.

Out of respect for the yellow-zone work we are planning, let's begin with your outermost features of self and work inward to the core. We start with aspects of self/identity. Take this as deep as you can. Sometimes, people answer flippantly, and that isn't what we're looking for here. We want to examine the choices you've made as well as the history, biology, timing, etc., that goes into each aspect of your identity because you can't connect with others when you don't know how you are perceived.

ASPECTS OF IDENTITY

What do other people see when they look at you? What is your race, ethnicity, and culture? How do you define your gender? How would you define the roles in your life? What activities represent who you are? What work do you do? What does your family look like? What is your socioeconomic status? How would you define your sexuality? Are you religious? What religion do you believe in? These questions and more make up your identity.

Your relationship with your identity is important, and we will explore this idea. First, we consider who you are on this fundamental level, and what you feel about your identity. Every therapist knows that when a patient reacts strongly to something, it's usually something they should explore.

Aspects of Self

Please look at the chart "Aspects of Self." This exercise will help you to work through different parts of yourself. It is meant to be a guide for deeper thinking around the notion of self-awareness. I listed several components of identity—though it is certainly not an exhaustive list. The list is meant to get you started. As you can see, there is plenty of room to add your own identity pieces and work through your thoughts. Look. Work it through. I purposefully did not define the concepts as they are constructs and everyone may look at this slightly differently. Also, it may seem as though there is repetition—I disagree. There are many facets of identity, and each represents a different side. If it seems too obvious, take a deeper look. If something doesn't apply to you, simply move along to one that does. If you have a strong reaction to an aspect of identity, spend a minute with it. Why? What's coming up for you? What information does that reaction offer about that word/potential aspect of who you may be—or who you are sure you aren't? Next, jot down how you define yourself, the impact each part of your identity has on you, and others.

Define aspects of self.

Consider how aspects of your identity impact your experience.

Consider your how your identity impacts others.

Aspects of Self

Race

Socioeconomic status

Sexuality

Gender

Partner

Employee/Professional

Physical self

Sex

Familial status

Partner

Parent status

Educational level

Stressors

History

Behavior

Choices

Mental health status

Health status

Housing

Addiction

Coping skills

Religion

Sacred beliefs

Physical practices

Friendships

Reputation

"I don't know about too many things, I know what I am if you know what I mean. Do you?"

—Edie Brickell

If you have the time, ask someone close to you to describe who you are using ten words. You can give them the same starting place (the action above) and compare. When we conduct assessments for children, psychologists get what we call "collateral data." This is parent, teacher, and friend information to help draw a clear picture of the person. I also do this exercise (the original action plus asking others to provide their reactions to one another) when I work with companies.

People find out something new about themselves every single time. It is great to evaluate yourself, and even more fun to get data from outside sources as well. Take it or leave it—but as they say, the facts are friendly. It doesn't hurt to find out more about how people in your life perceive you and whether their perception matches your own. Communication can break down in that gap.

Identity Is (Largely) a Choice.

"You write your life story by the choices you make. You never know if they have been a mistake. Those moments of decision are so difficult."

—Helen Mirren

Identity, like most complex constructs, has internal and external aspects. Psychologists try to better understand complex constructs like identity by breaking them down into time and components.

Whether you realize it or not, you've largely chosen who you are. All those choices about what to do and where to be, what you wear, who your friends are, what you consume (information, food, things)—these have shaped you, and you've made many choices. Even when you have forced choice, or bad/yucky/shit-tastic choices, you still make decisions. For some people who feel they've made good choices, good on them. And for others who have made good choices given less appealing options, even good-er on them! For those of you reading who feel that you haven't made as many rewarding choices . . . take another look and find at least one path you've chosen that has brought you something you are grateful for in this moment.

I don't mean your ethnicity, phenotype, ancestry, sexuality, gender, or many of the other aspects of identity that you can't change; I am referring to which parts of yourself you express, what gets hidden, when you "pass" as something else, and how you choose to share yourself with the world.

Who you are to the world and how you feel about your identity shapes your perception of every interaction. The identity we discuss here is a rough outline and practice to consider the basics of your current self-awareness. The action you just completed flushes out your basic ideas about who you are and brings them into your present awareness.

Now we have ideas about your intelligences, learning style, risk/comfort levels (I love traffic lights), and aspects of self. You are drawing closer toward self-awareness! Thanks for coming this far! Now let's see if we can decipher how well you know *you*, and in what areas. This clarifying exercise will allow you to visualize what you may or may not know intrinsically. Knowing more about yourself = good. Let's play with those traits by moving them around a little!

Human Development for Beginners

When you parent a baby, you answer a lot of questions about what we call developmental milestones, which are markers along the normal trajectory. For instance, when did your baby walk, talk, lift their head? Later, doctors ask social questions about making and keeping friends, language, and ability to connect with others. All animals, including humans, follow a typical growth pattern called a developmental trajectory that begins with conception and ends at death.

Development is so integral to you that psychologists assess your development at every intake appointment for all ages. We use the developmental trajectory to help us understand whether we have a patient who is outside that normal curve, in which case prevention/intervention may be required. As we begin to talk about healthy human development, it is essential for you to internalize two new theorems:

Theorems

Development is rarely linear.
Nothing is universal.

You are probably familiar with the notion of physical development, and again, if you've raised a child, you know a little about social development as well.

Sometimes, parents get worried about developmental timelines and expectations, but they are loose guidelines based on statistics. They exist, as I said, to help us see outliers and offer services where necessary. Let's apply the theorems above to the work we are going to do. There will be some parts of yourself that may not be as advanced as you would have thought, and other places where you're more developed than you realize.

Identity Development

The Making of *You*

- Values
- Personality
- History
- Time/Space
- Group memberships
- Intelligences

You are more than your basic physical and social development. There are countless aspects of self, as we've discussed. For each of those different parts of you, there is a process of identity development. Name any aspect of *you*, as we just discussed above, and I'll show you a developmental trajectory. As Simon de Bouvier said, "One is not born a woman; one becomes one." She was referring to the process of both physical and social changes a person goes through (and endures in some cases) to become a woman.

It is like this with all the aspects of identity. According to social scientists, everything from the physical to professional and all that's in between, each new piece of the puzzle that is *you*, must be developed. Many of these have been studied, documented, and operationalized so we can look at a person who identifies a certain way and compare that to their development. Remember, those are only guidelines. The positive thing about making clear outlines of the order in which people tend to develop is that we can compare! And thus more deeply understand a shared process. Because although there is infinite variability, there are also finite outcomes. That's a head exploder, but it's true. Think about it. Most people grow a certain amount. Most people choose a political affiliation; whether the choice is "nothing" or one or the other, it's a choice. The road may be winding to get there, but everyone is getting to basically the same few places.

You tend to loosely follow unspoken guidelines in your development of each new thing we do, believe, and are.

For now, let's stick with some areas of yourself that have been carefully researched. Let's consider those very important aspects of identity; after all, those are the parts most people see and evaluate first.

Existing Models of Identity Development

Race

Sex

Gender

Sexuality

Ethnicity

Political affiliation

Work identity

Worldview

Specific professions (counselors, pastors, doctors, etc.)

Religion

These are pieces of identity we just discussed. I'm here to delve into a few with you, and others you can research on your own if you're interested.

Simply Google some aspect of yourself and add "identity development" after it. *Feminist identity development.* Yep, there's research. *Parenthood?* Yes. As you can see, we won't be able to discuss them all here, but you are on a path of development for all the parts of who you are. We will discuss identity development again, in greater detail, in chapter 5 as well.

Learning more about your own and others' development helps you to see where you might fit together—and where you are different. The nonjudgmental knowledge of these processes can help you understand when disagreement occurs. Instead of reacting with emotions, you gain renewed perspective to allow differences. You can then connect better from where you are to where others are— like a children's matching exercise. When you only *feel* these differences and assume the other person is wrong, rather than in a different space, it is harder to create a bridge. The ability to see differences in developmental trajectories and meet people "where they are" is a secret that psychologists use every day. And now you can too.

"Make the most of yourself for that is all there is of you."

—Ralph Waldo Emerson

PERSONALITY THEORY

Your personality is one of the aspects of self that develops over time. In fact, it is unethical to diagnose a child with what we call *personality disorders* because we know the child's personality isn't set. I would argue it is never finished, but it is true that most development of your personality occurs before you are in your mid-twenties. Just like the rest of you, your personality develops.

Everyone loves to learn more about themselves. Psychology is a perennially popular college major because nothing is more interesting than learning about how you and others operate. When talking about self-awareness, a great place to start is to learn more about personality.

Your reactions, what you seek, how you present yourself, what matters to you—these are all the aspects that make up who you are. Of course, in this book we will dig into the nitty-gritty of identity. Let's start with your personality. In psychology, we love to break big concepts down, and personality is a gigantic notion. It doesn't get more complex than *who you are*. And yet, we can operationalize all that complexity into five traits. We often use the "big-five" model of personality traits to conceptualize each individual. This is where we begin.

The big-five model is sometimes called the five-factor model or the OCEAN model, and that's because the five factors are an acronym for the word OCEAN (openness, conscientiousness, extraversion, agreeableness, and neuroticism). We could spend a year exploring your personality (this is often a large component of therapy)—and it's a worthy endeavor. Let's work through some basics of personality theory so we can begin to use these psychological secrets to build a shared language and understanding as you move deeper.

Big-Five Personality Traits

Take a minute to read through the five traits and consider where you may be for each. If you are interested in doing a deeper dive here—and I get it—there are a ton of free (and awesome paid) personality assessments online. My advice is to look up a big-five personality test that will overlay with what we discuss here. Also, big-five measures are based in current psychological theory. Sure, put the book down, dig into who you are and how you operate. I'll see you later. And when I see you, you'll know yourself more, and isn't that really the point of this entire book?

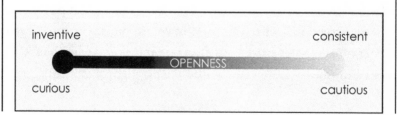

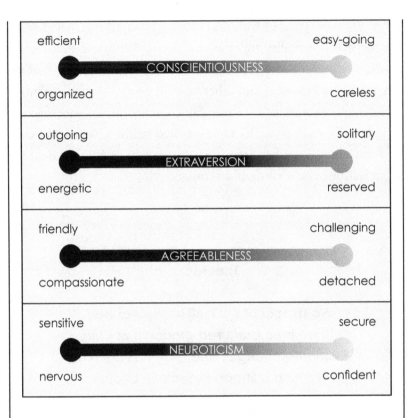

When you are ready—look at the factors above and please think of a recent situation in your life that caused stress. Work through the traits, consider how each may have had an impact on the outcome of that situation. Take notes, consider, sit with it.

What was the situation that caused you stress?

How did your personality traits play a role in the situation?

Traits aren't good or bad. And *nothing* is linear! Psychologists use the big-five personality traits as shorthand. We know that certain clusters of high or low placements on each continuum means we can anticipate behaviors and other ways of being. As social scientists and therapists, our aim is to simplify complex things—not evaluate or judge. We want to understand, predict, redirect, help—and clear understanding is the first step. I encourage you to adopt this stance when learning about yourself and others.

Theorems

No aspect of yourself is good or bad.
There is no preferred grouping of traits.
Everyone changes and grows all the time.
Nothing is linear. Especially people.

Keep these theorems in mind and evaluate your ways of reacting to stimuli; how might your personality traits interact with your ability to connect with others in deep and meaningful ways?

EGO DEVELOPMENT AND DEFENSE MECHANISMS

According to Freud, the goal of life is to be able to engage fully in love and work. Difficulty in either of these areas are where most people suffer and struggle. Obviously, connecting with others is key to each of those tasks, and intimacy is the optimal outcome. Psychologists love to talk about the ego. But we don't mean it the way you probably think about it. To me, and most psychodynamic therapists,[2] ego is synonymous with the core of you—the most precious (and fragile) interior bits. Defense mechanisms exist to protect the fragile and essential ego.

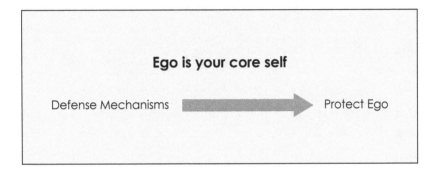

Ego is your core self

Defense Mechanisms ⟶ Protect Ego

Your ego is the very center of who you are, deep inside, under everything you layer on through time. Unlike your identity or personality, ego is much more intimate—so precious that it can be difficult to even look at it. The problem is that when you can't look at your own ego or how your defenses function, you repeat patterns and find yourself disconnected when you would rather be closer. This is one of the most tender areas you have . . . and so, to look closer here, we are going to use some basic psychological education to add information. You will retain a learning stance and look at yourself with grace and kindness. You are learning, and you can use this information to make more informed choices about how you interact with others.

What does a healthy ego look like? I like to imagine all things on a continuum, since nothing is black/white and most things are gray.

---

2   Psychodynamic therapy is a branch based on the work of Freud. He called his work *psychoanalytic*. Psychodynamic is a more modern approach that incorporates current thinking such as more equality between therapist and patient. Many people react strongly to Freud, and that is understandable. However, his early work and cutting-edge thinking has shaped our society (e.g. the notion of the subconscious, therapy in general, etc.) and has led much of the therapy world since its inception. We can be critical of the man, and some of his theories, while also valuing his work and contributions. Psychodynamic therapy—which focuses on childhood, going deep, figuring out root causes—is largely based on the work of Freud, and it is a beautiful process for many people. We can leave your desire to have sex with your parents out of it.

It is like this in mental health too—we don't think in terms of good or bad, right or wrong, but rather more like healthier and less healthy.

I would like to introduce the metaphor of a dimmer switch versus a light switch to you. A light switch is binary: on/off. A dimmer switch has a sliding scale. I would like you to add a dimmer to your switches—all of them. You don't have to use a dimmer if you have one, but the option of flexibility is always a good thing. When you look at ego, you can consider what is healthy or less healthy on a continuum rather than a fixed point. There are very few parts of healthy human beings that are static, ego included. Sometimes you think, *How I react is just how I react*, but you have so much more power than that over your thoughts, feelings, and behavior—that's where the dimmer switch comes in. Rather than snapping the same old reaction on or off, let's be more thoughtful and deliberate.

Healthy ego is tied to your defenses just like your physical health is directly correlated with your immune system. An over- or underactive immune response will lead to catastrophe, and the same is true of your ego. A healthy ego allows for the natural ebb and flow of relationships, while an overly zealous defense system leads to an inability to attain intimacy because of walls that are too thick. On the other end of the spectrum, a weak defense system can lead to a fear of being subsumed by "the other." Weak ego is the cause of both overuse and underuse of defenses. Weak ego doesn't encompass the entire ego, all the time. Remember, these are sliding scales. It makes sense that people are not always weak *or* strong . . . healthy *or* unhealthy.

You can have a weak ego in one moment, related to a sensitive or underdeveloped aspect of yourself, and be healthy in many others. Upon inspection, you'll find that the patterns you repeat are directly related to those aspects of your ego that are overdefended or underdefended. Identify those places for growth, explore the past pain, and engage in a new pattern based on deeper understanding rather than reactionary defense.

Here are some of the metaphors I use in my work, to help create a construct in your mind for the gigantic notion of *self* in relation to others. Let's return to the immune system metaphor.

Ego is made of a billion components, like the cells in your body. Like a cell, there are outer walls and a protected and essential inside piece. Within the nucleus lies your DNA, and without it, you aren't yourself. In a healthy cell, the wall is permeable to allow nutrients to flow in and waste to flow out, or the cell dies. Unhealthy or damaged cells can be breached—the wall is too thin or thick. Consider your ego and its many facets. Your use of defenses may be appropriate in many cells. At the same time, there are cells that aren't optimal.

This is human nature.

The concept of ego and its use of defenses in relation to your ability to connect deeply with others is so important that I am going to offer one more metaphor. Choose the one that sticks for you.

I often talk with patients about their ego as a stage and the rest of the world as the audience. Your defenses can be thick, like the gorgeous velvet curtain—letting nothing meaningful in or out. I sometimes think of this as the actor who pokes their head out to tease the audience—a head with no body, a connection . . . sort of. At other times, there is no curtain when the action on stage happens. There is free flow between stage and audience. The last component is the most subtle. Sometimes, when the script calls for a dream or memory sequence, a special see-through curtain called a scrim is employed. A scrim is a lightweight and translucent fabric. It allows the transfer of action, but it *is* a curtain. You can't just walk through it.

A mix of all three types of curtains is what you're aiming for! The goal is to be the stage manager in your own life and to have the ability to choose which curtain to employ and when. You can't be open, closed, or guarded all the time. You must be all three when appropriate.

Deep exploration of defenses and how or why you operate based on these mechanisms are the underpinnings of much of therapy. As you can see in the healthy-ego continuum and the metaphors above, the ego must be healthy enough to allow movement of nutrition (love and attachment) while keeping out waste (unhealthy or toxic people, things, or experiences). This is a deep dive into your inner world. Please watch out for reactions or remembrances that may need more attention through your support scaffolding.[3]

Ego and Attachment

I hope you allow some reactions to the ego metaphors described here. I always have big reactions when I consider my growth areas. Pick a metaphor and explore your defense/attachment style. I'll ask you to sit with it. Consider it. Work it through in any ways that feel relevant for you. This is where the work is. I'm proud of you.

Herein, we are introducing the notion of "ego." As an academic at heart, I must make y'all aware that we are wading into a field of study that *defines* itself by being deep and never ending in complexity. The exploration of your ego and her defenses is as vast and rich as the sea. We depth psychologists believe in the never-ending fluidity of human emotion and the disciplines that grow from it—psychodynamics, attachment theory, and all the subdisciplines therein are worthy of your time and exploration. For now, let's peek in the windows and doors of these houses, and I'll be happy enough to know that you are now perhaps a little more aware of the words we psychologists put to the ways you react to situations in your life. If you're satisfied here, me too! If not, you

---

3   Support Scaffolding = therapist, friends, family, teacher, clergy, lover, social media, neighbors, any people, creature, or systems you can depend on to help you as you grow and change. Like a building under construction, everyone needs some support scaffolding to keep them in place and to help them be their best.

can seek a depth-oriented therapist, grab a book, take a class, or go down the Freudian rabbit hole on Google. Either way, enjoy.

> **If you don't know who you are, how can you expect to connect deeply?**

Blocking Emotions

It's time to delve deeper into why and when defenses get too rigid or transparent. You simply cannot connect as impactfully with others when you don't know what you're projecting. Self-knowledge can require a walk down a tricky path. I am here with you—though it also may require some work with a therapist, friend, art, a retreat, etc. We just don't know what may come up, and sometimes it helps to have a guide and/or companion.

I'll introduce you to a good friend of mine, and one of the best teachers in existence: defensiveness. When you feel defensive, you shut down. You must learn to recognize how defensiveness feels for you! If you already know, then yay! This will be straightforward for you—though I'm pretty sure defensiveness knows some tricks you may not yet be aware of.

A large component of psychodynamic theory, and therapy in general, is the idea of defense mechanisms. We will discuss what the defense mechanisms are and how they work in a moment. Before a defense mechanism is deployed, you have an emotion. This leads to defense mechanisms, and then you have a new emotion, one that is easier for you to sit with. I call these big, solid, keeping-out-discomfort emotions *blocking emotions*.

Defensiveness often arises from shame and fear, so let's start there.

Think of a time when you felt shame or fear and hold it at the front of your mind. Vivid experiences will be helpful while we work through defenses. We focus here on these two blocking emotions because they so quickly come up with your defenses without your approval.

Let me introduce you to the "Path of Fear and Shame":

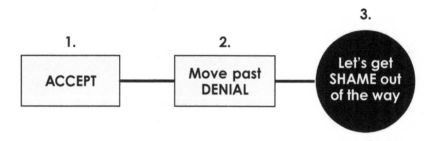

1. ACCEPT

2. Move past DENIAL

3. Let's get SHAME out of the way

Theorems

Shame is largely intolerable.
Shame often feeds the need for unhealthy coping skills.
Working to metabolize/destabilize shame is a
great gift to yourself.

After you *acknowledge* shame and try to learn the lesson it's teaching you (generally, knock that off), you can and should *let it go*. The secret of shame is simple—it doesn't do any good after the information has been shared.

There is only a corrosive effect to holding on to shame. No growth happens when you wallow in it. Yuck.

Shame has a best friend. It's fear. They are the BFF blocking emotions. I call them *blocking emotions* because they are old and useful emotions meant to protect our egos, basic to survival. And like many things, they are required but dangerous in excess. We will discuss blocking emotions in detail later.

Blocking Emotions

SHAME + FEAR.

Important. Often Overdone.

All the reactions you have to shame are likely identical to your way of responding to fear. Either way, both are teachers, and both are often swiftly dealt with by your defenses. I bring this to the forefront because frequently identity discussions circle around to your fears: Will you lose yourself? Is making room for another going to take from you? Will you or your loved ones be hurt? These are all based on the fundamental (and important) human fear of scarcity.[4]

- Will I (and my family) have enough?
- Will someone hurt us?
- Why do defenses exist?

Your defenses know all of this. They know it so well that they would rather you skip right over the learning/change-reaction piece straight to *ignoring* shame by inserting your favorite defense mechanism. This way the cycle can continue.

---

4   See chapter 4 for much more on how fear impacts your decisions and ways of connecting with the world around you.

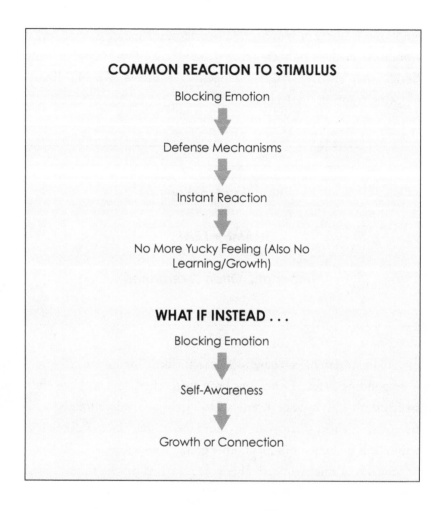

Blocking emotions can teach you how you react to distasteful or potentially threatening information. Here's the thing: if you have no awareness of your comfort (or discomfort) with the nitty-gritty, it is nearly impossible to achieve deep connections with others. And human beings *need* intimacy. It's what helps you thrive.

Now that you know *why* we have these essential defenses, let's talk about what they are and how they work.

DEFENSE MECHANISMS

12 Defense Mechanisms: Sigmund Freud

1. Compensation: Strengthen one to hide another.

2. Denial: Refuse to face a negative behavior.

3. Displacement: Take it out on someone else.

4. Identification: Attach to something positive.

5. Introjection: Conform feelings for approval.

6. Projection: See your faults & foibles in others.

7. Rationalization: Excuse and justify mistakes.

8. Reaction Formation: Pretend you are different.

9. Regression: Act much younger to feel better.

10. Repression: Putting things into darkness.

11. Ritual & Undoing: Override negative with habit.

12. Sublimation: Divert negative into acceptable.

Based on the 2017 work by Kevin Everett FitzMaurice.

Defenses are very powerful, and they serve an incredibly important task—to defend you from anything that might make your ego take a hit. Therapists spend an incredible amount of time exploring why these defenses exist and how to be more aware of them so that instead of an automatic response, you can make a choice about how you'd like to move forward. For instance, would you like to change something about yourself, or reject the data as false? Either way, it's generally better to allow the information to enter your consciousness than to push it away out of fear.

Theorems

Defenses are essential to your well-being.
Defenses can be wonderful teachers.
Defenses, like all things, can be magic in moderation.

Sometimes defenses don't *look* like defenses. Remember, they are well-oiled machines and very good at their jobs.

Defensiveness can look like these things, using reading this book as the example:

- Avoidance: This chapter isn't worth my time. I know myself.
- Zoning out: What did I just read? I'm bored.
- Denial: None of this applies to me. I don't put out anything into the universe except what I intend to.
- Shutting down: I need a nap.
- Getting angry: Who is this woman? She doesn't even know me. Ugh, I don't have time for this.
- Feeling sad: It's too much to look at how I've impacted others.
- Anxiety: Oh my goodness, what am I about to find out about myself?
- Projecting: She is the one who doesn't know herself. Clearly.
- Intellectualism: I know the way I'm reacting is simply my neurotransmitters overreacting.

There are about a zillion more interpretations of defenses, and figuring yours out is a huge step toward becoming more self-aware. It can be dicey work. Just remember to be kind to yourself, honor your defenses for their amazing work, and allow where you are to be satisfactory. Remember, you can't be open if we pull you so far outside of your comfort zone that you're standing in the red. Stay yellow, my friends, and self-knowledge will grow from that stance.

Defended

For this activity you can use the more casual description of defenses listed above as examples, or use the worksheet below with actual defense mechanisms, or both—your choice.

Consider the last time you heard something you disagreed with. How did you respond? Internally (thoughts in your head)? Externally (acted some way)? Did the way you react serve you well?

Now I'd like you to imagine (or remember) a comment directed toward an aspect of your identity. Reaction?

Lastly, please put stars beside your go-to defense mechanisms.

Avoidance

Zoning out

Denial

Shutting down

Getting angry

Feeling sad

Anxiety

Projecting

Intellectualism

We are setting up a clearer picture for you of who you are inside and outside, encompassing how you react to blocking emotions (which often arise given new, construct-shaking information), and how comfortable you are with risk. We've thought about how you learn, in what ways you're smart, and of course, we already know that you're here to grow and connect better with others.

Now that you are a little more aware of your personality type, aspects of your identity, your ego, how your defenses operate, and how they will likely interact with your journey through this book (and life!!), we can start digging in a little deeper. PS: knowing your defense techniques is generally helpful in connecting with other humans.

CHAPTER 3

Understanding Self and Others (Awareness Deep Dive)

E veryone lives within systems—you impact the systems, and the systems impact you. This is a chapter to help you understand who you are to others and what role the various aspects of your identity play in how successful you are in intimacy land. We will utilize aspects of narrative therapy, explore your values, and consider how fixed or fluid you perceive the world around you. Everyone can be more self-aware. Here's how!

"Remember, always, that everything you know, and everything everyone knows, is only a model. Get your model out there where it can be viewed. Invite others to challenge your assumptions and add their own."

—Donella H. Meadows

Are you ready for three new psychological secrets? These will round out the awareness component of your emotional success. The secrets are *systems theory*, the power of *personal narrative*, and the importance of *evaluating your values*.

Here, we take the picture of self as individual from chapter 2 and put her in the wider world. Have you ever played a video game? In chapter 2, we built your avatar; now we move into the game with all its complexity. How well do you play with others?

Think about how you learn, change, and take in new information based on your learning and personality styles we discussed in chapter 1. Then, consider what you need to do to get yourself ready to be as open and non-defensive as possible.

This chapter will require you to look at yourself as part of a system, and to do that fully, you will need to be as calm and centered as possible, interested, and prepared. These two self-awareness chapters (chapters 2 and 3), hold the key to everything after. They are the foundational work for transporting yourself into self-awareness—a place I'd really like to hang out with you.

> *"Nothing exists except atoms and empty space; everything else is opinion."*
>
> —Democritus

Everything, large and small, is made of space. From wee atoms to the vastness of the universe, what there seems to be is a lot of empty space. Whether or not all that space is devoid of anything is up for debate, but we do know that all this space continuously expands and contracts. It is powerful and, minimally, filled with potential. After all, if you split an atom, you get an atomic bomb.

I'd like you to consider all that space for a minute. Look down at your arm, think of the space between cells, within cells, and then deeper—to the space within and around atoms. All the potential in that vastness right within you for growth, possibility, change, and connection.

SYSTEMS THEORY: QUICK AND DIRTY

Systems theory is complex and gorgeous. It winds through the natural sciences and right into psychological theory. Once we talk about it here, you won't be able to unsee it; it will be everywhere for you.[5]

Here's how the theory works—everything balances out. It's basic relativity brought to both small and unthinkably vast concepts. Let's start with the smallest first. An atom operates as a system. Inside, subatomic particles whiz around in the vast space that makes up an atom. It's a system!

Systems theory is applied academically to both the living and engineered parts of life, perhaps because nature operates on systems theory. And as science largely works from nature (the only model we know), technology also has systems theory as an underpinning. It is everywhere. To manage the vastness of this concept, let's start with your life.

As I said, systems theory is vast and impressive. We don't have time for *all* that right here. But we are smart people, and we can create a framework to understand the concepts and apply them to meaningful change. Simply put, systems include components, processes, and functions. Systems interact, overarch, and move independently all around you, all the time. Starting with your body as an example, your circulatory system is currently running alongside your nervous system (you are reading a book *and* your heart is pumping) all while you breathe (respiratory system) and maybe go to the bathroom (endocrine and digestive working together!). You get it. Separate systems work together to make up a larger system—your body. That's the basic gist of systems.

Let's look at some of the systems you find yourself in. Let's return to Urie Bronfenbrenner from chapter 1.

---

5   Bonus psychological secret: Have you wondered why you see a blue Honda every-where right after you buy one? This is called the "availability heuristic." Your brain ignores *a lot* of data—so when you bring something to your awareness, you notice it even though it was there all along. There aren't suddenly more blue Hondas; you just acknowledge them now. More on the importance of these brain tricks and how they impact emotional success later.

Bronfenbrenner Model

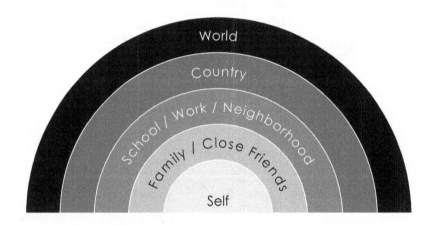

Bronfenbrenner used different language (literally—he was Russian), but he felt strongly that people operate within systems and that the pressure and experience of being in different systems impacts human development in profound ways. He called it ecological systems theory, and if you're interested, you can look it up. Enjoy!

As you can see from the chart, there are five systems listed. You may or may not be aware of the bazillion systems always surrounding your body, like the natural world, technology, the news cycle, etc. But for here, let's focus on these more concrete systems where you can work toward greater self-awareness and connections with others.

Components of a System

Self

- Physical body
- Thoughts, feelings, and behaviors that make up who you are and how you experience the world around you.
- Place where you live
- Identity
- Experiences

Family and Close Friends

- Nuclear family (yourself and a partner and/or children you may have or your parents and any siblings)
- Extended family such as cousins, aunts/uncles, grandparents
- Close friends who are supportive and available for your needs and you theirs

School/Work/Neighborhood

- The school where you or your children attend and the community surrounding the place
- Where you work and the people you work with, for, and around
- The neighborhoods that you are a part of at home, school, and work, as well as the neighborhoods you travel through as you live your life
- Your greater community/the city or county you live in
- The digital community you are a part of
- The work you do
- The things you are learning/training you receive

> ## Country
>
> - Where it is physically located on the earth
> - The topography/natural resources/geography
> - Citizenship status
> - The identity (usually a caricature) of a typical person from your country
>
> ## World
>
> - The physical planet
> - All the countries and people who inhabit the earth

"You're not thinking fourth-dimensionally!"

—Doc Brown (*Back to the Future*)

The psychological secrets in this chapter are somewhat theoretical. You'll have to think dynamically to engage deeply. I hope you can see how complex systems theory is. And how it beautifully helps to simplify such incredibly complex constructs. Imagine the systems moving like clockwork amongst themselves, and interwoven as well, and then let's add in another ingredient. We haven't discussed it yet, but *time* plays a huge role in every single aspect of your life and can adjust systems in its magical and often invisible ways. For instance, memories impact the self, and yet we also know that institutional memory can alter experiences for whole groups of people.

Epigenetics also shows that experiences can remold your genetic code and thus impact the future.[6] The past obviously has shaped the

---

6   If you are unfamiliar with the study of epigenetics, I suggest you put down this book and explore the topic immediately. You're welcome. If you have, and want to talk, send me a message because I want to talk more about it too.

larger institutions in which you live in innumerable ways, as well as your considerations, hopes, dreams, and plans. In systems theory, time and space must always be considered to flow and move you in seen and unseen ways. When you begin to explore your own experience of the systems of your life, I will remind you to always keep history and future dreams front of mind.

In a more concrete way, can you see how physical space is listed as a component for every single system? It cannot be understated that *physical space matters*. There are entire fields of study on the built environment as well as careful consideration for urban, new urban, and rural living— and how to plan thoughtfully for the abundance of humans living everywhere. You cannot separate yourself from your physical world as it impacts your life, and you obviously impact it right back. This book and, actually, the entirety of human existence is futile if humans ignore the obvious way in which they interact with the planet and fail to take action to halt the climate crisis. On a smaller scale, where you live is directly tied to privilege and power the world over. In fact, home dwellings are one of the primary denotations of wealth, regardless of society. Physical space is tied to privilege and bias in all ways—and I'll ask you to consider how the very places you and your ancestors have called home have shaped your worldview and life experiences. So take systems, overlay time and place, and let's see what happens.

How Do the Systems Work? What Do They Do?

When talking about the systems of the human body, the discussion turns to processes and functions of each, and how they interact. It is the same with the systems in which you exist.

The chart "Components of a System" lists *some* of the *parts* of each system. It does not include processes or functions of the systems. It is not a finite, finished, or complete list of components but a place to start your thinking to help you on your self-awareness exploration. The process and function of the systems I will leave to you, to consider from your point of view how the systems function—and to what end. To help you grasp those processes and functions, here are some questions you can ask yourself when considering your systems:

- Do you feel safe?
- Is there a safety net for your basic needs if you cannot meet them?
- Do you feel valued?
- Are you supported or undermined?
- Are there means for you to effect change?
- How does your existence alter the system?

Systems Theory and You

Review "Components of a System." If you want to grab the whole thing to work on, do it, or choose one system and work from there. Get some paper, space, and whatever level of privacy you require to dig deeply. Start by taking the components and making them personal. Consider what those components look like to you and in your life. Remember to consider time and space in your responses. Also, give yourself a break when you need it.

You never know what may surface when you begin to explore yourself in relation to your world.

If you'd like, you can draw boundaries around each system. Are they transparent, interacting, connecting—and what does that mean for you? Also, you can add arrows showing how systems in your life seem to interplay. Play with it, mark it up, and create something that gives you some awareness. Enjoy.

Components of a System

Self

Family and Close Friends

School/Work/Neighborhood

Country

World

With all of that, let's start working through your identity as a human being within these systems.

Let us never forget that not everyone is given the same glorious shining path. Privilege and bias are real, and they give people different systems in which to operate, and different paths to choose from. Those of you who've experienced more bias than privilege are saying, "Wow, thanks for finally saying that," and those of you who have a pile of privilege are either acknowledging it or are in denial. If you feel denial coming up, remember, you know it's telling you something. Are you experiencing fear? Shame? Maybe. Maybe not, but it's always worth exploring. No matter what your reaction is, it's part of your story.

PERSONAL NARRATIVE

Let's talk about stories. Do you know anything about narratives or narrative therapy? A narrative is the story you tell yourself (and others) about who you are, where you come from, and where you're going. If you had a strong response to the discussion of privilege above, it's likely I rubbed up against a personal narrative in the wrong way. Perhaps the "story of you" doesn't include privilege, and everyone has a difficult time accepting revisions to their narrative. The power of the narrative cannot be overstated. Visualizations, stories, fables—these are all so powerful because they are quick and clear images that some would say appeal to human beings' universal knowledge as a species. Or as Jung[7] called it, the *collective unconscious.* In narrative therapy we ask patients to write the story of their lives, going as far back as they'd like—meaning, perhaps, back in time to their ancestors. Some belief systems adhere to a multiple-pathways or past-lives rule, and in that case, going way backwards may be a necessary step (as the Indigo Girls suggest in the song "Galileo").

According to GoodTherapy.com, narrative therapy helps patients in three distinct ways:

- Helping people objectify their problems
- Framing the problems within a larger sociocultural context
- Teaching the person how to make room for other stories

Wow! Can you see how those goals are so amazingly aligned with ours? Let's unpack that a little.

Helping people objectify their problems. This is always a helpful place to start because what you want to add, always, is more light than heat to a problem. If you can take a step back and assume a bird's-eye or top-down view (rather than standing in the middle of it), you can generally start to consider what you can or want to move around to live the life you want. Changing perspective also helps you to get space from a situation in order to manage your emotions in the moment.

Framing the problems within a larger sociocultural context. First of all, narrative therapy grows from ideas of feminist therapy (among others).

---

7   Jung was a student/friend of Freud's, and although the two had a passionate and productive relationship, it ended abruptly when Jung became too entranced in the "mystical" world for Freud's taste. Both operate with a psychoanalytic mind, and both contribute to the field of depth psychology.

Examining how you navigate the world within your sociocultural contexts is one of the main tenants of both feminist psychology[8] and this book! How wonderful that while you take that bird's-eye view, you also look at what is all around you and how you interact with those systems and they with you! Fabulous!

Teaching the person how to make room for other stories. This is amazing! When you move from that bird's-eye view back to feet on the ground, there are very personal experiences happening all around you—and making room for other people's stories rather than projecting your images onto them is, again, one of the basic tenants of this book and our work together.

How can you explore your narratives? For our purposes, I will ask you to consider writing your whole story,[9] though just looking at the highlight reel will be enough to keep you heading in the right direction. If you do want to review your story with a professional, many therapists would be happy to do so. You can seek someone who specifically focuses on narrative therapy. Everyone benefits from looking at the shorthand they have created about their lives, and the stories they tell themselves about who they are.

---

8   In 2017, Jeanne Marecek defined feminist psychology just the way I understand it: "Feminist psychology is a subfield of psychology concerned with gender, sex categories, and sexualities. It includes both academic researchers and practitioners (i.e., psychotherapists and counselors). Feminist scholarship is often fueled by a commitment to social justice. Feminist psychologists have challenged cultural beliefs about innate female nature, and also invidious stereotypes about various groups of women. It has brought to light the lives and experiences of women and girls across the social spectrum. Feminists have also examined the part that gender plays in the distribution of power in society. In clinical psychology, feminists have insisted on the connection between psychological suffering and social context, with some focusing on experiences of sexual abuse and intimate violence." There is much more to read, especially in subfields (e.g. feminist therapy), but this sums up beautifully the complex idea of a theoretical orientation quickly.

9   If you want to write your autobiography, I suggest a few parameters. You can start with a word count, theme, or specific focus—or a mixture of these. There are also excellent writing prompts one can find online to help you start the process.

Theorems

The stories you tell yourself become facts.
These facts shape how you perceive the world around you.
How you perceive the world impacts how you present yourself and how you see others.
You act on what you perceive.
Those behaviors/decisions become your life.

Your inner voice, for example, is a direct result of your narrative. I don't want to delve into your cognitions here, but I can tell you what you already know: how you talk to yourself becomes your self-image, a key component of your ego and ego strength. So, the story of your life, as you tell it, is deeply tied to your core self.

These thoughts also influence how you react to people like you and not like you, as well as new situations. You can see where this is going . . .

Your Life Narrative (abridged)

Please take a moment and think of the big-five[10] events in your life. If there are more, narrow it down—sometimes if you group into themes, it can help. If there are less, let there be less. If you want to ignore me and write a zillion, do it. I chose five because it's manageable, and it will help you see enough to be meaningful.

Sometimes writing big events can be triggering—so before you begin, be in a safe space and consider your support scaffolding. We are doing deep and important work, and sometimes, like fracking, digging deep can make earthquakes. Be loving with yourself and honor that you are taking steps to connect better with yourself and the world around you—a noble cause. Try to be as open and defense-free as possible, and to not judge what you write or make value statements about your life from your list. As always, creativity reigns: write, draw, make a song, dance it out, meditate on it, walk away and give it space—whatever works for you.

Now that we've got the big-five moments of your life, let's work with those events/storylines. When you think of those big moments—how do they . . .

---

10   Please don't confuse big-five life events with the big-five aspects of personality from chapter 2. I don't know why psychologists like five; it's a nice, odd number, I guess.

Overlap with your idea of your identity?

Learning style?

Personality?

Aspects of self?

Defenses?

Impact your level of openness/ability to open?

Apply to your ability to connect with others?

Alter your current levels of empathy?

You are the central player in your life narrative. Sometimes you allow yourself to act in a supporting role, but that is a choice. In your narrative, you create stories about how you get to the places you get, and why you have or have not achieved your goals. As the protagonist in your story, you impart meanings to your successes or failures. For instance, if you have a strong "I've gotten to where I am with no help" narrative, my mention of privilege likely upset you. That makes sense! Of course, the world and the systems you live in have a role to play, whether you choose to acknowledge the stage on which you exist. It's time to step outside of yourself and look around.

Self-Disclosure

*"Life is like photography. You need the negatives
to develop."*

—Ziad K. Abdelnour

We are pulling together all the work you've done to this point—identifying your intelligences, learning styles, aspects of your personality, and identity exploration. We've tackled defenses and now have some basics about your personal narrative. As I've mentioned before, people are complicated. I love it, like a real wood-burning fireplace: popping, making good smells, and being a wee bit dangerous. That's you!

In therapy, there are lots of different viewpoints on whether therapists ought to talk about themselves. When I teach, I always tell graduate students that if their client has to ask if the therapist is okay, they've gone too far. In other words, there is a lot of gray area. As a feminist depth psychologist, it is part of my orientation to be authentic with my patients. That means if you ask me a question that won't impact our work, I can answer it briefly, and it will build our rapport. It feels disingenuous to me to flip a question back on a patient if the answer won't disrupt therapy in any way, and I can quickly get back to the work at hand. Along that way of thinking, I've asked you to do so much, and it's inauthentic to deflect a simple question when honesty will do.

My Big Five

My big-five narrative is more like a big *one*. I mean, when I sit with my narrative, sure, there are lots of things, though it often boils down to my hip. Maybe it's because it has been a part of me since the beginning, or because it has had the greatest opportunity to shape my world. Or both. I haven't always been able-bodied, and my hip would tell you I am not still.

I was born with congenital hip dysplasia.[11] I had a bunch of surgeries, and one or two didn't go as planned, so I got lopsided. Then we met Dr. Timothy Ward at Children's Hospital in Pittsburgh. I was eleven. He told me I could stretch the right leg or chop off a growth plate in the left leg. I was sure I wanted to be stretched. I didn't want to be short. Unexpectedly, I met a boy in the waiting room the day we were doing pre-op appointments, and he had one leg pulled up and resting on a chair. There was something that looked like a bird cage wrapped around his leg. When I looked closer, I saw that it was also going *through* his leg. I remember the nausea I got in that moment— and that I have now in recounting the experience.

The unspoken rules in children's hospital waiting rooms were as follows:

- Never flinch when looking at another kid and their scars/ wounds/disabilities.
- Expect to be asked what is happening with your body.
- Respond directly and include most-recent surgery and outcomes.

But that child's leg had me breaking rule number 1, and I couldn't ask what had happened. Thankfully my mother has never met a question she didn't want to ask, and this is how I came to know that the device on his leg was the stretching process I was about to start. His mother offered that it was more painful than it looked (I remain incredulous on this point) and that it was often infected. And now I am happily two inches shorter than my genetic code stipulates.

That surgery helped for a bit, but then my right hip (the problem all along) started getting worse as I grew, and the deformity of my hip socket became more pronounced. At sixteen, I went back to Dr. Ward, and it was now time for a larger surgery. I had a major operation and

---

11   Saying "born with" and "congenital" is redundant, but I didn't know congenital meant "born with" for the longest time, so I still say both.

then couldn't walk for several months. I scooted along in a wheelchair and then crutches. I was pulled out of school for half of that year.

At that time, I learned a lot about developmental asynchrony, being out of step with my peers, and I'm not sure I ever really stepped back in. Throughout childhood and adolescence—and even now, at close to middle age—I see my body differently from my age cohort. To me, every day when I run or use my body, I am grateful and do not take it for granted. I know what it is to be in pain, and I know that it isn't just children who don't know how to react to a person who isn't walking. When someone asks me, "Why did you become a psychologist?" I tell them about my hip. Being developmentally asynchronous from a very young age (five years old in body casts) can teach you a lot of useful things about yourself. It also tells me that the way a person presents is not always how they identify. And if we can remember one thing together, let it be this:

It never hurts to be kind.

By this, I mean with yourself and with others, when you have a choice about how to think of someone, how to speak to them, or how to conceptualize who they are as a person. If they have offered their preferred way of being seen in the world, embrace it. For so many, this starts with knowing who you are. I offer my story because it is a window into my self-awareness—a self-awareness that I would like you to increase in yourself. When you have unfinished business, your defenses arise to protect your ego, and then it is more difficult to be kind.

E-VALUATE

Values = core beliefs you use to make choices

Kindness is one of my hugest values. The things that matter to me the most are distilled from my big five, and we all operate this way. We have these transformative experiences, and from them we glean messages about huge, overarching things.

Theorems

Your narrative shapes how you see the world.
Values come from the lessons you take away from your life narrative.
Values impact your every decision.
Values are distinctly personal, though people often feel they are universal.

Huh. That last theorem gets you sometimes, doesn't it? You get stuck in thinking that your values are universal . . . *and yet they aren't.*

Some of your heads are exploding right now. Others are nodding. There is smugness and self-assuredness and that feeling in the top of your chest, almost to your neck, that means stubbornness. Not much good comes from that feeling and the resulting behaviors. So, let's push through and move right back to an open stance if you can. Values are not universal. Of course, most believe in some basic rules—don't kill other people, for instance. But think of the varied and deep value sets people hold and you'll see pretty quick that everyone has vastly different ways of seeing what the "important" things are.

Some Common Values

What we eat

How we eat

Eating animals

Abortion

Religion

Sex

Where we sleep

How we work

Accumulating vs. distributing wealth

What constitutes success

Who we love

Appearance of ourselves and loved ones

As you can see from the image above, human values touch on the most basic human functions. Over millennia, constructs were built and designed for various reasons that people as individuals and entire civilizations (helped along by the systems they created) adopted as *Truth* with a capital *T*. And yet you can see that throughout history and across geography, these "Truths" are varied and distinct.

What do I mean? If you have a culture that survives on agriculture, values will center on the protection of farming, and so on. Humans take the next step from believing what they value to be universal to then trying to *force* it to be universal. Obviously, we've entered philosophy land. For our purposes, I'd like to ask you to consider how you might take your values and try to lay them over other people, ways of being, cultures, etc., like tracing paper over the wrong sheet.

Laying your values on others gives you a false image, and it also isn't going to help you connect better with the people around you.

It isn't just you; everyone does this. Bias is part of this, as it's born from your visceral beliefs. Values come from primal thoughts. We try our very best to pass those values on, and so they have history and heft to them. We built our systems on those values—adding more gravitas.

Just for now, I'd like you to step back and look from that bird's-eye view, like you've done before, and see the diversity of values in all the systems of your life. Is it possible for your way to be the only way that is true? If you hold to that without allowing respect for the individuals around you, it surely will be hard to connect in a deep and meaningful way.

E-valuate

Please take a moment to list the values most important to you. You can choose how many; just pick a number that you can work with, that feels relevant to you.

Next, please consider what you do when your values come up against something threatening.

Last, answer this question: Do you believe your values represent Truth? Consider defenses, personality, intelligences, and personal narrative in your response.

When you look at your values and responses to the action above, what reaction do you have? Can you engage with someone you respect about their thoughts and see if your responses differ? What would it mean to you if they do? Can you see how your values and beliefs about what you hold true impacts your ability to connect with others?

My responses to every single action in this book, and that last one, would be vastly different if we compared me at twenty years old and me now. My life experiences, training, and general openness in my personality has utterly changed my responses. I began with responses that would have been certain and meant I eschewed entire ways of being/ thinking. I wanted to connect better with the world around me, so I had to transform. These are paths and questions only you can answer. If you can't respect the values of others, it will be hard to connect deeply.

Respect is a component of love.

You've concluded the self-awareness portion of the emotional success equation. We have a clearer version of you to take forward. Prepare to engage in the get-yelled-at-from-down-the-hall-just-for-being-you kind of education. You know where your defenses lie; try to stay in the yellow zone. Find insight from new information. Get educated.

Thank you for being open to exploring who you are—your personality, identity, intelligences, learning styles, values, personal narrative, and defenses. We've covered the deep and the shallow, small and large, known and maybe previously unknown. With all of this, we are ready to talk about how you can educate yourself. Let's add shared language and some information to the mix! Onward! To education!

CHAPTER 4

Check Yourself Before You Wreck Yourself

Connections are less meaningful if you lack the tools to successfully communicate. Education gives us a shared language to explore complex topics. In this chapter, we will fill your toolbox with psychological know-how! Let's explore identity development, the importance of in-group/out-group phenomena, unconscious bias awareness, and privilege. Emotional success depends on knowledge of many kinds of people and ways of being.

"Education is the most powerful weapon with which you can use to change the world."

—Nelson Mandela

There were three ways I learned to be a psychologist. One you already know: getting yelled at down the hall. Second was traditional classroom learning: ten years of graduate school, and some of it stuck. The most salient of those lessons I share with you in this section: the third and final variable in the emotional success equation, empathy, I honed by doing therapy. I've tried to thoughtfully bring you through each of those experiences to increase your chances for emotional success.

Education can look like many things, but without a level of shared knowledge, empathy and social skills will only get you so far. People have big reactions to the word *education*. You might be flooded with memories, associations, thoughts, and feelings—assumptions about what education means and the direction we might head together.

Here, we take your new and improved self-awareness and sprinkle on more psychological secrets. We will focus heavily on identity as it is the thread that pulls together all of you. Identity is private and it is also public. Education here includes the theories that explain the way your identity translates to the groups you are a part of, and what that means.

Psychologists know education provides space from deeply emotional topics. In therapy, we call this intellectualizing—to take something emotional and overthink it. We would rather you didn't do this on our couch, but the ability to shift from heart to head when you want to is a key to emotional success. If you don't have education around these intense subjects, you're left with reacting only by what you know, and everyone can learn more. Education gives you perspective on how you can connect better with others by understanding certain human phenomenon.

Let's take your increased self-awareness and add more facts that help psychologists frame some of the hardest things about humanity. The psychological secrets discussed in this chapter are learning theory, social identity development, and unconscious bias awareness. We move from the inside toward the outside here. Let's take all those moving bits of you, add new ideas, then plunk you into society.

We start your education with the basics of how you learn. In chapter 1 we discussed types of intelligence and learning styles. These all fall under the umbrella of what we call "cognitive psychology." Cognitive psychologists are very interested in how people think. Part of how people think is learning. This doesn't sound sexy, but you'd be surprised how much cognitive psych surrounds you in your daily life.

Marketing theory, for instance, is built on these concepts. What ads you see, how social media operates, where you choose to shop—all these choices are influenced by marketing, whether you admit it or not.

I want you to be in on the secret. Therefore, we will start with learning theory. We build on your awareness of self, intelligences, learning styles, and general ideas about how this all develops. Remember, learning styles and intelligence are about how you obtain and process information. Learning theory is what your brain does with it next.

LEARNING THEORY

Academia is almost my religion, and my personality is so open that my father says my brain might spill out. I'm inclined to love new ideas.

Once you are self-aware about how you function in your interior world, you need to internalize a shared language and understanding to increase your emotional success. Education can be formal, in a classroom. This is what many people think of when I say "education." Let's broaden your understanding to include any ways you gather new information. You are educated when you travel, read, talk to new people, watch a documentary, and remain open to different experiences.

I understand the "ugh" reaction to *education*. I love school now, and I enjoyed it as a small child—but everywhere in the middle was rough. By sixth grade, social difficulties, surgeries, and harder material dampened my enjoyment. I began to prefer extracurricular adventures. I spent most of my downtime memorizing Madonna songs and dreaming about the future. This went on throughout middle and high school, until I was lucky enough to go to college and find out I could study things that made me feel excited. Suddenly, I was a dedicated student.

This makes sense because when things are too hard or you aren't interested, your ability to remember things is weakened. On the other hand, when you are excited and open to new ideas, you make and store memories directly into long-term storage (which has no limit and never expires!).

> *If you are interested and open, you are going to learn and retain more information.*

Learning helps you to live better. As you build new neural pathways, your brain gets better at making connections; thus, your intelligence and understanding of your world grows. The idea that cognitive decline is synonymous with aging is simply not true. When people create a culture where the elderly are kept away from new information without being integral to daily life, depression, loneliness, and cognitive decline tend to soar. Is this universal? No! Though it is common and is also a good metaphor for everyone. If you keep the *new* at bay, your mind will literally work into its same old patterns, and, eventually, it will be difficult to learn.

> *When we learn it tickles our brain.*

Think back to your personality and learning styles. If you tend to be quite open, you are more likely to take an active approach to education. Based on what we know about memory, you're also going to retain more information. In France about 100 years ago, there was a very hardworking psychologist named Jean Piaget. He came up with an idea to explain how people take in new information called *schema* (among many other theories that we use as the bedrock for developmental psychology to this day). Schema is what we call places in your mind where you store new information. According to Piaget, it takes work and time to create new schema.

When I teach about cognitive psychology in my Psych 101 class, I refer to schema as boxes. Imagine as a baby you've got all this information to process—you need a sorting system. There are boxes laid out everywhere, and you're making new boxes all the time. You get a piece of data: a ball. You make a box called *Ball*, and it includes everything round, colorful, fun. Later that same week, you go to a pumpkin patch. Momma picks up a pumpkin and you point and say, "Ball!" See how that classification system happens? That's because you built a schema for *Ball* and then try to shove everything in there; that's called assimilation.[12] When the new item doesn't fit, you must accommodate, and build a new box. You do this a zillion times a day—building new boxes, shoving ideas into boxes (mostly right but sometimes wrong), and generally sorting your way through the world.

There is no quality control system to see if you put things in the right boxes—aside from your own continued learning. I hope you can see how schema can quickly translate to relationship satisfaction. Once you make a box, it is real work to stop packing it and to create a new one. The implications for lack of continued learning are staggering. Instead of new pathways, you form shortcuts, which become "ruts." These are patterns, and you get stuck. When you stop learning, your perception of everything you see and hear is colored by outdated and underinformed thinking. You cannot have emotional success without continuously learning about how people operate. You must also engage in the less formal but ongoing education of individuals in your lives. Educating oneself is a never-ending walk into curiosity park.

---

12   The term assimilation has been used to discuss the importance of oppressed cultures to assimilate to the dominant culture for centuries. Let's note the history of the word and try, as we can, to apply it in the way Piaget presented, to mean "pull together" rather than what has largely meant "whitewash" to many people and cultures.

Assimilation	Accommodation
Saw this round orange thing for the first time (pumpkin).	Existing Schema: She has a round orange ball.
Existing Schema: She has a round orange ball.	Someone points out that this is a fruit called a pumpkin, though it is round and orange.
Child will call this round orange thing a ball.	Realizes that all round orange things are not balls.

As you work through this chapter, this book, your life, you'll either be assimilating this new information into boxes you've already built or creating brand-new schemas and connecting the ideas with other things you already know. Either way, it's work, and again, being open to it will yield the best results.

You're either assimilating and accommodating, or you are shoving things into schemas where they don't fit. Education is a handy tool to help us create new schema without having to work through all the hard stuff with other humans, and also to help us have appropriate ways of approaching others in order to be most open to each new situation and person. If you constantly try to fit human beings into the schema you developed long ago, you can easily see that deep and meaningful connections are unlikely.

Create New Schema

Before we move on, let's assess how open you are to this new information and to assimilating/accommodating. The outcome is less important than knowing where you stand as you begin. Take a deep breath, and please answer by making an X on the continuums as fast as possible, then step back and review.

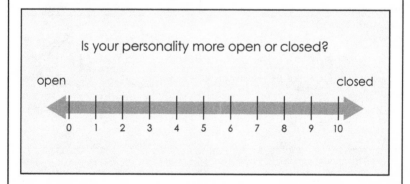

Is your personality more open or closed?

open   closed

0   1   2   3   4   5   6   7   8   9   10

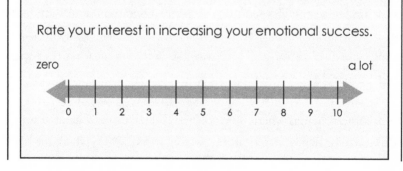

Rate your interest in increasing your emotional success.

zero   a lot

0   1   2   3   4   5   6   7   8   9   10

What is your desire to connect more deeply with the people in your life?

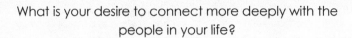

How much do you like the word education?

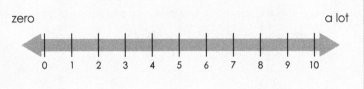

How much do you like the word assimilating?

How much do you like the word accommodating?

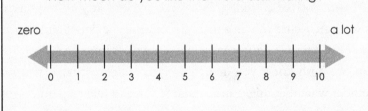

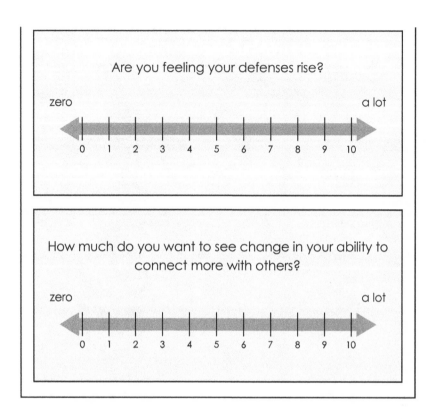

Thank you for engaging. Now take a glance at your responses to know if you're currently in a place to continue, or skip it and return at a more open time. I don't want to waste anyone's time, and if you aren't open, we both know you aren't going to remember what you read. Consider what that might mean, and feel free to make up other words to use if education, assimilation, or accommodation have negative connotations for you. Unless your responses reveal a readiness to take it in, put the book down and go do something else. It will still be here when/if you find yourself in a more open stance. When you are ready, we are going to make new boxes.

Now we know how your brain takes in information and that whether you are more likely to prefer assimilation or accommodation is largely based on your personality type. Does that make sense? If you are more open versus closed, making new boxes is likely your way of operating (accommodation), while the more closed or rigid among us will likely prefer to add new info to boxes they already have (assimilation). The aspects of self and identity all play and work together. Let's take what we know about identity and development from chapter 2 and add some education onto that self-awareness. We have schema/boxes for these concepts; now let's fill them up, and maybe make some new ones too!

SOCIAL IDENTITY THEORY

"In the social jungle of human existence, there is no feeling of being alive without a sense of identity."

—Erik Erikson

Take a step back. All the different aspects of your identity function at the same time and space within systems you are a part of—like your body and all the small and large operations occurring at the same time. It is complicated. Here's another image to show *how* complicated you are, using a slightly different model that allows us to see the pure complexity of human development.

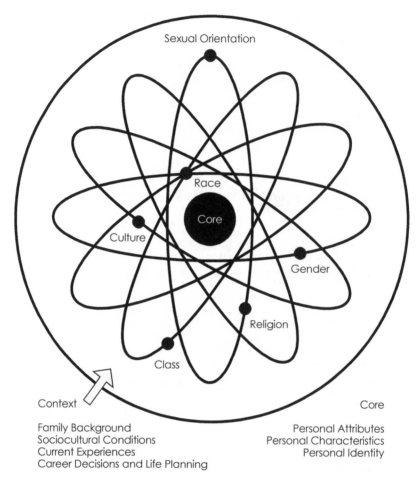

Adapted from the work of Jones and McEwen (2000).

Of course, this entire process and all the movement shown here has been summarized into one theory, to help discuss the concepts without your brain leaking out. I want you to know this foundation is to help you understand that you can be quite accomplished in one area of development and perhaps need growth in another. And so you can adopt the notion that everyone is working, and perfection is never the goal. Thoughtful progress over perfection—that's my motto.

How you navigate development of all the parts of yourself is complex. And it is essential to your success as a human being. How does this complicated, constantly changing ecosystem—*you*—interact with the world? In 1979, British social psychologists Henri Tajfel and John Turner created *social identity theory* to summarize all the moving pieces, and to talk about how the many processes add up to some essential human interactions. They take the complex model of yourself within systems and simplify it to two components: *personal identity* and *social identity*.

Personal Identity = How you see *yourself*
Social identity = What *groups* you belong to

Social identity theory is amazing, and I could've started the book here, but it is important for you to see the bigger picture of where the theory comes from. We had to build all the schema first: aspects of identity, personality theory, development of all these—all the things that make up "personal identity" that we have explored together. And now we will assimilate/accommodate social identity development into ideas we've worked on together. We are going to build new ways of seeing who you are and where you belong—a.k.a., your social identity.

Whatever groups you belong to make up your social identity. There are identity-based groups (good thing you just explored aspects of identity) and group memberships based on other factors. This is obviously not an exhaustive list, just a starting place.

Identity-Based Groups

Race
Ethnicity
Sex
Gender
Sexual orientation
SES
(Dis)ability
Culture

Other Group Memberships

Actual groups
Geographic area
Age cohorts
Alma mater
Sports teams you support
Religious affiliation
Country/social club
Hobby
Political affiliation
Values

Exploring Social Identity

Let's revisit your identity. Please consider the group memberships chart above as well as aspects of self that we worked on in chapter 2. As always, try to answer from your gut. Visceral responses are the most honest. Answering in this way helps us to get intrinsic ways of thinking rather than more "buttoned-up" responses. We can't get to the nitty-gritty if you clean up the mess before we get it in the open. Try to be as honest as possible. All humans engage in groups to survive and thrive. I already know you love your group best, and there's no reason to deny that here. (Go Steelers!)

Please list the groups you belong to:

Now, please go back to each of those groups and think about these questions:

Do most of your friends also belong to these groups?

How does membership in this group make you feel?

Do you celebrate or hide your membership in this group?

How have your feelings about membership in this group changed throughout your life?

> How do you feel when you think of the "opposite" or counterpart to your groups (e.g. liberal/conservative)?
>
> Has group membership ever given you something you didn't earn or, in reverse, a problem to solve that otherwise would not have existed? Both?

This exercise can be more difficult than it seems. I made a joke about "Go Steelers" at the start of the exercise—when really it is so much deeper than team affiliation. When you look at the sports teams you support, for example, it might seem surface level, but teams often represent much deeper meanings and a sense of belonging than you realize. In Pittsburgh, the expectation to love the Steelers, an American football team, is so strong that every Friday during football season, the entire town dresses in team colors. The Steelers are tied to our history. Celebrating the team links us to one another and our past. When actual steel production (and jobs) dwindled, for a long time the team was the only way the city found success. This has been true of many sports teams throughout history. Domestic abuse calls increase 10 percent when any home team loses. When "their" team loses, the abuser's defenses come up, and they act out. That is how tied sports/teams/group memberships can be to your essence of self, your ego.

That's just sports. When I think about groups I belong to, I love being Italian (though I'm only 25 percent), I love France, I'm liberal (surprise!), an academic, a psychologist. It's funny—just writing those words makes me feel proud, warm, happy, centered, and connected. When I think of the "opposite" of some of those, I feel angry, uncertain, and warm in a bad way. You can judge those reactions in yourself—which you know will lead to shame, guilt, shutting down. Or you sit with them and acknowledge that your reactions helped people survive when clans ruled the world and membership equaled a chance to keep living and passing on DNA. It doesn't get more basic than that. Let's take this information about yourself and layer on some more education to focus the picture even more.

Social Identity Theory in Your Life

I love social identity theory because it sums up so many of the concepts we've worked through in a clear way! In your life, you go along with your personal identity as well as your social identity. Both are key to how you see yourself and the reason that your parents don't want you to hang out with people they don't approve of: you become like the people around you. Human beings are so social that their brains are hardwired with special neurons called *mirror neurons.*

Mirror neurons help you identity how people act and what you should do in order to fit in with the group. These special cells are what make babies interested in the human face more than any other sight. Have you ever noticed yourself sitting the exact same way as the person you're talking with? Mirror neurons! They help you fit in because being part of the crowd equals success. When you use your mirror neurons, they multiply! The more you engage in deep connections, the better you get at connecting!

This makes evolutionary sense. Human beings realized that when they stick together, their survival rates are higher. People who are pushed out of the group are more likely to die. It cannot be overstated how essential to survival your social identity is. Let's use this theory to better understand what it means to be part of a group.

Social identity has personal and social components. Let's talk about how it works and what it looks like in real life. Psychologists use social identity theory to explain how groups interact. Humans use social identity in three ways. The first is called *social categorization*—your personal and social identities we've discussed throughout. You could also call this *aspects of identity* and/or *group memberships*. Social categorization is the work we've done in this chapter and book to this point.

What do you do with those memberships and identities? We call this *social identification,* which allows you to easily sort everyone else. Of course, you don't just have a team, right? You play other teams, and the competition is a key aspect of continued support of your team! Each time you win, your group is bolstered, you celebrate, have rituals, feel close to the other fans. This is called in-group.

Everyone else is out-group.

You have your social identities and social identification (who is in/out); then you begin to compare. This is rivalry, presupposing traits of the "others." Now that you can quickly sort others through social identification, you begin to employ *social comparison*—which ranges from thinking another team stinks all the way to unthinkable acts like genocide.

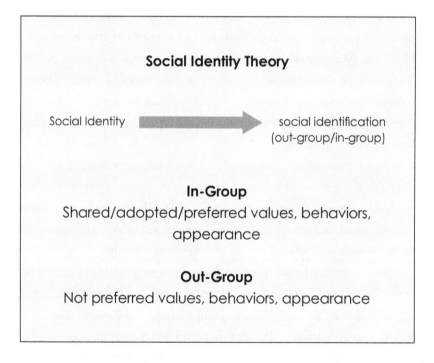

Social Identity Theory

Social Identity ➡️ social identification (out-group/in-group)

In-Group
Shared/adopted/preferred values, behaviors, appearance

Out-Group
Not preferred values, behaviors, appearance

When you think back to your own group memberships, you can now refer to yourself as in-group/out-group. It is natural to seek other humans who you think are "the best" and then to emulate the way they think and act. You can begin to see how you naturally value people like yourself and are more wary of "others."

Theorems

Belonging is good.
Someone is always on the outside .
On the outside = isms[13]

In-group and out-group are also words that describe dominant and oppressed groups. Using the list of identities we started with earlier, let's be clear (based on the research) about which groups are dominant and which are oppressed. The chart isn't up for debate; the values of the dominant groups are prized above the oppressed group, whether you agree or not. In fact, in the case of most identities on this list, the dominant group is in fact the minority (see White, male, Eurocentric, etc.).

---

13   Rac*ism*, sex*ism*, heterosex*ism*, etc. I call these the "isms." This is the "othering" of fellow humans through social comparison and the use of in-group/out-group membership to benefit the dominant group. When you see *isms* written through the book, I am referring to this phenomenon, not just the ones listed here.

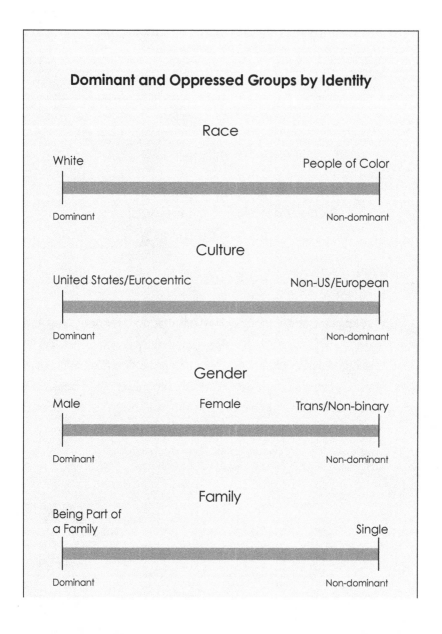

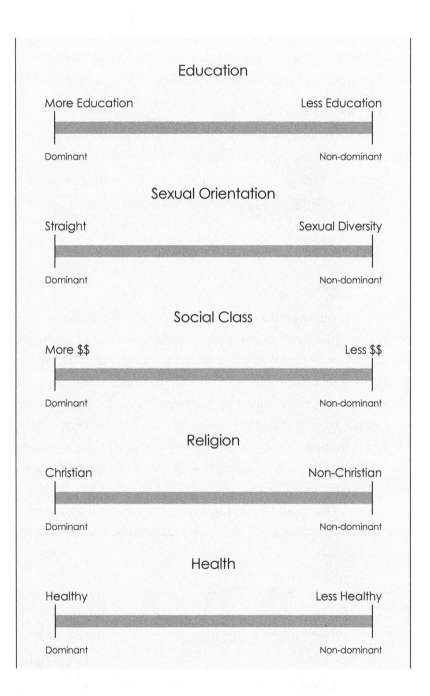

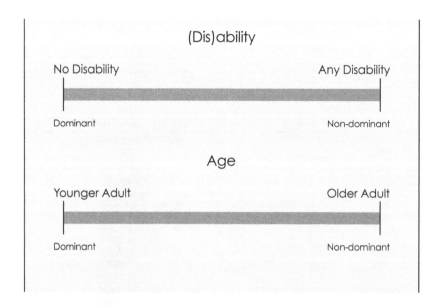

Anytime people are part of the dominant group and use a stereotype of the oppressed group to ensure the dominance of their own group, that is promoting an *ism* (remember, racism, sexism, etc.). Examples: telling racial jokes meant to make a group look bad; retelling a story where a stereotype is a central theme; engaging in discussions about how women aren't as skilled in math or able to be good leaders; making fun of or limiting someone due to a physical limitation; expecting that an elderly person is incapable of a task due to their age; assuming someone's religion equates to certain beliefs; believing that all people really want to have children and have negative feelings if they aren't a member of a couple, etc. All these behaviors shore up the status quo, and the status quo is the chart above.

Theorems

All systems want to maintain status quo.

Whether we are discussing your family, school, community, or gigantic social systems, all systems in nature work toward maintaining homeostasis. It's like nature has a cheeky quote painted on the wall in her living room: "If it ain't broke, don't fix it." The problem is, while that is a great system in nature, humanity gets a little bungled up. It feels to me as though culture and technology move faster than human brains can keep up. People have glorious, tangled webs of interaction, but their basic functioning resembles caveman reactions at times. We are here together in this book to navigate the webs and sort through those jumbles.

Carl Jung often discussed the idea of the *collective unconscious*; when I see films and books representing an idea repeatedly, it speaks to the things everyone is generally afraid of, deep inside. Zombies, for instance—"us versus them," right? Ghosts, any war film—it's always *us* versus *them*. The ironic thing is that at the end of the day, all human beings have the exact same needs and wants. Which is how these scary tropes work. They are based on universal fears.

All human beings want to be safe and loved. And for their clan to be safe and loved.

When you throw in fear, greed, power, poor choices, anger, impulsiveness, etc., you get all the heartache that exists. When you keep your shared needs in mind, the work of connecting with others becomes easier. I hope you are beginning to see how group membership strengthens you and at the same time can limit those who may be "out-group." Let's work on this.

BIAS AND PRIVILEGE

Humans are social creatures. Everyone does their best when they have social support. Without feelings of belongingness, you can die. With constant reminders of being out-group, many people live harder and less fulfilling lives. This is bias. When you get more resources, help, or are propelled forward by your group membership, we call it privilege.

- Out-group = Oppressed Group ➔ Bias
- In-group = Dominant Group ➔ Privilege

These equations are true for all the groups to which you belong. Small and large groups, from classrooms to governments. "You're either with us, or against us." Some group memberships you can make, add to, or change, while others are intrinsic to who you are, and there's nothing you can do to alter them. And don't forget, since human beings are gloriously complicated in some ways, and part of many different systems, you belong to more than one group at a time!

Intersectionality = Multiple group membership (*at the same time*)

You don't belong to just one group, do you? Whoever you are, you're more than one thing. All those different pieces are called *intersectionality*. If you refer to the infographic "Multiple Dimensions of Identity" in this same chapter, you can see the complexity of all the various ways you interact with the world. This is what intersectionality looks like! Failing to understand multiple-group membership (intersectionality) is why many people find the idea of White privilege, for example, confusing and thus reject the idea (it may also have to do with shame, fear, defenses, or denial, and that's okay too). Let's say you are White and struggle financially. If you have low socioeconomic status, you belong to a group that experiences bias and oppression, even though being White has benefits. Both things are true at the same time. The existence of one aspect of identity does not cancel out the other. Intersectionality is a burgeoning area, and there is much to read and discover; please, go and dive right in. When you're ready, let's look at how your social identities look from a bias/privilege perspective.

Intersections

Refer to the list of identities below. Please look and circle which applies to you—or if neither are quite right, put off to the side how you identify. If you are not on the continuum, it usually means that it is not a dominant trait. Once you have completed the list, try to just sit with it. We are simply collecting information now, and we will take plenty of time to process this work throughout the next chapter especially. If something surprises you, note that, because you've been living with these identities most of your life. That's one of the funny things about human beings; we can be oblivious to our own reality because, as they say, sometimes you can't see what's in front of you. Don't overthink it. Just select where you are, and let's be educated about that reality.

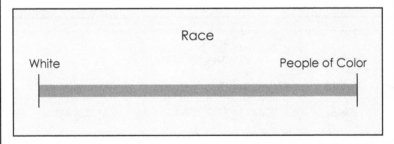

Race

White   People of Color

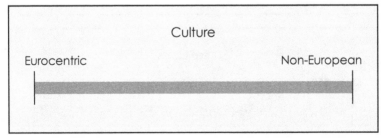

Culture

Eurocentric   Non-European

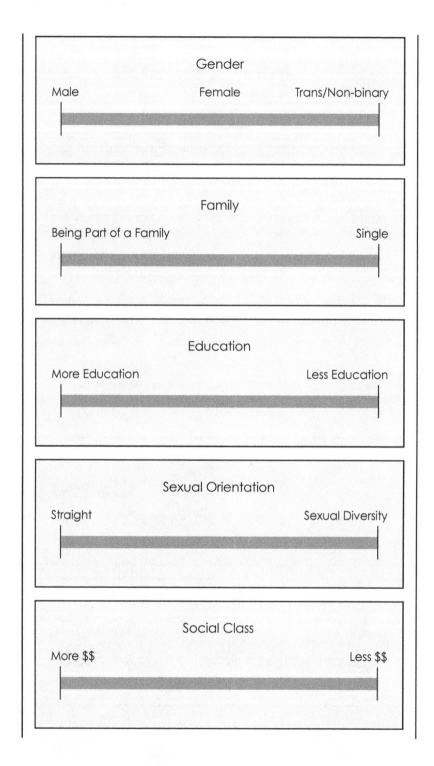

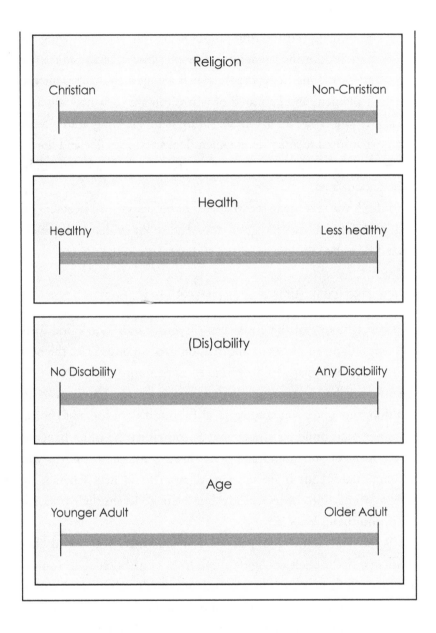

I hope that by looking at where you are in the in-group/out-group, oppression/dominance chart above in an objective way, you have gained some knowledge and yet remain open to the journey. No matter where your *X*s are, everyone experiences variation on that chart. Some are almost all toward one side, while others are smacked up against the other end of the spectrum. And just knowing this, acknowledging the reality of these differences that impact people's lives in great and terrible ways (and everything in between), is such a huge step that I want you to take a moment and be proud of where you are right now. Because no matter who you are, if you are sitting here, knowing a little more about what social identity development looks and feels like and how it operates to keep some in charge and others controlled, and you can be honest about it all.

I think you're ready to see what gifts or burdens your placement on each of those identities has given you. And to know that each person has a different constellation of bias and privilege in their lives.

Unconscious Bias Awareness

Sorting is one of the great tasks of your mind. Your mind sorts through billions of pieces of information each second. Does the new information assimilate, or do you need to accommodate for the new idea? Remember, accommodating takes more energy. Isn't it easier to put things in a box you already have? Even if it's not the best choice, it's easier than building a new box. Accommodating often happens in the front of your mind and is not always automatic. When you accommodate, your brain must work to create a new schema. By shoving things into boxes quickly, bias helps to lessen the workload. Thus, your brain loves it.

Remember, status quo, path of least resistance. Your mind likes shortcuts. So implicit thoughts come from your brain stem (quick, assimilate information into a preexisting box!), while explicit bias generally involves your conscious mind (hmm . . . that idea doesn't quite fit; I think I need a brand-new schema). It looks like this:

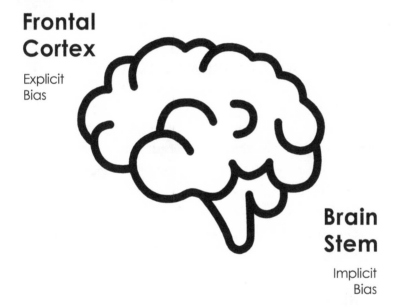

Implicit Bias = Unconscious

Explicit Bias = Conscious

Frontal Cortex

Explicit Bias

Brain Stem

Implicit Bias

Unconscious bias awareness training is big business in Silicon Valley, and in corporate culture in general. I'm weary of this trend because many times people will learn they have this unconscious bias (even though it's been there all along, helping you to live and thrive) and suddenly they feel *shame*. Shame, then denial, then *no more communication*. There's research which illustrates that when you introduce the idea of bias but then don't frame the new understanding with additional education, you are left with a bunch of shamed, denial-loving executives and techsters.

If the information in this chapter has you feeling defensive, take a step back. I'm here to offer secrets to help you reach emotional success, not have you shut down. If you are defensive, consider we are just talking about concepts. No one is judging *you*. If your defenses have risen, it is because you've taken some information personally. Try to separate that reaction if you can. Remember, the ability to see these psychological secrets without getting too emotional is the central theme of the book. If intellectualizing the ideas helps you to engage and consider new information, you are accommodating. Congratulations!

IN-GROUP (DOMINANCE) + BIAS + ACT ON BIAS = ISMS

Why are we pulling together so much about who you are and how you operate in the world? To help you navigate all this new data. To use it to connect more deeply with others, versus shutting down. Everyone has bias. And when you have in-group status (dominance) *and* bias *and* you act on that bias . . . that's where isms are born. To be in-group is *real* power, and that is why you must know yourself. You're ready to see some of your own bias. The best way to do this is to tap into your unconscious mind.

Implicit Awareness Tests

Have you ever taken a *Cosmo* quiz? Or one of those quizzes on Facebook that will tell you which Harry Potter house you belong to? One of the reasons those are not reliable or valid is because the person taking the test can see the outcome. Often, you'll take these sorts of quizzes realizing, *Oh, if I pick the picture of the mountains, I'm probably going to be in Gryffindor* . . . See how you're trying to shape the outcome? Scientists don't want you to shape the outcome of their measure, or it's ineffective.

Therefore, when studying bias, psychologists at Harvard came up with the Implicit Awareness Tests (IAT). The IATs force you to quickly make choices based on implicit (back of brain/unconscious) responses to questions. This way, you can have a clear answer as to where your biases lie. You can't cheat the system. IATs have been proven to be reliable and are therefore the gold standard when assessing bias. The IATs now measure dozens of different types of bias a person can have—and I want you to learn a little more about your own bias before we close out this chapter and move on. Anytime I consult with a company, we use this exercise as a starting place for important conversations around the inevitable bias everyone has. You can use it to start discussion with the people in your life as well.

Implicit Bias Awareness

Please go to the Harvard Project Implicit website. Read through the goals of the project, the type of research being conducted, and anything else that feels relevant to you. If you feel continued interest, you can click through to take a test. You do not need to include your contact information, and it is free of charge. At the conclusion of the assessment, you will be given a summary of results based on current research in the field. I would like to ask you to engage in at least one of the tests to answer the questions below.

Which IAT did you take?

Why did you choose that one?

What reactions did you have to taking the test?

Did the results differ from your expectations?

What do the results tell you about how you connect with other people, specifically the people impacted by that particular bias?

I hope this exercise has helped you to see where some of your own biases lie, and how they may impact how you connect with others. I can't make it clearer— every person has bias. Feeling shame or guilt over your results will only make your ability to connect with others more difficult. Remember . . .

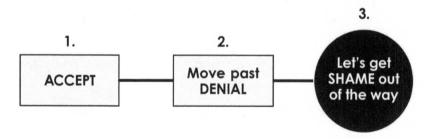

YOU'VE CHECKED YOURSELF. DON'T WRECK YOURSELF.

We are moving away from the path of fear and shame. At this point in your journey, your arms are getting heavy with self-awareness, self-knowledge, and psychological secrets—concepts to help you process what's next. Next is the part of the discussion that will require every bit of work we have done to this point; it is the chapter where I offer up more theories, theorems, and statements that explain how you shape your world and one another's experiences.

Now you know a little more about your personality, defenses, areas of growth, what general identity development looks like, and whether you might experience oppression or be in a more dominant role in the systems of your life. And we have assessed the surface of where some of your biases may lie. Let's take it all and move on. You're ready.

CHAPTER 5

Hot Topics in Humanity 101

Welcome to the meat of the book. This is it, people. The moment I have been building up to and preparing you for in all the ways I know how. If this book were a yoga class, this chapter would be the heavy work, and the rest of the book is closer to *shavasana* (the lying-down, connecting-with-the-universe time). Every single aspect we have discussed to this point will come into play. Your aptitudes and intelligences, yep. Personality type, yep. Values, yes, yes, yes. Defenses . . . *yes*. All your history, attributes, aspects of your identity, narrative, ancestors—it is all here, and I'll ask you to somehow keep it front of mind, hold it in your working memory, be able to acknowledge when you see a roadblock, and, without judgment, press forward.

This chapter is designed to move you from a general understanding of personal and social identity development toward how they impact your life and the people around you. Psychological secrets in this chapter include racial identity development and the theory of moral disengagement. As a metaphor, your goal is to be more cognizant of the air you breathe and to make a choice about what you let in and give out.

Everyone can be more loving and less "lazy" about their automatic thoughts. Let's engage your core principles that make you want to connect with other humans and do this! Some of you may think you are "already there" . . . huh. I have found that like much of development, this process is cyclical. I think I'm past something, and then, hello! Here I am having an unwanted automatic thought again. I'm pretty sure everyone can improve. I know I can.

All therapists-in-training take classes with a focus on identity. I've taken those classes as a student and taught them as a professor. The course is designed to alter your perspective and completely shift your paradigm from wherever you are in your identity development to a new level. Programs that train therapists tend to utilize these courses as guideposts to discern whether students are prepared to be multiculturally competent in their work. To be multiculturally competent means you are compelled to constantly consider and openly explore all aspects of culture and identity with your client, and that you also continue to do this work with yourself. The importance of multicultural competence cannot be understated. Without multicultural competence, the counselor could do harm to potential clients. It is a big deal.

Success in the "multicultural" class looks like openness, lowered defenses, willingness to learn from others, and a basic understanding of racial and sexual identity development models, as a start. You obviously can't be released into the therapy wild if you don't have these skills. I've always thought it would be helpful for students to know what faculty *really* are looking for—openness, willingness to assimilate *and* accommodate. Aren't these goals *everyone* ought to share, regardless of profession?

OPEN AND WILLING TO LEARN

What does emotional success have to do with multiculturalism? Everything. The goal of high emotional success is to connect better. Identity is the thread that holds your personal and social lives together.

It is a string straight from your ego to the systems you live in. Honestly discussing all the parts of identity in a calm, clear, and open way that lets you move past fear and shame is the *only* way to find emotional success. Everyone experiences bias and privilege. If you ignore people's differences (and you can, if you have privilege), meaningful connection is impossible. In fact, if you think you're connecting but fail to see where your bias/ privilege may push up against the other person, connection will falter. If you are part of the dominant group, you may not notice this! When you do notice, this is what is meant by "woke"[14] . . . as if you've been sleeping in a matrix-like dream of privilege. Even if you are woke, you will still make missteps. Continue to work. Be open. Acknowledge what you don't know. This is the string that ties your ego to the world. It will get tugged. Keep going.

Like all those therapy students, I ask you to be open to bias and privilege in your life. You will move to the other side of the chapter slightly changed, and more able to deeply connect. No small goal, but it can be done. We are about to do it.

How we impact the world
How the world impacts us

Here, we add two new psychological secrets to our toolbox. These are challenging for graduate students who focus on inner growth all day, so give yourself grace if this is new to you! Together, we explore a specific aspect of identity development—racial identity. Of all the types of identity development, I chose this because it is that important. Secondly, we will take the in-group/out-group knowledge you've built

---

14   I've seen words like *social justice* and *woke* be used in a negative way lately. To me, these words make me feel kind, like my purpose is to connect. I suppose by reappropriating the words and making them seem small or even silly reveals that others don't see these words as positives but rather something to make fun of. I'm not sure how making fun of something leads to increased communication and connection. If you're poking at something you disagree with for a cheap laugh, or to belittle someone else, I'd ask you to consider why. It might grow your connection with your in-group peers in the moment, but does it make you feel good? Just wondering. It doesn't usually make me feel good when I do that.

and discuss what psychologists call *moral disengagement*. Together, these two new psychological secrets will round out the education variable in our emotional success equation.

I've asked y'all before to consider systems theory. Please pull it to the front of your mind. Consider the narratives of your life within the systems all around you. You don't act the same everywhere you go! This is called *code switching*, and it is normal. Although you are basically the same, different aspects of your identity surface if you are at home, work, house of worship, or out with friends. Let's explore some life events that you maybe didn't include in the big five but are worthy of further exploration in this context.

Earlier, I asked you to "intellectualize" anytime you felt defensive. Now, let's switch gears, and if you are ready, let's all try to move closer to emotional reactions. I wanted you to grasp the concepts before we added heat. Now we are turning on the fire. You're ready. Your defenses will likely kick into gear. Good for them. They're doing their job. If it helps you, you can switch back and forth between using your defenses and attempting to remain open. Just please try to be aware of those defenses. Jot them down, or just watch them go by, without judgment—in fact, maybe with gratitude. Attempt to stay in the yellow zone here, so if this is too easy for you, figure out a way to dig deeper, and if it's in the red zone, take a step back.

As always, this work may bring up thoughts and/or unfinished business that require a therapist. If so, seek a helper and make an appointment. When you have the appropriate support scaffolding in place, go at your own pace.

Discussions of identity can be triggering. Identity trauma is real. Racism, sexism, homophobia, intense bullying, etc., can lead to suicidal thoughts, and sometimes suicide. This topic is not a light one. If identity has been a difficult area in your life, please get support.

On the other hand, if this exercise brings up nothing for you, I suggest you aren't being open enough with yourself. It is unlikely you have never experienced both positive and negative reactions from others in your life related to your identity, no matter who you are or how you present to the world. This exercise is not a place for self or other judgment but a way to sort through the reality of experience so you can be better prepared to meet yourself and others where you—and they—are, and to connect better in that authentic space.

Leave your (self) judgment at the door.

Exploring Bias and Privilege in Your Life

Take a minute to think of some defining moments in your life. It may help to look back at your responses from earlier exercises in chapter 4 ("Intersections" or "Implicit Bias Awareness," for example). Imagine how your responses may be different from other people's—your neighbor, a coworker, a person in a different country. If you don't feel like you understand the task yet, it may mean you need a little more information, and that will come in the next few chapters. If that's the case for you, you can circle back around to this action after some more reading. Give it a try now, please, and see what you've got. Then you can always revise and update because everyone is growing here.

Describe instances when an aspect of your identity has led to you experiencing something negative (ranging from uncomfortable and/or distressing to trauma/abuse and/or ethically wrong treatment).

Describe instances when an aspect of your identity has led to you experiencing something positive (ranging from increasing your mood to more global/systematic benefits you may experience on an ongoing basis).

It can be grueling to think about moments you were treated poorly due to some aspect of your identity. This is what bias feels like.

You may have received something you didn't earn thanks to something you can't control. This is what privilege looks like.

Everyone experiences a mix of *both* bias and privilege!

> If we discuss Black Lives Matter, for instance, and you're not Black, it doesn't mean White (or any other) lives don't matter! #blacklivesmatter was created because the oppressed group (in this case) is aiming for equality . . . safety. When any oppressed group requests equality, please choose to see that as a bid to make things fair—not to get "special treatment."[15]

Thank you for working through the exercise. It will help you to consider how your values are lifted or challenged when you meet the world. It will also tie your understanding of your place in the world to your narrative. You can see that your narrative and values have some overlap with experiences of injustice or unasked-for gifts you have

---

15   While I'm in love with a retired NYPD police officer, it is important to note that "blue lives" and "Black lives" are not equivalent. A profession (being a police officer) is chosen and can change throughout life. A race (being Black, indigenous, or a person of color) is *not* a choice and is central to one's identity.

received in your life. Often, I see people forget that intersectionality means we experience *both* bias and privilege! Everyone does to greater and lesser extent, in different parts of their lives. It doesn't work out to be even, but I want you to know that all people do experience in-group *and* out-group dominance/oppression at times. Bias and privilege have altered your path. I would like to tell you a little about how my path has led to my own perception of bias and privilege, my values, and is deeply tied to my personal narrative. Sometimes when you hear another person's story, it can help you open to your own experiences without judgment. I offer this information about me not as good/bad or right/wrong way to be, simply as information about me and what I've experienced as an example of one human being trying to connect better with others based on who I am and where I come from. I hope it is a helpful narrative in prompting you to look at your own life.

A Story of Privilege

I start with my ancestors. I am an American to the extent that I have four grandparents who were each 100 percent whatever they were. Respectively, they were each Italian, Polish, Swedish, and German. The Germans came to America in the 1700s, and all I have left of the German heritage is one of my names. I don't know much at all about the Swedes; there's a story there, but this isn't the place or time. That leaves us with my maternal side—who were very recent immigrants, spoke the language of their motherlands, and felt deep pride in sharing and enjoying as much of the culture as they could with all of us many cousins. I *feel* Italian and Polish for these reasons, even though I grew up being identified as German and Jewish—and for a decade of marriage had an Irish name. These cultural connections shape my identity.

My parents both were the oldest in their families and proudly achieved the first associate degrees of anyone who had come before, as far as we know. They left the town they were raised in and which we visited often, on long car rides with grown-up talk that my brother and I absorbed. All that talk was filled with expectations and group norms our little family created. I used to feel I had been given all the amazing chances in my life because of my hard work. While I have worked hard, I now realize so much of my success was the result of my parents' toil, not my own—good choices they made about school districts, and their sacrifices, parental involvement, and giving us any opportunities they could find. I grew up thinking all of that—the great schools, safe neighborhood, chances to excel at things I am good at, loving support, and endless high expectations—were normal.[16] And the gift and privilege of it all was lost on me.

Seeing even beyond my family and community systems to the privilege I experienced as a White, straight, cis person was obviously not going to happen. Don't forget, for those of you who read the book in a linear fashion, I had this bum hip throughout my life and have always felt enormous pride in my ability to overcome those physical limitations. I felt in many ways as though I had made my way on my own merits, and I did . . . to some degree. In my twenties, my life narrative simply didn't allow for the idea that a pile of gifts I had never asked for had propelled me further than I could've gone on my own. In fact, not much had ever held me back.

I've alluded to this before; I'll iterate here fully—I was sure I was not privileged, and I felt "colorblind." The reason I believed I wasn't racist was thanks to holidays with my grandfather. He used family gatherings to share his endlessly racist views, using slurs and stereotypes over mashed potatoes. In middle school, I started standing up to him. Year after year, we were kicked out of holidays. Standing up to my grandfather felt huge to me. My parents didn't like how I spoke to him, but they backed me on what I said. I felt empowered and self-righteous. Who knows what my motivations were, but I felt in my heart that I wasn't racist.

---

16   Here's the funny thing about "normal." Humans tend to only see what they see. What your life is, you assume as "normal," and everything else is "not normal." Obviously if everyone feels this way, no one is "normal." Privilege happens when you are a part of the dominant group, so your normal gets forced on everyone else, even if that isn't what they prefer or what their culture, values, or history dictates.

In graduate school, faced with my own racial identity for the first time, it was very hard for me to begin to understand that I am actually . . . racist. That everyone is. That in-group and out-group leads to natural bias, and pretending it isn't there just makes it worse. Remember, push past that fear and shame; let's get denial out of the way. Because all the while I spoke up to my grandfather, I remained unaware, and thus complicit in, systems-level preference for White people over people of color. My ignorance, denying oppression still exists—that's racism too. It was difficult for me to imagine racism existed because I didn't *want* it to. I wanted it gone, and I imagined it was because I couldn't stomach it. The idea that people had been held back by it, or the idea that I had been propelled forward because of it, led to shame. Fear. Denial.

You can see how my narrative led me to believe that I wasn't privileged, I didn't act/feel/think racist thoughts, and I had earned everything I achieved just by my hard work.

A Story of Bias

In addition to realizing I experience privileges due to my race and socioeconomic status, I also came to understand that others have bias against me as a woman. Whereas I began life thinking all was fair and equal, I eventually began to understand my own intersectionality.

I grew up in a semirural, very White, solidly middle- to upper-middle-class town. Our schools were clean, safe, and new. Through a series of fortunate events, I ended up at a small, private women's college. Pushback from my family was immense. It was too expensive. Everyone said I would become a "lesbian feminist" . . . How's that for a one-two punch (in fairness, I was open to one and now identify as the other)? I took out loans and moved into the city. Ironically, through the privilege of my magic school, I became aware of bias in my life. Seminar classes with women authors from a woman's perspective grew my understanding. I suddenly saw that women experience bias against us. I hadn't known there were words for the differences I saw and felt around safety, expectations, societal norms, or representation in leadership.

I got mad. I'm still mad. Things I blindly accepted became painful, like religion and politics. In my own family, discussions became heated; sometimes they still are. I felt like someone had made me aware I was living in a fantasyland. Again, I rewrote my narrative to include this part of my story—a piece I didn't ask for or want but chose to acknowledge.

These awakenings into bias and privilege occurred for each aspect of my identity—and they continue to shift over time. This openness, sometimes painful but always liberating, I wish for you.

YOUR NARRATIVE

Again, I offer this brief narrative of my intersectionality as an example of one person's journey. As we've discussed, it helps to frame your experience to better understand your narrative, which colors your perspective and impacts your ability to connect with others.

Have you rewritten your narrative over time? What about a narrative considering the intersectionality of your identities and how they work in the context of your life? There may be parts of you that require development, and that's normative. Just keep swimming.

The next few actions build on one another. Let's approach the ideas of identity, bias, privilege, power, oppression, and dominance from different perspectives, with techniques to gain insight. My advice is to work through them all at once, with enough time to then sit and process them as a group of exercises. There are three in this sequence that work together. I've added extra room for reactions after the third one in the set is complete. Enjoy your growth, and good for you for doing work toward greater knowledge and connections.

(Re)writing Your Narrative

Please rewrite your life narrative as it relates to bias and privilege. I just offered mine to you— the where/how/when of what I've believed and why I felt I didn't experience bias or privilege. I know there's a story in you of how you've gotten to where you are, and whether race/sexuality/sex/gender/religion /physical health and ability/heritage, etc., played a role, and how. You have a clear identity story surrounding your experiences of bias/privilege, and now is a good time to write it down.

After you write it, please read it. Where did privilege/bias play a role? Are there places you didn't notice that point toward being a member of the dominant or oppressed group? Let's explore.

I hope working through your narrative from this perspective gives you new information. This work is essential to emotional success, and it is ongoing. No one is perfect, and everyone can grow. It happens to me all the time. A few weeks ago, I was working in my daughter's school, making thumbprints. I was working with all the little children, one after the other. Finally, I worked with a little girl who is Black. She wasn't talking much, and I realized on the third or fourth thumbprint that I was assuming that this child needed extra help. Sure, it was partly because of her silence. But let's be honest—it was her quietness combined with her being Black that led my mind initially (unconsciously) to all sorts of conclusions. I had assimilated her into a stereotype, which is just another word for schema. Without activating my frontal lobe, I unconsciously applied bias and decided she was poor, not very smart, and needed extra help. (!)

When I finally engaged my frontal lobe and realized the boxes I'd put her in, I felt like someone had hit me in the stomach. I stood up and took a second between thumbprints. I looked at this young girl, felt the fullness of the moment—my privilege and power over her in a million ways—and saw how it can all unfold, keeps unfolding. If she were White, I don't think I would've started helping her, which was effectively holding her back. And that is the truth. I may have assumed poverty, but isn't that another bias I have based on my history, my narrative? And so there it was. I reset and let her go, as I had with *Every. Single. Other. Child.* And guess what? My bias had been wrong. Here she was making perfect little thumbprints, and my White, dumbass self had been holding her back, expecting the worst. Whoa.

I could offer up all the excuses I thought of then and now. This was my defenses at work, and although some of them may be true . . . the facts remain. This at best is a *microaggression*. Microaggressions are moments like this—when no one gets "hurt" but assumptions are made, and dynamics shift. Isms are perpetuated by microaggressions (e.g. sexism, able-bodiedism, etc.).

Here's how—and why—my recalibration wasn't just overly sensitive "political correctness"[17] but rather essential for her well-being. Imagine people assuming you are incapable and not as intelligent, and constantly compensating by either doing things for you or not asking too much of you. You can see that over the course of a lifetime, this will alter your trajectory. What's more, when microaggressions are hurtful, we call this the "death by a thousand cuts." Moving along in life and then being reminded of the bias against you, even in supposedly safe spaces, is disturbing and exhausting.

Microaggressions build up and can lead to depression and other mental health difficulties. You can blow off a microaggression, as the oppressor or oppressed; that doesn't make it any less real.

---

17   Again, a term that was originally meant to mean something like "considering other people's preferences" that is now a punchline. I will reiterate that I consider being "PC," "woke," etc., to be another way of showing kindness to someone else. It costs us nothing and makes someone else feel good. Why not? I love a love party.

I share this with you for so many reasons. First, I've tried to do this work on myself a lot, and look what still pops into my brain when I'm busy, frazzled, or distracted. Everyone has work to do. It's not just race—*it could be any area where your biases show up.* Unconscious thoughts hang out with you all day, every day. I want you to know that even though it's normal to have bias, we can stop! Think! Change the trajectory of our actions, thoughts, feelings midstream and work toward connection. In this case, that meant me getting out of her way. Even as I write this a few weeks later, I feel shame creeping in and the desire to just cut these paragraphs. But that wouldn't help. That's me jumping into the fear shame/denial merry-go-round. So, for now, I leave it.

Now, it's your turn to be vulnerable and open. It's the only way to change and find deeper connections. Let's take those rewritten narratives I asked you to write and move to a more specific place.

Consider your various identities and how they operate in the world. Keep your rewritten narrative front of mind, being as open as possible, and let's see where we can get together. This is a less free-form, more specific way to get at these ideas of bias and privilege in your life.

Now it is time to literally draw a picture of who you are. In this chapter we've gone from the big story to the core beliefs that come from your story, and now to how other people see you in the world—the basic aspects of your identity that other people and systems bump up against every day.

Let's bring together all we have experienced so far together—what you now understand about your own defenses and ability to be open, systems theory, identity, and how these abstract concepts become very real features of your life. Let's get specific about who you are as a person and how you are seen by others so we can help you connect better and attain emotional success.

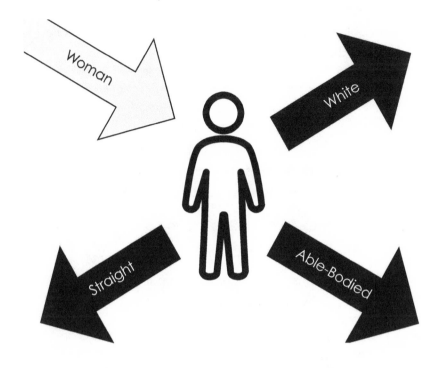

Let's pretend this figure is me. The white arrow pushing in on me represents a bias I experience. I am a woman. In this society, there are more benefits to being male than female. I have privilege. I am White, cis, mostly able-bodied, straight, and middle class, to name a few. These are the arrows I push out on others. Because I get privileges, it pushes on others. You can see that each person has their own makeup of bias against them as well as privileges they experience *at the same time*.

Privilege

Please draw a stick figure of yourself. Remember to include (1) arrows pointing in as bias you experience, and (2) arrows pointing out as privileges you have.

Let's look at all the actions in this chapter for a moment. Please consider them when answering the following questions.

Big Re-action

Are there any patterns or awareness you came to as you moved through the actions?

Did the process feel connected to you, or as though one built on, changed, added to another? Why or why not?

What feelings or reactions came up for you as you worked through the process?

Did any changes begin for you, or do you feel you are in the same place as when we began the actions?

My goal here is to get us buttoned up as much as possible and on the same page to move forward with additional education. The next part of the chapter is what the multicultural theories courses dig into.

SCIENCE OF IDENTITY

As I discussed earlier, identity development/formation is a huge and glorious area of study. Psychologists want to know more about each process, and that requires narrowing and then being more specific. Remember, there are developmental models for nearly every aspect of identity. We focus on racial identity models here because this psychological secret is *that* important to your emotional success.

Identity is always in the room, and if you come to awareness around this topic, it will naturally spread to other areas of identity development.

Identity Development Models

Racial

Black/African American Identity Model

Asian Identity Model

Latino/a/x Identity Model

Indigenous Identity Model

Multiracial Identity Model

Biracial Identity Model

Transracial Adoptee Identity Model

White Identity Model

Sex

Gender

Sexuality

Ethnicity

Health

(Dis)ability

Political affiliation

Work identity

Worldview

Specific professions
(counselors, pastors, doctors, etc.)

Religion

Age

Why Are All the Black Kids Sitting Together?

In the late 1990s, Beverly Daniel Tatum wrote a book called *Why Are All the Black Kids Sitting Together in the Cafeteria?*, and if you haven't read it yet, you should (she also authored the person of color racial identity development model below). The book describes racial identity development in people of color. Understanding racial identity development is key to emotional success because race is all around you and often one of the first things you notice about others . . . or that others notice about you. When I hear people talk about race, I can usually assess where they are in their racial identity development. If you're unaware of where you are, you're more likely to make inaccurate or harmful assumptions about people different from you. One assumption I've heard often is that Black people are racist because they group together in large gatherings—like school cafeterias. In reality, there are many reasons this occurs, including safety and a desire to surround oneself with similar people. This is a stage of racial identity development! It's not a slight to other humans; it's a natural progression. As they say on 1980s TV, the more you know.

The dominant group *cannot* experience the ism.

Black people aren't being racist when they sit together. There is no such thing as *reverse racism* or sexism aimed toward men, etc. This is simple. You may experience a slight, but the continuum doesn't change for one person. Please accommodate for this idea. Isms are system-wide, not person- or even small-group-of-people-wide. If you are a member of the dominant group, you don't get to say you experienced an ism. You didn't. What happened to you was not systematic but an unfortunate moment of bias, brought on not by an entire system but by one or a few people. Until the dominant group and oppressed become equal, there is no such thing as "reverse" anything. That's just life. In that aspect of your identity, you experienced privilege your entire life. A few instances of bias in that area don't cancel a lifetime of privilege, whether you knew you had privilege or not (even if the bias was something big like not getting a job or losing a friend—though unfortunate and unfair, it still doesn't permeate your entire life). If you have a reaction to that, please circle around and check your defenses. Also, look at whether you aren't assimilating and accommodating for this new information.

Often, people claim reverse racism when members of the dominant group can't understand why they are excluded from a place, gathering, etc., made up of members of the oppressed group. The initial reaction of feeling excluded often makes most of your defenses pop up. Remember, defenses are here to protect your ego, and fragility leads to breaks . . . not connections. It is totally natural for groups to want to create their own spaces—stadiums, sports bars, clubs; it happens everywhere. The dominant group sets the values, aesthetic, medical knowledge, leaders in every field, policies, style, behaviors, expectations, and social norms for whatever they have touched, throughout time. Therefore, if, like me, you grew up and existed most of your life in White-only, Christian-only, straight-only (it seemed), able-bodied spaces, then it doesn't feel like there are any dominant/oppressed differences; it just seems like it is "normal." Privilege is your reality matching with the dominant group, so you don't even notice that there is an in-group/out-group experience. Privilege is being in-group and not even being aware that others are on the outside, either forced to assimilate or not succeed in the paradigm created by the dominant culture. When you assume your worldview is *the* worldview, you deny yourself opportunities to both connect deeply and see what exists beyond yourself. I, like many people, grew up only seeing my world and assuming it was the entire world. But I was wrong.

Most of the world is brown, for instance. And not Christian. You get the picture. If you've gone your life feeling comfortable in most of the spaces you exist, it may not make sense why someone would need their own space, away from you. But if you're reading this and you have experienced bias or oppression, you've probably already skipped ahead. If you're still with me, please imagine a world in which everything is different than it is—flipped. If you are in an oppressed category, switch it. If you experience lots of privilege, switch it.

That's how others live, every day, in the setting you're imagining. Whoa. Right?[18]

Identity Development

Let's add some education to these ideas to build our shared language. All aspects of identity go through processes to reach wholeness or completion of a stage. Your process depends on whether you're the dominant or oppressed group. I'll offer two here so you can have a deeper understanding.

In graduate school at Boston College, I had the great fortune of meeting Dr. Janet Helms. Her work centers on racial identity development, especially for White people. Additionally, she helped me personally become a better person by being patient with my ignorant self. For a quick comparison, please see the following chart adapted from Amelia Hubbard's work, which strives to create best practices for Biology teachers. This image can help us better understand the types of racial identity development, based on one's racial make-up.

---

18   For more, watch *The Color of Fear* https://www.imdb.com/title/tt0484384/ the whole way through. It will be worth your time.

White Students (Helms, 1990)	Students of Color (Cross & Vandiver, 2001)
1. Contact Unaware of own race and little to no concept of racism	**1. Pre-encounter** Internalization of racist messages (personal significance unrealized)
2. Disintegration Aware of racism and uncomfortable with this topic	**2. Encounter** Coping mechanisms vary
3. Reintegration Victim blaming used to cope	**3. Immersion/emersion** Desire to be with members of own race and to learn more about African American experience
4. Pseudo-independent Pull between feeling that change must happen and confronting one's own discomfort	**4. Internalization** Reframe internalized messages with positive self-image of one's race
5. Immersion/emersion Seek out white role models who typify "anti-racist" stance	**5. Commitment** Commitment to solving problems faced by one's race
6. Autonomy Comfort in multicultural settings, positive association with change	

Whatever your identity, it helps to know where other people are too, so let's all look at both models. Try to acknowledge any defenses that come up, and simply read the information. Each status listed is based on factor analysis from reliable and valid measures. That means that many people were asked questions about identity, and these are the common themes that repeatedly came up. Read through both lists. Where are you? Are you surprised? Angry? In disbelief? Did it confirm what you already knew?

Let's break it down a little. First, as always, development is *not* linear. Phases may be long or short, depending on how much work a person does. For y'all, who are actively working, the stages could happen quickly.

Exploring Racial Identity Development Models

Please read through both models above to answer the following questions.

Thinking of the model that applies to you . . .

Which stage are you in?

Is it the stage you want to be in?

Were you surprised by the stage you are in?

What do you think you can do to maintain your current area or move along in your racial identity development?

Is there anything that scares you about moving forward in your development? What might be holding you back (e.g. defenses, expectations of those around you, narrative, personality, learning style, systems you are a part of)?

Thinking of the model that does not apply to you, name something(s) the model brought to your attention you weren't aware of.

How can understanding this model a little more clearly help you to understand how others react to you? General reactions to the model?

When you add information and take away your gut reactions and feelings, you can approach these conversations with calm openness rather than fiery defensiveness. Growth does not come from defensiveness—or, in many cases, ignorance—and neither does connection. Gaining some education about racial identity development specifically, and identity development overall, has given you shared knowledge. These are concepts to be understood, new schema to place your experiences. Knowing why people react as they do, and what they might be working through, can certainly help you to connect better. Becoming more aware of your own developmental trajectory helps you to build your emotional success. Congratulations.

The next psychological secret answers the question "Why do good people do bad things?"

MORAL DISENGAGEMENT
(WORST-CASE SCENARIO)

"Do unto others as you'd have them do unto you."

—The Golden Rule

All human beings want to be safe and loved. And for their clan to be safe and loved. This is humanity's deepest desire and life's work. No one is perfect. Small and large indiscretions occur daily. You are a glorious mess. Everyone is. We have discussed what privilege and bias can look and feel like in your life—what most people have seen and feel on a regular basis, what you think of when you hear terms like *bullying, isms, harassment,* etc. These small moments happen within systems and ultimately impact the trajectory of people's lives, but they don't usually seem dramatic or huge in the moment. This is part of why they can so easily be ignored or diminished if it isn't happening to you. Horrific moments such as hate crimes, shootings, or jury reactions to police brutality directly impact one group more acutely than another. Even inhumane acts such as genocide happen every day, somewhere on earth. Unthinkable as they are, these too can be washed away from your daily existence if they aren't outside your window or knocking on your door. You know atrocities exist, but your mind does its best to protect you in your daily life.

There are biological reasons you don't focus on the pain and trauma of others. Evolutionarily speaking, you would note the information: person gets eaten by bear. Terrible. Your brain assimilates the information: don't go near hungry bear. Then the memory leaves the front of your mind and is only recalled when it is needed. Cortisol, which heightens your experiences and gets you ready to fight or flee, is also poison in large quantities. It isn't good for you, physically, to continue to relive something terrible after the lesson is learned. You need enough cortisol to react, remember, and then it ought to leave your system.

Trauma is when you have an experience and can't regulate the retention of memories/reactions, and the moment continues to feel acute for much longer than the actual event. Your body/brain is not built to live in heightened states on a continuous basis. Remember, nature wants status quo. Homeostasis is the goal. Therefore, when you see or hear something disturbing happening to another human being or group of people, it is natural to want to build defenses around the situation so you can go on with your life, feeling safe and secure. It isn't good or bad; it's how people are wired. However, for the sake of connecting better to others, you must sometimes force yourself to sit in an uncomfortable reality to better understand the complexity of another person's life. In this section, we are going to spend time in the far end of the out-group continuum: what are the worst things that can happen when you don't think, when you look away, or when you impose in-group/out-group thinking without education or empathy.

Why does it matter? Bullying works by focusing on one person in a group—and then people extrapolate what they've seen, and everyone who is in-group with the person being bullied now knows they'd better behave a certain way, or else. While the term is somewhat of an understatement, can you see that everything from harassment to hate crimes to genocide are forms of bullying? This means that the people who are in-group with the attacked person or people walk around with fear that what happened was a warning *to all people in that group*. For instance, when a mass shooter targets women, Jewish or Black people, etc., all people who have that same identity have been targeted. Does that make sense? And within that group, fear and worry can grow. This is why hate crimes are so heavily punished—when you focus on identity when going after someone, you impact all people with that identity.

We talk about this end of the out-group continuum here because some groups of people are carrying around more identity-based trauma than others. It is a privilege to feel like your group hasn't been targeted and you therefore don't have to worry about being a victim in this way. To communicate and connect, you must be more able to bring this worry and extra emotional burden into your conversations. So, let's create some shared knowledge around these horrible things, so you can talk with openness rather than fear or defensiveness, just like you talk about anything else. When you have the appropriate knowledge, you can hold even the worst things.

Psychologists call the extreme othering of the out-group in order to engage in atrocities *moral disengagement*. Albert Bandura is a psychologist I admire very much. He had quite a career, and then he turned his incredible intelligence and thoughtfulness to the study of why "good" people do bad things. Moral disengagement is born from an ism plus power. It is a place where terrible things happen in the name of the "greater good" . . . but really for the sake of the "greater group." What happens when an out-group moves from oppression to something worse? Hate crimes, bullying, genocide—all forms of "othering" lead to human suffering. They all come from an in-group/out-group dichotomy. You must understand the very end of the continuum—how the dominant group can operate to ultimately control the oppressed. It may seem farfetched, but this is the way bullying works, just on a grander scale. You only have to treat one person badly in front of others and, voilá, people fall in line. Remember, humans are wired to be part of the crowd. Sometimes this works against us.

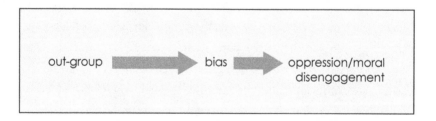

When you feel a threat to yourself or your group, you tend to act out in potentially dangerous ways. If you think of Hitler or any leader who wanted absolute control throughout history, look no further than step one of moral disengagement: get people to feel afraid of the "*Big*

Bad Other." Before we move on, please consider whether in your life you have a group you are currently fearful of. I'll make a list of common tropes, and you can see if any apply to you. You may also think back to the IET activity that helped you know more about your implicit biases, as bias can lead to fear, as we know. If this list doesn't work for you, think of one that will illicit yucky feelings and work from there. Yucky feelings can lead to fear, and that stops people from connecting. Let's bring these reactions into the light and examine a little deeper.

- Criminals
- Muslims
- Poor people
- Men at night
- Women
- Rich people
- Military
- Immigrants
- Powerful men
- Homeless people
- People of color
- Law enforcement

Seems to me there is someone on that list that probably makes you feel threatened. The people you fear, or who are threatening to your values, are other. Please think of them when looking at the chart below (based on the work by Professor James Detert and his groundbreaking work on 'Competent Courage' in the workplace).

Mechanisms of Moral Disengagement	Definition
Moral Justification	Portraying violent acts as serving a higher social cause
Euphemistic Language	Using sanitizing terms (e.g. martyrdom operations) so violent acts are seen as mild or benign
Exonerative Comparison	Comparing own acts of violence to extremely heinous or outrageous acts of violence
Displacement of Responsibility	Placing the responsibility for the harm one causes on other groups
Diffusion of Responsibility	Obscuring or minimizing the casual role played in the outcome of violent acts

As you can see from the chart, individuals "other" people all the time; it isn't just horrific things that demonstrate this tendency. Can you see how you use these mechanisms to defend behaviors? When we talk about moral disengagement, it is another way of saying that people dehumanize others in order to deal with the cognitive dissonance that arises within them when they know something is wrong. People's humanity is so strong that one has to dehumanize someone to hurt them. This is moral disengagement. There are very few people who can cause harm to another person without somehow telling themselves that the other person is sub or less than human. Think about the example of a firing squad. Classic example of diffusion of responsibility. Separating people from their humanity is the first step, and I hope you can see that bullying, belittling, and lack of empathy are all steps down that terrible trail.

A Recent Example of Moral Disengagement

I have thought many times about what example to use here, and I refuse to pull up the Nazis for two reasons. First, in hindsight most agree it was a terrible, unthinkable way to behave. People are almost universal on that point . . . now. At the time, though, they didn't know how to act, and moral disengagement was employed all over the world to keep people from believing it was as bad as it was; some still can't believe the atrocity of it all. Secondly, I would prefer a recent example because you are more likely to feel hot and bothered and *real* about it since it is a current situation, and I want all that realness that you have about identity to come right up to the surface.

I'll use the example of separating children from their parents at the border between the United States and Mexico. Before anyone assumes this is a political issue pointing at one party or another, I assure you this policy has long roots and continues at the time of this writing. It is also very difficult to provide an example of moral disengagement that both elicits "big feelings" and isn't polarizing. No matter where you stand on the issue, it's a great example of action you certainly wouldn't want to happen to you, and yet for various reasons (othering), many have defended the decision. Remember, moral disengagement helps you to allow things to happen to other people you would never want to happen to you or your loved ones. Let's work it through.

FACT: Children are separated from parents at the border, and thousands are not reunited with their families.

- Moral justification: They were here illegally.
- Advantageous comparison: I/my family/some ancestors came here legally.
- Distortion of consequences: They can go somewhere else for asylum.
- Denial: Children aren't being separated from families/conditions aren't that bad.
- Diffusion of responsibility: It is the only way to protect our borders. The law must be upheld.

People tend to employ moral disengagement when they feel afraid, and the first step is to take the out-group and treat them as nonhuman or "other." Can you see that "othering" Mexican people is what racism looks like? Making them seem like dangerous people coming to take your job, your home, maybe even your life—this is a timeless process that makes other people seem like less than human so you can justify separating families and detaining people who may actually need your help. When someone is threatening you, or you perceive them to be a threat, you throw up your defenses, don't you? It's a basic human response. Whether or not it's true, it can help to see how moral disengagement is the epitome of "clan thinking."

Moral Disengagement

out-group ➜ bias ➜ oppression/moral disengagement

Please look at the example of children separated from their families above. Let's talk about your reactions. Do you agree with my premise?

If not, I still want you to try on the idea of moral disengagement. Pick something else and work through the problem. Another recent example would be the Russian invasion of the Ukraine. If you use this example, look at how Putin has attempted to engage in moral disengagement by othering Ukrainians and placing them as the aggressor.

Whatever you choose, please describe the situation you are going to work with:

Describe the dominant group and the oppressed group

Describe what happened. Can you discern the mechanisms and phases of moral disengagement for your scenario, as I did above in the example? You can use the chart "Moral Disengagement" to help you work through this action. There are also many videos on YouTube as well as articles and an entire book about this topic if you're interested in learning more.
Were you surprised by the stage you are in?

Actions

Moral justification:

Advantageous comparison:

Distortion of consequences:

Diffusion of responsibility:

What do you think is the space between bullying, hate crimes, and moral disengagement?

Have you ever felt yourself engage in moral disengagement?

Have you ever felt yourself condone moral disengagement?

How can you assimilate/ accommodate your existing schema to incorporate an understanding of moral disengagement?

Thank you for working through this action. When you can see moral disengagement happening, you can find perspective. Terrible things come from dehumanizing. Now, more than ever, these themes are central to a fair existence for all humanity. If you are in a position of dominance and experience privilege in any domain, it is your responsibility to help restructure the systems that hold some up while they push others down. Everyone deserves to breathe.

EDUCATED

This section took you from understanding cognitive schema through development, identity development, bias and privilege, and understanding your own experiences of dominance and/or oppression and pulled it all together. We also spent some time examining the worst-case scenario of human behavior when in-group/out-group is taken to extremes, and how that impacts groups of people on a daily basis, directly and indirectly. We've highlighted the importance of bringing instances of moral disengagement into conversations with others and creating space for identity-based trauma in your heart. Just because you don't experience something doesn't mean it isn't real. What is happening in the world around you deeply impacts everything from your physical health to your mood, and horrible things that happen far away are no different, as we will discuss in the next chapter. Humans are wired to connect, and it makes no difference to your mind whether the person is close or a world away.

You now know that in-group/out-group can influence your behaviors, thoughts, and even feelings about yourself and the people around you. There are *so many* resources on each of these topics—I'm happy to guide you toward them. Another way is to look at some of the themes and dig into Google/Google Scholar/YouTube to learn more and to better educate yourself.

With shared language, and additional awareness, you are ready to move forward, knowing who you are and how you're experienced by others. Watch those arrows, friends; they can be sharp. Ready for something new? Let's go!

CHAPTER 6

Empathy Is Transformational

E mpathy is not a magical ability. Reading, writing, arithmetic, empathy—these are all skills acquired through learning and practice. What does empathy look and feel like? How do you define it? What can you do to welcome empathy?

"It takes a long time to become young."

—Picasso

Did you know that children as young as six months old know the difference between right and wrong? Developmental psychologists have been able to determine (with the use of awesome "games" and cameras) that infants have early understanding of those who help and those who hurt, and they prefer the helpers. Moral judgment in infants is a burgeoning field, and an interesting one that speaks to human beings' innate desire to connect with and be helpful to others.

This means you were born with an innate sense of wanting to connect with others. Over time, you build up your social and group memberships, creating in-group and out-group scenarios in all the systems of your life. In this way, you grow a sense of "us versus them," somewhat losing your general desire to connect with others. Emotional success means you are aware of what limits connections with others. You won't have emotional success if you don't want to connect, no matter what group memberships you have. In this chapter we will consider how empathy feels, looks, and when empathy is difficult. The psychological secrets I will share are the universality hypothesis and what empathy looks like in therapy.

What Is Empathy?

Empathy feels like love.
Empathy looks like kindness.
Empathy can feel impossible.

All three are true. We are moving from awareness and education now into love land: empathy. Empathy is so key to emotional success that nearly half of the book is dedicated to the exploration and growth of it in your life. As I said in my TEDx talk,

---

Empathy helps us to see the world from another person's perspective. Without it, we have awareness and information but no real attachment to other people.

This chapter is an introduction to empathy. I'll ask you to use what Buddha called *shoshin*—beginner's mind. Consider how you feel when you begin something new: open, bringing in and noticing everything, without feelings of expertise or preconceived notions. I realize we all know a little something about empathy. At the same time, please suspend that knowledge, open up all of your existing schema around the idea of empathy, and let's start unpacking to see what we've got.

What Is Empathy?

What is empathy to you? Please create a representation of empathy—a drawing, a paragraph, a word map, or whatever feels best to you—to begin to unpack your feelings around empathy.

Then, please put an X on the spot that feels most comfortable for each of the continuums provided.

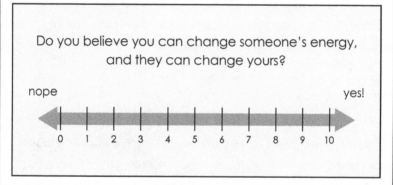

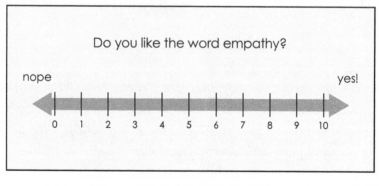

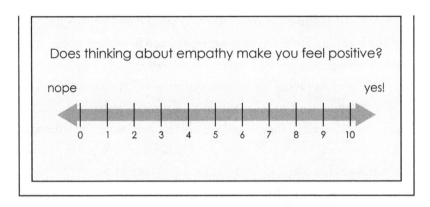

If empathy feels good to you, you are more likely to do it. And the reverse is true as well. Everything we've explored—your personality, intelligences, ego strength, defenses, identity, values, biases, life experiences, group memberships—contributes to your empathetic style. I want you to be aware of how empathy feels and looks *to you*. To me, empathy is warm gooeyness. Empathy exemplifies the idea of opening rather than closing, of letting go and letting things flow. This is my philosophy, and I want to share it with you. Let's begin with the most basic ways you can engage in empathy.

The Platinum Rule

In general, letting go and being open can be difficult. Empathy asks you to do this to the extreme. Not only are you asking yourself to be vulnerable, but you are also creating space for another person's experience to enter. In therapy, when I think of empathy, it feels like I've created a whole new room, a place I go where my mirror neurons are simply firing and helping me to be as close to the other person as possible.

Empathy is flow rather than restriction.

Empathy allows us to unlock the Platinum Rule.

Let's take the Golden Rule a little further now. Sometimes people will pat themselves on the back for employing the Golden Rule but still end up with an unhappy person on the receiving end. This is because the Golden Rule needs an update.

The Golden Rule: Do unto others as you'd have done to you.

The Platinum Rule: Do unto others as you'd have done to you . . . *if you were them.*

There is a lot of room for misconception here. Let's clarify. Have you given a present or tried to help someone, only to realize that they aren't as happy as you imagined they would be? This is often because you thought of *yourself*—what you would want (the Golden Rule). What if, instead, you considered or asked what the other person would want?

How to use the Platinum Rule:

- Find out through open communication, when possible, and/or education, what the other person wants.
- Put yourself in the other person's shoes.
- Engage in activities that support the other person's needs/wants as much as possible.

You can employ the Golden Rule without using empathy, but it is impossible to engage the Platinum Rule without it. Want an example? You aren't feeling well, and someone who cares for you makes their favorite chili. What a sweet gesture. Your friend made it for you because when they aren't feeling well, their grandmother makes chili to cheer them up. This is the Golden Rule in action. Lovely.

Only problem is . . . you hate chili. It hasn't come up in the relationship, for obvious reasons, but beans give you gas, and you try not to eat beef. Oh, and you don't like spicy food. Hm. But wait! Let's see if we can correct this situation: Instead of the Golden Rule, your friend uses the Platinum Rule. The friend asks you what you would like instead of assuming, or considers that you don't like spicy things; they also noticed that you order turkey sandwiches when you're tired or sick. Your friend may not like turkey sandwiches, but this is your party, after all, so turkey sandwiches this time. You feel heard, cared for, loved, and your friend can eat chili.

Obviously, this example applies to all sorts of things. If you think back to person-first language in the very first chapter, you have a great way to use the Platinum Rule! It doesn't necessarily matter what *you* would like to be called, or how you would like people to utilize pronouns; the loving response (that costs us nothing!) is to offer what the other person would prefer.

Is the Platinum Rule something you can always use? Nope. Do you always have all the information about what other people want/need/ like? Nope. Isn't it also great to have things to aspire to, to help you connect better with others? Yep.

The Platinum Rule is one way to see empathy in action. There are others.

Empathy = Being Aware of the Humanity in Everyone

What does empathy look like? Empathy isn't sympathy because to be empathetic you must see yourself in the other person's situation.

Many times, people confabulate empathy and sympathy. But sympathy is ego driven, and it separates you from others because sympathy is something you give someone, not something you engage in together. Empathy and sympathy are like a mini in-group/out-group experience. With sympathy, you see the other person and you feel for them. Empathy is when you work to put yourself in their shoes.

Sympathy often looks active.

Empathy often looks inactive.

And in the stillness, empathy transforms everyone.

One is not better than the other. You need both. Sympathy is what helps you to make food when someone needs to be fed (but please, no chili), give advice, tell a story that helps someone feel better. All of these are important. Sometimes, though, what can help the most is simply being heard, seen, and validated in your experience. This is what empathy looks like.

"People have said, 'Don't cry' to other people for
years and years, and all it has ever meant is 'I'm too
uncomfortable when you show your feelings. Don't cry.'
I'd rather have them say, 'Go ahead and cry.
I'm here to be with you.'"

—Mister Rogers

I see you.

I hear you.

Your thoughts and feelings are valid just as they are. Let's sit in this moment without trying to change it. Just be. Together.

You being you.

No judgment.

Me working to feel how you feel, not how I would feel.

That last part might seem confusing. I'll tell you a story and hope it helps bring us to the same page. In graduate school when I was training as a therapist, I noticed something strange in the therapy room. When I focused 100 percent of my attention—including internal thoughts, awareness, and energy—on the patient, the room would sometimes get wonky. It was as though it would fade away, or the patient would suddenly seem very large in the room and the rest of the space would become "fuzzy." It scared me at first. Then I realized the feelings associated with it were warm ones. When I voiced the reactions I had in those sessions, it would strike a chord with my patients, and we would make great progress.

I started to welcome this experience and realized that it is a beautiful version of what Freudian psychotherapists call "counter transference." In the beauty of pure and ego-less focus, it is as if information passes between humans that our conscious mind would miss. I began to describe these phenomena to students, supervisees, and peers as the "Indiana Jones bridge."

In one of the Indiana Jones movies, he is confused because he has followed all the rules and feels stuck. He stands on the edge of a precipice and needs to cross to the other side. Suddenly, he takes what looks like a suicidal step forward. In fact, it is a bridge camouflaged to look like the abyss. Although the particulars of those movies are lost in my memory, that scene stuck. In the moments where I have engaged in deep empathetic posture with a patient, I take steps on that invisible bridge to say the things that don't make rational sense, may not seem connected, and seem to pop into my head out of thin air. It never stops being scary. No one wants their patient to look at them and feel like the connection is lost, however, universally it seems to work. More than that, the response can be one of shock because it is attached with what they were thinking but couldn't or didn't say. Empathy can lead you to "being on the same brain wave" in almost unfathomable ways. Everyone has this ability to almost magically connect, and that's what I want to bring into your focus right now.

EMPATHY IS TRANSFORMATIVE

You don't need to be a therapist to have this amazing experience. It can happen anytime human beings focus solely on the present moment and make an opening for the other person's experience. You know these moments and call them magical, because they are. Examples include quiet moments with your babies, intimate and loving sex, playing sports when you feel in concert with teammates, dancing with sustained eye contact, and so many more. People long for those intimate connections. They are available to you if you are ready to commit to greater connections. Sustained focus and open hearts are all it takes. I am not a mind reader. But when you deeply and intimately open to another person without distraction or ego, with all those mirror neurons firing, you can connect in ways you may not understand logically.

This is empathy. Attempting to be with the other person, in the moment, and not focus on one other thing. You do this all the time. Whether you're walking across invisible bridges or experiencing shrinking rooms (which I now know is something many therapists experience), you've likely noticed that when you are with someone you like, you find yourself sitting in the same position. It goes so much deeper—you end up looking like the people you love. Sounding like them. Your values and purpose in life can become aligned. Remember the mirror neurons? Human brains are built for deep and meaningful connections.

We don't discuss this often, but did you know that therapists benefit from the therapeutic relationship too? All that glorious deep connection we get to engage in all day at work? It is transformational. It is impossible to let all that in, connect with another person on such an intimate level, and then be the same. I don't know a lot about metaphysics . . . or even regular physics, but I've come up with tons of theories about all that S P A C E between atoms that we discussed earlier in the book. The energy you feel is real, and when you allow energy flow between yourself and another human being (or animal, or natural space like the woods), something truly divine happens. Whatever the divine is for you, everyone knows that feeling of wholeness, completeness with the universe and themselves as one; that is the magic of being empathetic and truly open to another person. It is sacred to me. And it is surely transformational.

People ask if the trauma and sadness I hear impacts who I am, how I operate in the world. Of course it does, though I've learned to work through that content in productive ways. What I am left with is transformation. Love. Energy transfer. Those deep connections are the secret gift that anyone can have when they are deeply open and empathetic to another person. They are my purpose in writing this book and sharing it with all of you. It is impossible to hate or hurt another person when you feel empathy for them. I see empathy diminishing, and it dims the light of the world. Empathy is transformational. You become someone a little bit, and they become you a little bit. It is very difficult to hurt someone if you are connected.

What Does Empathy Feel Like?

I studied art history as an undergraduate and love learning more about history today. Art history is history, illustrated. And history is really a group of stories that reveal human nature, which I obviously love to study. Furthermore, art is an expression of humanity—often left to our own interpretation. At the start of the book, I promised I would use many different ways to share information with you, based on various intelligences and learning styles. I share this art now as a way to bypass your thinking and aim for your heart. Be open; let it work.

Please take a moment and look up the painting Guernica, by Pablo Picasso. What reaction do you have when you look at this painting? What do you see? Whether it is familiar to you or new, you are having a reaction, and I would like you to note it. Sit with it for a few moments. You may know who painted it, what it is based on; you may have a response to the abstract nature. I ask you to focus on the emotion of the piece.

When I was twenty, I was lucky enough to study art in Paris, France. I stood in front of this gigantic painting and couldn't breathe (it is *huge*—takes up an entire wall of a very large room, imagine that). Our professor was Greek, spoke primarily Italian at home, and we were living in Paris . . . speaking a lot of English. You had to *listen* when she spoke because all four languages worked their way into her lectures. On the day we stood in front of this painting, I didn't have to work hard. I knew what she said, and I felt her passion. This was a deeply European woman, with love and family spread across the continent, and she told us the story with calm sadness.

Guernica

Between the World Wars, Europe never settled in. The ugliness of the Great War unsettled humanity. Like a half-finished argument, it festered and bubbled, a not-really-dormant volcano. Atrocities and openings for dictators were created.

Resentment, fear, and shame swirled in the air. The moral

disengagement, use of "othering," and extreme in-group/out-group rhetoric that propelled Europe through World War I remained steady until it simply refocused and intensified.

Like many people, when I think of World War II, my mind comes to Germany and the Nazis. The war started in many places at once. In Spain, fascists were aided by the Nazis. In 1937, Hitler dropped bombs for an entire day on a small Basque town called Guernica. A few months later, Picasso was asked to paint an image representing anti-war sentiment for the Paris International Exposition because he was the most famous Spanish painter (and a bit full of himself, but then, he was Picasso).

He painted *Guernica* as an act of rebellion for the home country he'd fled. The painting was shocking, for its abstract representation of humans as well as the violence. Think of Picasso as an early Martin Scorsese. The painting was so powerful that he stated it could not be viewed in Spain for many decades. It has only recently been on exhibition there.

When you look at Guernica, see the story there. With the perspective of time, you easily take the side of the people in the painting—a small town ravaged by daylong bombing meant to show force. After the bombing, the German Nazis and Spanish Fascists blamed the atrocity on the opposing forces, knowing how inhumane the actions had been. I bring this to you because here it is. An abstract painting. Of an event that occurred over eighty years ago. You aren't looking into anyone's eyes. It isn't even a photograph. When you break it down, it is simply a representation of humans and animals. And yet a reaction rose within you for the people in the painting. That's empathy.

Empathy looks like connection. It looks like growing closer. It looks like selflessness. It looks like listening. It looks like focus on the current moment; like seeing the other person, without judgment. It looks like these things because these are the components of empathy.

EMPATHY FOR EVERYONE

People often attribute magical qualities to skill sets—intelligence, athletics, leadership, EQ, math, music, artistry. Often, you assume the person possessing these qualities was bestowed these gifts at birth. And yet, I know plenty of people who, throughout their lives, have followed what came naturally and found themselves uninspired, bored, or full of regret over a lost opportunity to explore other interests. In addition to your innate attributes, psychologists who help people look for dream careers are equally invested in a person's interests. The place where ability and interests meet is the sweet spot for success and joy in any task.

"Change is not a threat to your life, but an invitation to live."

—Adrienne Rich

Theorems

Skills can be learned.
Empathy is a skill.

Maybe you can't catch a ball, run a marathon, or decipher multiplication of fractions (is it just me?)—and then again, you could be wrong.

Argue for your limitations, and they're yours.

Yes, you are good at some things and great at others. If you never practice and you believe you won't succeed, you certainly won't. A platitude worth considering: if you don't think you will succeed, you'll be right. That's sad. And defeatist. But that's not why you're here. You want to be a better human and connect more deeply with the people all around you. That is why you will succeed.

The Universality Hypothesis

Darwin proposed the idea that if you can read emotions successfully, you have an evolutionarily advantageous position. One hundred years later, the *universality hypothesis of facial expressions* (universality hypothesis for short) is the foundation of psychological understanding of emotions. Across humanity, people share seven main emotional responses on their faces and in their hearts: happiness, sadness, fear, disgust, anger, contempt, and surprise. Amazing.

People are wired to love people. Remember mirror neurons? On a cellular level, human brains are wired to match other humans. There is a section of your brain made just to help you connect with other people. Sometimes, with autism or other diagnoses that may make it difficult to match up with other people, we expect to find fewer of these mirror neurons. In these cases, we can help people make connections by working around any deficits and building new pathways. Therefore, whether your brain is full of mirror neurons or not, everyone is wired and ready to connect. If you want to connect, we can find a way.

Here is a photograph of a person smiling. The picture might make you want to smile . . . and you don't even know them! Let's explore your innate ability to feel what others are feeling.

Can You Feel It?

We are going to take a field trip online. For each of the emotions below, I would like you to please go to your favorite search engine, type it in, and then take some time to react to the images you see.

Anger

Pick an image that speaks to you. Take thirty seconds or more to look at it. Then please answer these questions:

How do you feel?

Other reactions?

Disgust

Pick an image that speaks to you. Take thirty seconds or more to look at it. Then please answer these questions:

How do you feel?

Other reactions?

Surprise

Pick an image that speaks to you. Take thirty seconds or more to look at it. Then please answer these questions:

How do you feel?

Other reactions?

Sadness

Pick an image that speaks to you. Take thirty seconds or more to look at it. Then please answer these questions:

How do you feel?

Other reactions?

Contempt

Pick an image that speaks to you. Take thirty seconds or more to look at it. Then please answer these questions:

How do you feel?

Other reactions?

Happiness

Pick an image that speaks to you. Take thirty seconds or more to look at it. Then please answer these questions:

How do you feel?

Other reactions?

Why do you think these are the seven universal emotions easily understood throughout all of humanity?

How does it feel when you can't read someone's expression?

Are you easy or more difficult to read?

How do you think being "easy to read" may impact your ability to connect deeply with others?

YOU ARE EMPATHETIC

You already have empathetic skills! You use these abilities every day. We can hone them together and help you to make even more purposeful use of these innate capabilities. Get ready to feel all the feels! You are going to grow your empathy more than you knew possible.

If you can't be kind and loving to yourself, you will need your defenses, and empathy will be challenging. This is classic "oxygen on the adult face first" behavior, and it's necessary for survival. If you can't practice self-compassion, it will be impossible to be compassionate to anyone else. What you see in others reflects yourself; the cells that help you connect are called *mirror* neurons, after all.

Empathy requires a ton of energy, resources, feelings of general safety, and a sense that the world is a fair and loving place. There could be 1,000 reasons you don't have this worldview. And those reasons, no matter how valid, will keep you from connecting with others. I ask you to explore your defenses and consider appraising them. That is all.

Let's start as close to home as we can. Again, if you can't give yourself empathy, it is impossible to give it to others. Time for a self-check-up. Remember, if you feel something come up and you need to work it through, employ your support scaffolding.

Inward Empathy

Please answer the following prompts:

Describe your love for yourself.

Discuss how you show yourself compassion.

Describe the feelings you have about yourself.

Do you often feel blocking emotions?
Do you know why?

Review your responses. What reaction do you have to what you wrote? Is there more room for kindness? Do you apply the Golden and Platinum Rules to yourself?

If you notice you aren't kind to yourself, it may be time to explore why. You can't empathize with others if you don't have empathy for yourself. You deserve to have empathy for yourself.

Do you remember the example I just offered about me connecting deeply with my patients? Here's another piece of that puzzle. When I was pregnant with my children, I had a very difficult time engaging in that empathetic practice that had become so integral to my work. My defenses were sky high, and I found it difficult to allow information and energy to flow freely. When negativity or potentially upsetting content was shared by a patient, I found myself literally shielding the baby, and thus myself. I'm not sure what the patients I saw then would say about their experiences. I certainly sought supervision and worked to control my urge to defend my belly. I was surprised to find myself so viscerally responding to energy I was once very comfortable with. I share this as an example of how integral defenses are, even when you aren't aware of why you are not as vulnerable as you'd like.

When you feel defensive, it is harder to connect. When you need to have your own needs met because you experience a deficit, it is harder to connect. Your urge to protect and take care of yourself necessarily cuts off the ability to connect with others, even if it could potentially be helpful.

If you think of how people often disconnect from others who may need compassion, you'll hear the defensiveness in their rhetoric: "I had to work hard for what I have. Why should they get things for free?" That says to me that someone feels they have worked hard and *not* gotten what they deserve, and they still struggle, or struggled for a long time and continue to have strong feelings about their hardship. When you add fear to a feeling of not having needs met, defenses are natural.

Let's return to the dialectical we discussed earlier in the book, and consider that someone else getting help does not preclude help for you as well. When you feel your own needs aren't being met, it is natural to find empathy difficult, and it is complicated. At the same time, you can move past those unconscious reactions toward greater awareness and control over how you meet each chance to show empathy in your life.

Empathy is warm, loving, and when you are unblocked, it flows. It offers both the giver and receiver much, and it is what helps connection to flourish. It is transformational on all sides. Simply being aware of its properties and limitations can help you to become more open to the skills that add up to empathy. Let's work on those skills.

CHAPTER 7

Mastering the Empathy Equation

> **Empathy = Enter the Other Person's World +**
> **No Judgment + Understand Feelings +**
> **Communicate Understanding**

E mpathy is an expression of love.

Empathy is so powerful that I've spent half of a book preparing you for it and the other half discussing it. In this chapter I will share psychological secrets about building healthy boundaries, theory of mind, and the empathy equation. We will break down each of these secrets into skills you can use.

I *love* empathy. The word, meaning, feeling, the idea of it. Empathy is one of the deepest expressions of love. It requires you to be fully present—to put aside your distractions, thoughts, and worries. Next, you must hollow yourself out to make room for the experience of the other. It's not a mirror, as some people suggest, but rather an expansion of space—an addition of who you are through a loving osmosis.

EMPATHY IS A LOVING OSMOSIS

After you engage in the empathetic transfer of feelings, you must make sense of what you now hold. If you feel with the full range of human emotions, you are better equipped to define feelings when they plop into your awareness. Finally, you must let the other person know that you get it—that you are picking up what they are throwing down.

How many times have you said, "I didn't know you agreed with me!" or "I thought no one else felt that way." These statements imply someone wasn't told that they had been seen or heard. They didn't know empathy happened; so it didn't do its full magic work. You must let the other person *know* you are in it with them or, frankly, my friends, it is all for naught. And that doesn't deepen any connection.

That's it. You've just mastered the empathy equation. If empathy is a skill, that means we can break it down into manageable components. It makes sense that a nursing scholar (Wiseman, 1996) would be a leader in this field. Nurses are, generally, empathetic. Many times, when I've been at my worst, a nurse has lovingly done something to make me feel better that would ordinarily make me feel too vulnerable, like bathing me or helping me to the toilet. Sometimes empathy can feel like that: too close, maybe even a little gross.

Sometimes empathy is called upon when the details are hard to hear. We call all that nitty-gritty of a story the *content*. Sure, the content is sometimes interesting, or upsetting—as a therapist I've heard lots of words that might distress anyone. But I know what matters is the emotion behind the information, and my empathy is what moves the relationship. It is the same with everyone, in any deep transfer of emotion.

I'm not saying don't listen to the specifics of a story. In fact, there is an entire chapter dedicated to being good at this skill. I am saying don't get hung up on collecting information when you haven't finished the empathy equation. A simple therapist rule—focus on empathy, not curiosity. You may end with less facts, but the connection will grow. And from connection comes magic.

Distance Loving

Let's talk about the amazing fact that empathy can happen for you from thousands of miles away, with people you don't even know. I mean, that's *magic*!!! Remember the painting I showed you in chapter 6? You can feel empathy for people in a painting who died before you were born in a place you may have never been to (or heard of). Human beings are awesome like that. It might seem like we are talking a lot about one-on-one conversations with people you love, but empathy is bigger! Empathy is the glue that holds humanity together. By offering it to another person from far away—even if it means you simply send them a prayer, send light and love, sign a petition, write a note, send money—a human connection is made, and everyone benefits from the positivity of shared positive energy.

EMPATHETIC BOUNDARIES

Like anything, you can overdo it in empathy town. Let's set ground rules as we dig deeper. Over-empathizing can be as detrimental as not connecting at all. What are some appropriate boundaries? While people often think of boundaries as thick and impenetrable, there ought to be more nuance than that. You can't shut everything out and thrive. You do better with movement in and out. You need input, even at the cellular level. Think back to the analogies we talked about earlier—of the cell wall or a scrim in theatre. If boundaries are difficult for you, as they are for many, take the time to explore this in whatever ways you can.

Empathy is a deeply emotional and intimate experience, when done correctly, and you must be able to acknowledge when things have moved from safe to a less healthy place. This can be different for everyone. You must know yourself and be able to identity when firm boundaries need to be in place. Conversely, when do you put up walls that keep you from intimacy? If you sponge up other people's feelings, building appropriate boundaries may be difficult. But it is necessary.

Appropriate use of boundaries is best when taught young. However, sometimes caregivers model unhelpful behaviors. The bad news is that you often revert to the ways of loving that you were first taught. Good news—you can relearn healthier ways to connect. When I talk about love and intimacy, I always like to say it's like a dance. Very early in your life, before you could speak or walk, you danced *to the music of love.* The music-of-love dance is a metaphor for all the emotions, behaviors, and thoughts that automatically begin to play in the background when you fall for someone. In case you haven't noticed, people repeat patterns throughout their lives—and one of the biggest places they do this is in relationships. You learn your very own music of love dance from your families of origin at a very young age (sometimes before you have words!) and then, without intervention such as therapy or self-reflection, you repeat those patterns as you grow. If you have a joyous dance that lets you be free and your whole glorious self, yay! Most people have some funny little twerks in their dance caused by a too close or too far away partner (parents). If your dance is not what you'd like, you might become conscious of this when you begin the music-of-love dance.

Change up your dance to fit the way of being intimate that fits you better. You can teach your children to enjoy a free and glorious dance by loving them and letting them have space when safe and appropriate. It's called authoritative parenting, which is somewhere between permissive and authoritarian. If you're interested, look it up because it is wonderful, interesting, and important.

If your music-of-love dance has you running away, building walls on the dance floor, or maybe the opposite—trying to inappropriately climb on the lap of your partner, for instance—then you might struggle a little with boundaries. Empathy is intimacy, and you'll need to figure this piece out to engage as deeply as you'd like (more about how to see and alter your music-of-love dance in chapter 11). Knowing appropriate boundaries that are safe and allow love can be tricky business, but it's worth the trouble. If this is an area of work for you, take the time to suss it out and create healthy boundaries.

Healthy Boundaries

Please answer the questions below to get an image of what you might do when you hear the music of love. Let's be clear about the status of your boundaries.

What is your reaction to the idea of the music-of-love dance?

What do you think your "dance" looks like?

Is your dance what you'd like it to be?

How does your dance impact your ability to be empathetic?

How does your dance impact your ability to connect with others?

If you'd like to change your dance, how do you think you might do this?

You need boundaries with the people around you, including those you connect with through the internet/media/reading, etc. For instance, teens have access to more personal information about their peers around the world than ever before. Sometimes all this empathizing can lead to increases in mental health difficulties; there is much that can be depressing in the world, and when you have personal relationships with friends around the globe, those events and circumstances can bring that sadness right into your heart—especially if discussions center on shared struggles or worries. Humans tend to "ramp each other up" (mirror neurons at work).

Therefore news "fasts," breaks from social media, or a pause on gossip in real life can be necessary. Let's not forget this. Balance in all things. If you tend to be an emotional sponge, proceed with this knowledge in mind and learn ways to connect without jumping down the rabbit hole. Shake up your music-of-love dance, even if it's with a partner from far away.

With all of this in mind, let's begin to master the empathy equation first shown at the beginning of this chapter.

**Empathy = Enter the Other Person's World +
No Judgment + Understand Feelings +
Communicate Understanding**

ENTER THE OTHER PERSON'S WORLD

You know how you can have a conversation with someone and be in sync? It is one of the joys of life. Sometimes, you fall in love based on being able to stay on the same page. It seems easy when it works; yet entering into another person's world requires a few big tasks and a zillion automatic small ones. People who have difficulty with social interactions know what I mean.

Theory of Mind

"Theory of mind is the ability to attribute mental states—
beliefs, intents, desires, emotions, knowledge, etc.—to
oneself, and to others, and to understand that others
have beliefs, desires, intentions, and perspectives that
are different from one's own."

—Wikipedia

In the late 1970s, an American psychologist named David Premack coined the term *theory of mind*. At first, it applied to animals who could identify themselves in the mirror. The term has come to define being able to attribute mental states to others, including emotions, intentions, hopes, expectations, imaginings, desires, and beliefs.

That is a lot. Not to mention that human beings do not always say what they mean and sometimes say different things in various situations. Although it may seem as though people are contradicting themselves, many things can be true at once (families tend to have the most challenging time with accepting these multiple truths about a loved one). And so here it is: you can juggle all of these bits and pieces. Some people are better at this than others, and frankly, being skilled in this arena is the general definition of emotional intelligence or EQ. It is a valuable and essential skill to help you connect better with the people in your life.[19] No matter where you start, anyone can master theory of mind.

To put yourself into someone else's world, you'll need to do *metacognition*, which is thinking about what you are thinking about. This recursive ability, to explore your own thoughts, is a truly splendid

---

19   Empathy is a particularly useful and rewarding business tool. *Harvard Business Review* offers several books each year on the "Best EQ Practices," which are based on empathy in part. We will discuss the importance of empathy in your professional life in chapter 12.

gift and one that you get better at with time and practice. Let's take a minute and consider where you stand on this empathetic variable.

Entering the Other Person's World

Let's remember the last time you had a chance to empathize with someone.

Imagine the last story you were told. When people tell stories, there is an expectation of listening followed by an appropriate response. When you engage in this process and fully tune in, this is entering into the other person's world. Please bring a recent experience to mind and answer the following questions.

Name the experience.

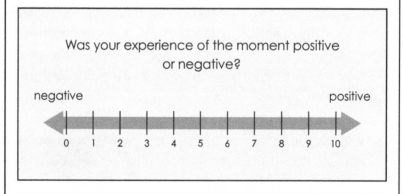

Was your experience of the moment positive or negative?

negative   positive

0   1   2   3   4   5   6   7   8   9   10

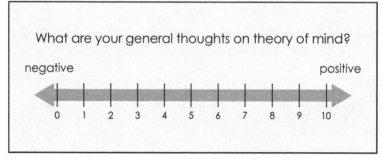

What are your general thoughts on theory of mind?

negative   positive

0   1   2   3   4   5   6   7   8   9   10

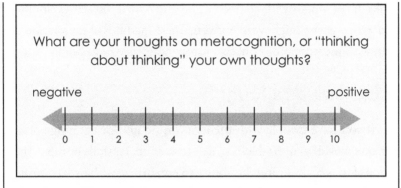

What are your thoughts on metacognition, or "thinking about thinking" your own thoughts?

negative   positive

0   1   2   3   4   5   6   7   8   9   10

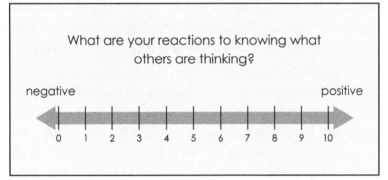

What are your reactions to knowing what others are thinking?

negative   positive

0   1   2   3   4   5   6   7   8   9   10

Does it feel safe to emotionally enter another person's world? Why or why not?

It helps to know where you might get stuck, so without judgment (good practice for the next section), please write a little narrative about your reactions and general thoughts on the practice of entering another's world.

Where you've been has as much impact on how you interact with others as your innate abilities. If you feel you've found a place where you're stuck, find a way to unstick it when you're ready. "Stuck" can mean the inability to engage enough or diving in too deeply to empathy land and feeling/getting lost. If you'd like to explore your reactions more deeply, this can be sorted in therapy, long talks with friends, journaling, walks in the woods with an open mind and a focus on self-exploration, and whatever else might work for you. These methods of exploration can help with incorporating concepts throughout the whole book.

Social Skills Are Taught

If you have trouble with theory of mind and/or entering another person's world, you can luckily turn toward social skills groups. These groups focus on building the ability to empathize with others through practice, all in a safe environment. We offer them for all ages. I've run many of these groups. They provide a wonderful way to practice the skills required to grow theory of mind and all the components of the empathy equation.

One of the reasons social skills groups are so successful is that empathy is a skill you can build. Sure, some people pick it up so fast it seems innate, but focused guidance in this area is a great help to people of all ages. If you have children in your life, it's never too early to build on that natural human interest in goodness, fairness, and connection by engaging in discussions around empathy. Very young children are ready to learn and connect better with others. Television programs such as *Daniel Tiger's Neighborhood*[20] have been shown to help children increase empathetic skills.

Skills groups and specialized children's shows work because they are based on the knowledge that humans want to connect and they love to repeat what is modeled to them. One of Daniel Tiger's favorite themes throughout the show is based on some simple questions that guide us toward that Platinum Rule:

---

20   *Daniel Tiger's Neighborhood* is a twenty-first-century show based on the genius of Fred Rogers (who happens to be my hero and is also from Pittsburgh). I don't know about you, but I can't hear "It's you I like" without catching a frog in my throat.

Teaching Empathy
Show a situation (on TV, in a book, in life, etc.)

Ask the child,
Have you ever experienced something like that?
How did it feel?
How would you feel if that happened to you?

And if you want to be advanced . . .
What would you want if that happened to you?
What should we do?

It's that simple. In fact, if you internalize these questions, can answer them honestly, and practice, before you know it, you will be entering the other's mind with ease and fluency.

Empathy = Enter the Other Person's World +
No Judgment + Understand Feelings +
Communicate Understanding

NO JUDGMENT

"If you don't have something nice to say, come sit by me."

—Alice Roosevelt Longworth (originally) by way of
Clairee Belcher (*Steel Magnolias*, 1980s version)

Judgment can be fun. In fact, talking about another person can build intimacy with your preferred friends. This makes a lot of sense if you think back to your knowledge about in-group/out-group. Here's a secret: when you gossip, you get a slight increase in oxytocin! Why do you think? It is because you are evolutionarily wired to engage in practices that help you remain in-group! So, as I said, gossip can feel good. What you are doing, after all, is building a connection with another person and solidifying your place in the group.

One clear way to establish that *we* are on the same page is to openly discuss (which has some risks) negative feelings about *them*. You already know this, but let me remind you—although it can be delicious in the moment, eventually gossip, or any other forms of judgment, makes you feel smaller and sometimes uncertain. This is because when you make judgments about someone else, the intelligent and big, glorious front of your brain knows that it is *you* who could just as easily be on the outside.

This is how bullying works, remember? Ostracizing certain behaviors, ways of being, or aspects of identity lets everyone know— those on the outside *and* those on the inside—that it is not okay to step outside of whatever norm has been established. When you judge others, it comes from your blocking emotions and the defense mechanisms that follow.

Judgment is pure projection—a classic defense mechanism. Think about this for a moment: when was the last time you engaged in judgment? If you feel someone's humanity and respect them as equal, it is much harder to judge. Sitting high on judgment hill, it is impossible to connect. And connecting is what it's all about.

Nobody's perfect. Just like bias is completely normal, so is judgment. Everyone needs an ego boost from time to time, and judging other people is an emotional bolster. Of course, it is unacceptable when judgment turns to bullying or hurting another person, or ventures even further down the continuum toward any of the isms. Thank goodness you have a frontal lobe that can tell you when you've gone too far.

You know that yucky feeling in your gut? That's not love speaking.

If you want to learn more about yourself, just look to what you judge the most.

Judgment keeps you from being close to others. It is a defense built to keep you from getting hurt. If you are deeply judgmental, I ask you to consider why. Has there been deep pain in your life? What are you afraid of? Revisit your defense mechanisms and consider how they serve you, or don't. If you'd like to make a shift, this may require professional help. People judge others because they feel threatened, or don't like an aspect of who they are. These can be deep things to explore and alter—a noble endeavor for all.

One of the key features of therapy is what Carl Rogers called *unconditional positive regard*. This means whether you agree with a person or even have an intense negative reaction to them, you must approach them with positive regard. Positive regard means offering respect for the humanity of the other person. This is true both of people who have committed heinous acts and those who have a different value system from your own. New therapists struggle with this. It certainly creates a treasure trove of unfinished business to explore and grow from. What you are left with is the knowledge that no one can heal and grow without love. And love is unconditional warmth.

You can't fully engage in empathy if you've brought judgment to the party.

I wouldn't be able to lose my ego and reflect emotions and feelings to my patients if I were sitting there feeling fearful or worried or disdainful—any blocking emotions that lead to defenses. Defenses are walls, and walls make it hard to connect. The same is true in your life. If you have judgment, you aren't employing empathy. It is impossible to hold both right at the same moment.

Theorems

Judgment and empathy do not coincide.
Empathy is a deep and intimate connection with
another person.

Judgment blocks you. Like shame, judgment is an energy that protects you, turns you away from connection. You know the way you feel when you get a blocking emotion; it's a turning inward, a loss of flow, a protective rather than connective stance.

Remember the blocking emotions from chapter 2?

- Shame
- Denial
- Projection
- Judgment
- Anger
- Distrust
- Fear
- Disgust
- Contempt

Defense mechanisms are born of blocking emotions. Please think back to your preferred defense mechanisms. Here's a reminder; plus, let's add on what happens after your (very necessary) defenses kick in.

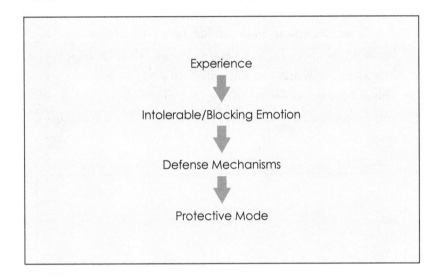

When you are in protective/defensive mode, you cannot connect wholly with another person. You cannot empathize if you are blocked as empathy requires an openness of heart and a silencing of mind to be fully able to experience the moment.

How can you tell when you are experiencing a blocking emotion?

Blocking Emotions

Please take a moment to consider how your defenses lead to blocking emotions. Look at the continuum below. In the space below, please write a recent experience where you had an intolerable emotion, your defense mechanisms arose, and then you entered protective stance. Afterward, please answer the questions provided.

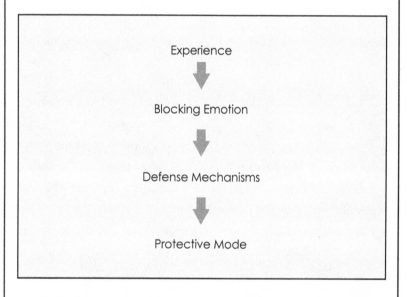

Experience

Blocking Emotion

Defense Mechanisms

Protective Mode

Consider whether the situation went the best way possible. What would have happened if you were able to notice the blocking emotion and ask it to settle in for a moment rather than acting on it? Could the situation have turned out differently?

How can you notice when you are experiencing a blocking emotion?

"When you judge another, you do not define them; you define yourself."

—Wayne Dyer

It is useful to notice when you experience blocking emotions. It is better to notice your reactions and make choices about how you act, versus replaying patterns without conscious control. At the same time, remember to respect your defenses—they serve a great and important purpose. Sometimes, you must be protective. I ask you to be aware enough to make a *choice* about whether you want to be protective or connective in any moment versus having unconscious reactions. No one wants that. It is certainly less likely to lead to greater connections when you put your lizard brain in charge.

What Is Empathetic Failure?

When you judge, it leads to empathetic failure. What does it mean if you fail at empathy? Empathetic failures in intimate relationships have deep and lasting impact on both the relationship and the individuals involved. Sustained or repeated empathetic failures often signal the end of the relationship. They can leave people feeling alone, confused, and unsure rather than validated, supported, and loved. When you fail to empathize, perhaps you can fix the current situation and move on; however, with repeated misfires of unmet needs, the relationship will suffer.

In therapy, we take this so seriously that we talk about ways to "repair" the situation if an empathetic failure is made by the therapist. Repairs include a discussion of the empathetic failure as well as a heartfelt acknowledgment and apology.

When you make empathetic mistakes, you must acknowledge them and try to repair. Everyone makes mistakes! The work of this book is to move you from a place of automatic responses toward thoughtful reactions—to help you see where some of your judgments and bias come from so you can be more objective; to choose your reactions and connect with others in a meaningful way. Judgment and bias are children of the same parents: fear and shame. With self-awareness and education, you will be able to move past that heritage and make room for empathy. *This* is how you will connect better.

"I don't think anyone can grow unless he's loved exactly as he is now, appreciated for what he is rather than what he will be."

—Mister Rogers

Without empathy, you cannot have intimacy or deep connections. You feel it when someone has "othered" you. Even if you are in a generally loving relationship, it hurts when someone pulls away and leaves you feeling judged or otherwise pushed aside. Blocking emotions are called this for good reason—they build barriers around you that keep out anything potentially harmful. Unfortunately, they also keep out the beneficial.

Human beings are creatures that need love. We know that cortisol (the stress hormone) raises heart rate in the moment and over time can lead to damage in your organs. The antidote to cortisol is oxytocin. Your body produces oxytocin when you are in a loving and safe environment. Did you know that when you hug someone you feel safe with (including your pet!) for twenty seconds, your body releases a flood of oxytocin? It also happens when you breastfeed or have an orgasm! This is because oxytocin serves as the hormonal glue that binds you to other people. It's so important to be connected in terms of evolution that oxytocin is related to forming memories! Oxytocin helps your mind to create memories and to transform short- to long-term memories,[21] heal your body, and calm your mind. It is truly a magic hormone, and you only get it through connection. Unless you'd like to only connect with people who agree with you all the time, you're going to have to leave some of the blocking emotions at home and get in the muck with the rest of us.

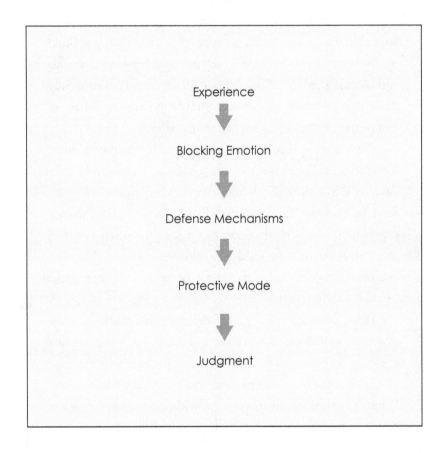

Experience

Blocking Emotion

Defense Mechanisms

Protective Mode

Judgment

---

21   Did you know that you have seemingly endless long-term memory storage? Some theorists believe this is because you need to remember a lot of things to survive, and to be able to pass important information on to future generations. You have a mega-chip processor in there! Enjoy!

Path of Judgment

We've done so much exploration together of who you are in the world, how you operate, and how all of that together impacts your ability to connect with other people. We are going to build on the actions you have taken regarding defense mechanisms and blocking emotions and bring it all together. You've already done the groundwork, so this should be easier. You're all emotionally warm and stretched out, as it were.

Which of the blocking emotions listed in the graphic from earlier in the chapter is primary for you? Some people know right away—"Oh, it's anger"—while others have to notice and watch for a day or two. Observe yourself like an awesome little science experiment and see what comes up for you when you feel uncomfortable or threatened. Knowing your primary blocking emotions is a great skill as they get between you and connection.

List your primary blocking emotions.

Please consider your "go-to" defense mechanisms that we discussed in chapter 2—let's bring them to the front of your mind. Now, please list your primary defense mechanisms.

Look at the blocking emotions and the defense mechanisms. What relationship do they have with one another? What reactions do you have to seeing them written here?

Please answer these questions:

How judgmental of other people do you think you are?

not at all   super judgy

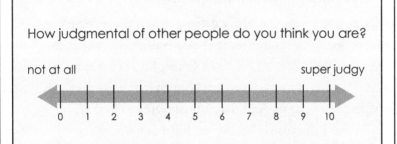

How judgmental would the people closest to
you say you are?

not at all   super judgy

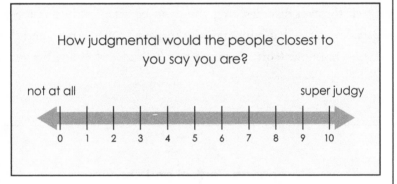

If you could *choose* how judgmental you are, what
number would you choose?

not at all   super judgy

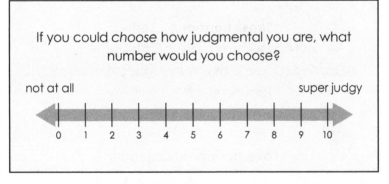

Do you feel that being judgmental has ever made it
difficult for you to connect with others?

not at all   yep

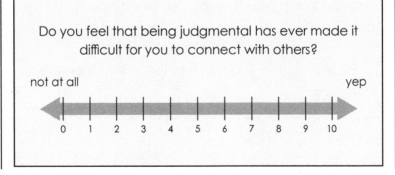

We've spent a fair bit of time exploring your reactions, go-to blocking emotions, and which defense mechanisms you prefer—all to see that one of the clearest ways these manifest is in judgment. And all of this, generally, to keep you from getting hurt. The funny thing about life is this great paradox: you must be open to feel the deepest intimacy, love, and connection. And that is the greatest risk of all.

We have discussed this before, but I want to make it even more clear as we have just done some good depth work. When you separate yourself through defenses, over time you become less intimate with others. We know that human beings thrive on togetherness, and that the stress hormone (cortisol) increases in solitude, while love brings on the healing power of oxytocin.

Comparing Cortisol and Oxytocin

Stress hormone: Cortisol
Increased heart rate and blood flow
Damage to organs over long-term exposure
Inability to think rationally
Difficulty converting experiences to memory

Love hormone: Oxytocin
Lowered heart rate and blood pressure
Healing to organs with exposure (short and long term)
Ability to think deeply and increase metacognition
and connection building
Ease in converting short- to long-term memory

Joining with others keeps your defenses, blocking emotions, and judgment in check, which is one of the keys to engaging in loving relationships. When you feel judgment, you hold it—even sometimes holding your breath. Alternatively, when you feel empathy for another person or group of people, there is a feeling of flow—of love. Over time, choosing love is personally beneficial.

Love is good for you.

While you need to protect yourself at times, flow of acceptance and empathy feels better and is healthier. It also can be so scary. It is a choice only you can make. Past worries/trauma/experiences as well as personality type can halt you from feeling open about people, especially people who are not like you. Remember that your fears are largely unfounded, and that love is better for your health.

Empathy = Enter the Other Person's World + No Judgment + Understand Feelings + Communicate Understanding

---

UNDERSTAND FEELINGS

I'm glad we just talked about blocking emotions and ways you defend against intolerable experiences/feelings because it's fresh in your mind. Our focus has been on how defenses stop you from connecting with others. They also stop you from connecting with *yourself*. The goal of therapy is to uncover the emotions that have been defended against due to the subconscious battle between what you *really* want/need and what you deem intolerable. The goal of psychoanalytic theory is to guide the patient toward insight. In other words, when your defenses protect you from other people, it is a secondary response to their actual job—to protect you from your own intolerable feelings. There are emotions you are most comfortable with, the ones that get ignored, and everything in between. The emotions you neglect are so foreign to you that you may not be able to recognize them in others. If you can't see them in yourself, how could you see them in someone else?

Before you can understand someone else's feelings, you must understand your own.

All the work we've done together, to know yourself and explore who you are and how you operate, has led us here. There are aspects of your own emotional experience that are less developed than others, and these areas can hold you back from greater intimacy.

In family therapy training, we were assigned a book entitled *Constructing the Sexual Crucible*—yeah, yikes, that's a doozy of a title! The notion of the book is that each individual will come to a long-term committed relationship with another person. Like a crucible in chemistry class, you enter a safe place (commitment as crucible), and through the chemistry of combining two lives, both are intrinsically changed (science!). The premise is that a lifelong relationship is a stage of human development! And without the experience of learning more about yourself through the pressure of the crucible, you do not get the opportunity to forge a new self. Whoa. Those ideas stuck with me.

Do I think you need to be in a lifelong relationship to get your own stuff sent back to you for review? Nope. To me, the crucible can exist anytime you open yourself fully to an honest relationship with another human being—*even if you don't know them that well*—and allow change to occur. For example, am I deeply changed at a cellular level through my marriage? Yes. The same is true of my relationship with my brother, children, parents, and dear friends who constantly blow my imaginary world up . . . in a good way. It goes further: When you enter a truly open and empathetic relationship with another person who you may not even know that well—or maybe even just saw on the news—you become changed. You learn about who you are in this way through seeing and allowing yourself to feel parts of the full range of human emotions that you aren't as fluent in. Through empathy, you can grow your human experience. You become different and more knowledgeable about your own feelings.

Full Range of Human Emotions

What is the full range of human emotions? Just as you have favorite colors, you have favorite emotions. I call it the *emotion rainbow*, and it has about thirty emotions. I like to think of it as a rainbow with different-colored bands, all important, essential, and varying in hue. Recent studies have found that basics such as anger and happiness may be "secondary" emotions, though I am perfectly happy to keep them here as primary emotions as no one wants to imagine a world without happiness, and I am willing to let anger come along for the ride.

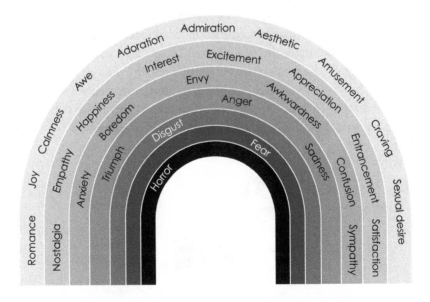

Just like there aren't any "good" or "bad" colors, there aren't good or bad emotions. Your brain is such a cool and somewhat mysterious place that you associate lots of different senses with facts, feelings, memories, etc. Though it may seem a little elementary to explore human emotions through the lens of a rainbow, I assure you science backs it. Those of you who are artistic in thinking and learning may appreciate the connection, and the rest can benefit from the adventure. New pathways = healthy brains.

Emotion Rainbow

One of the best ways to explore your emotions is to map out, quickly, what colors correspond to each of your feelings. Like many things, your initial and quick responses are best. Don't overthink it. If you did the Implicit Awareness Tests earlier in the book, then you've had some practice (https://implicit.harvard.edu/implicit/takeatest.html). If you haven't, bookmark the IAT page and make sure you take that journey. We know that the best responses, the ones that show you how you truly feel, are the fast, non-corrected answers. With that in mind, grab a pile of crayons or markers that represent the colors of the rainbow—and get going.

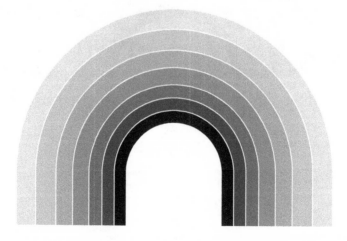

Admiration	Entrancement
Adoration	Envy
Aesthetic	Excitement
Appreciation	Fear
Amusement	Happiness
Anger	Horror
Anxiety	Interest
Awe	Joy
Awkwardness	Nostalgia
Boredom	Romance
Calmness	Sadness
Confusion	Satisfaction
Craving	Sexual desire
Disgust	Sympathy
Empathy	Triumph

Please color-code the emotions. After you finish, go back through the list and explore your reactions to each emotion—jotting down whatever thoughts come up for you as you hold each emotion front of mind. Enjoy!

Now you are more familiar with the emotion rainbow! You must know it for yourself, or you can't identify someone else's. Think for a moment: if ten people in a room completed that action, they would have ten different responses (this is actually a very useful group exercise to help people see the complexity of understanding feelings for themselves and others). If you don't take the time to know your own emotions—what your favorites and suppressed choices are—as well as all the options that exist and how you react to each, it can be very difficult to assess someone else's emotions.

If you aren't comfortable with the full range of emotions, you won't be able to use the Platinum Rule. Because no matter how much you may want to connect, if you can't engage in "emotion speak" with ease, it will be hard to see when someone shows you their rainbow. Everyone can practice emotion speak—it's vulnerable, good for you, and builds intimacy. Who doesn't want to go on a ride on the emotion rainbow?

How can you do this? Just like you have done here, explore your emotions. Let them come up and notice what you feel. Begin to name emotions. If you're brave and it is authentic for you, express these emotions to others. The more you walk in emotion town, the more comfortable you will be.

> **Empathy = Enter the Other Person's World +**
> **No Judgment + Understand Feelings +**
> **Communicate Understanding**

COMMUNICATE UNDERSTANDING

Someday, I am going to write a book entitled *They Don't Know Unless You Tell Them*. It's true. Many human conflicts come from psychic syndrome.

Psychic syndrome = Assuming other people are mind readers

Psychic syndrome leads to confusion, sadness, and less intimacy. This happens when you say the words all therapists dread to hear: "They know

I . . . (fill in the blank)." Of course, the other person doesn't know. You "think" and "hope," but human beings have short emotional memories. Especially when it comes to relationships. Therefore, you need to *tell people you love them.* Tell others when you love, hear, see them, and when you understand how they feel (more on psychic syndrome in chapter 11)!

If you don't tell the other person how you feel, it's an empathetic failure. You may feel empathy, but the message wasn't delivered. This can be a challenge when you aren't physically in the same space or don't know the person or group of people you are feeling empathy for. There are lots of ways to show empathy, just like there are a lot of ways to show love. I'll leave it to you to make a list and find ways to express your empathy to those both near and far in your own way.

Why is it so hard to say you empathize? For the same reasons it can be a challenge to express anything. It can be scary. Remember the love paradox? You need intimacy. At the same time, the risk is huge. Defense mechanisms and blocking emotions are to credit/blame for these roadblocks. Being able to be open and defenseless enough to communicate vulnerability requires every skill you have. You must be open without being too open and real without fear. When you take the vulnerable step of expressing emotion/shared empathy, it is one of the bravest things you can do.

Express Empathy

Without expression (in whatever way fits the situation), empathy can be lost to the island of good intentions, and an empathetic failure may occur. This is all right occasionally but does not lead to greater connections. If high emotional success is your goal, you'll have to become fluent in expressing empathy.

Please describe a time you've had psychic syndrome (you thought someone knew how you were feeling—and you wanted them to know—but they didn't).

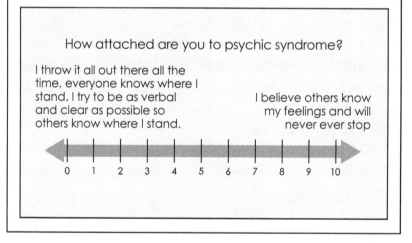

What was the outcome of this miscommunication?

Have you had psychic syndrome other times? Does it happen often? How might you like to change this in the future?

How attached are you to psychic syndrome?

I throw it all out there all the time, everyone knows where I stand. I try to be as verbal and clear as possible so others know where I stand.

I believe others know my feelings and will never ever stop

0   1   2   3   4   5   6   7   8   9   10

There are no perfect ways to express empathy. It is an alchemy of the moment, the people involved, history, vulnerability, affection, and a desire to be close. You sometimes hold back because of blocking emotions—fear, for example, that you won't be understood, or that you will look foolish. You might worry about showing empathy in front of your group for a member of another group and losing your standing—this is a big one.

"There are all kinds of courage," said Dumbledore, smiling. "It takes a great deal of bravery to stand up to our enemies, but just as much to stand up to our friends."

—J. K. Rowling

If you think of some of the bravest moments you've seen in your life or represented in media, the theme of showing empathy in the face of losing in-group status is *huge*. We cannot overstate the risk involved in expressing empathy during high-intensity moments. However, whether you fear expressing the wrong way, fumbling over your words, or losing your status in a group, there is simply no universal right thing to say. Sometimes, not saying anything but instead offering a touch or sitting beside the person in loving silence is just right. To avoid empathetic failure, you need to give empathy a try with an open heart and mind. You don't have to be perfect; you just have to be loving. Even if you fumble. Even if you need to repair a failed attempt.

GENTLE GUIDELINES

Now that we all agree that inaction is least preferable as it relates zero message to the other person, let's talk about some general guidelines that therapists use to let people know that they are heard. Feeling validated is one of the most healing experiences on earth. Let's try to give that to one another. Along that thinking, here are some things that let you know that you may not be empathizing but rather sympathizing, or something else. One good way to tell if you're empathizing: if you are thinking a lot, you probably aren't connecting as deeply as you can.

Things that might mean you aren't expressing empathy:

- Giving advice
- Talking a lot about your own experience

- Thinking a lot—being "in your head" (intellectualizing)
- Not feeling what they seem to be projecting
- Attempting to change the mood

While there is a time and place for each of these activities, empathy time is not the moment. As we will talk about in upcoming chapters, there is skill involved in being fully present with another person. Doing things that pull toward status quo—"Don't cry" or "Here's how you can fix it," or "Here's how I fixed something like that," the toxic positivity[22] of "It's not that bad," changing the subject, going silent, talking about something unrelated—are usually signs your blocking emotions and defenses have taken over. If/when this happens to you, and it happens to all of us, just back up, take a breath, restart. All you have to do is sit for a minute. Listen. You will find a moment to try again. Isn't that great? Just sit for a second. Calm. Slow down. And next thing you know, you'll be back in connection town versus the advice palace. I love that palace, but I don't want to go there if what I need is some validation.

I'm guessing you don't either.

You are ready to practice the empathy equation. Empathy is a third of emotional success. To enjoy emotional success, you need to be able to sit, listen, and shut out the world so you can tune in 100 percent to the person in front of you.

Thankfully, the next two chapters will guide you toward skills in both areas.

---

22   Toxic positivity is toxic if it doesn't allow the other person space to process the "negative" emotion they're experiences. There is a fine line, though, as gaining perspective is also important. The key here is to stay in step with the other person rather than trying to drive the emotion bus for them.

CHAPTER 8

One-Mindfully

Y ou can't empathize if you aren't fully present. When your own thoughts aren't managed, your "mind debris" becomes a barrier between yourself and others, inhibiting intimacy. This chapter will help you work toward being fully present in order to prepare the ground for empathy to bloom.

Empathy seems like a matter of the heart—connecting with others is an expression of love. But it requires your whole self. Mindfulness is an exercise of the mind. Without mindfulness, you can't practice empathy. The psychological secrets to achieving emotional success in this chapter are negativity bias, inattentional blindness, autopilot, and some of my favorite therapy tools. When you know what your brain is up to, you can steer the ship into calm water.

Mindfulness allows you to quiet yourself and offer empathy. Here are the tricks of the trade.

Mindfulness is everywhere. The buzz exists because it is cheap, available, and magical. Without leaving your home, or even your chair, you can rewire your mind and connect more deeply with yourself, other people, and the world around you. When you can't focus fully on the person in the present moment, you get in our own way too much to "enter into the other person's world." One of the great things about mindfulness is that it is accessible to all and doesn't require much more than determination and openness to the idea. The rest is up to you.

Whether you are sitting with people in real life, watching a TV show, or scrolling on social media, when your own thoughts, worries, reactions, judgments, etc., come to the front of your mind, you see through the lens of all that *stuff*. I call this mind debris. Let's clear the clutter you allow in your headspace so you can connect with others and enjoy emotional success.

WHO IS IN CHARGE OF WHAT YOU SEE?

Let's talk through how your mind works, and then we will focus on how to "do" mindfulness. There are so many reasons your mind is clogged with thoughts. Many are related to topics we've already discussed, such as personality, defenses, experiences, values, learning styles, etc. These realities have created special glasses for you—the lenses through which you see everything. Perception is controlled by your brain. All the sensory information that comes from your five senses (sight, sound, touch, feel, and taste) works as data points for your mind.

You already know that your brain must sort through millions of pieces of information every second. This leads to bias, as we've described—and that's due to the way your brain chooses what you see and how you see it. In fact, your brain has what is called a *negativity bias*. Based on millennia of successful evolution and survival, you remember the dangerous, bad, potential threats, etc., better than the good. The good won't necessarily help you to survive. After all, it just makes the living better, whereas transferring those negative experiences to long-term memory can mean the difference between life and death. Mindfulness helps you rewire and notice negative bias before you make life choices and decisions based on it. You're not just biased against other people as a way of protecting yourself; you're biased against anything that's perceived as a threat.

In addition to your brain coloring how you see everything with a negative bias, it even controls *what* you see! There is awesome research about what we call *inattentional blindness*, which means if you don't put your attention to something, you won't see it. The experiments that demonstrate this are powerful.

Imagine a room full of people watching a video of a basketball game. They are divided into groups. The researcher asks them to count how many points each team makes. Sometimes they pit the groups against one another to count the opposing team's score. Competition seems to really up the ante. People begin to focus, hard. Next up, a person in a gorilla costume walks right through the basketball court (could be another animal, though many are gorillas for some inexplicable reason; if anyone knows why it's a gorilla, please message me). The "gorilla" doesn't run, or even rush. In fact, the gorilla stops and looks at the camera before heading back off the court. Then the researcher stops the video and asks the participants how many points were scored. Some people—usually less than 5 percent!—look puzzled and confused; is he going to mention the weird gorilla?

Everyone else proudly states the number of shots scored. When a brave person finally speaks up and discussion of the gorilla ensues, most participants are in disbelief. Regardless of the near universality of this theory, time and again people deny it could be so and then, when shown the video again, believe it to be a different video. Every time, participants simply can't believe they didn't see the gorilla. Given evidence (the video), they remain in denial.

This is perhaps the most important point of all! It seems people are largely unaware of their limitations. How on earth doesn't everyone know about inattentional blindness and discuss their "blind spots" in common language? People seem to do the very opposite and deny these potential limitations rather than acknowledging them. Perhaps they could realize everyone must work together to see the whole picture. Everyone has inattentional blindness, specific lenses through which they see the world, and general shortcomings as human beings. What matters is that you work toward managing these possible constraints.

When I think of inattentional blindness, I am deeply struck by all I don't know—all I don't even *know* that I don't know! What is out there, or right in front of you, that you don't see/experience because you can't understand it and don't perceive it? Remember, data must be either a threat or a help to bring it to the front of your mind. I wonder huge thoughts about this inability to *see* the world around us—considerations about the smallness of our understanding, and more manageable thoughts relating to interactions with others. What are you missing due to inattentional blindness and being on autopilot?

Mindfulness has been proven to help you click off autopilot. This will increase your openness to what is in front of you. In this chapter we will discuss how mindfulness works, why it works, and how you can practice this magical skill to help you connect better with the world around you.

Mindfulness Matters (?) or (!)

Please take a moment and answer the following questions. As always, your fastest responses are the most honest. Let it fly, and let's see what we're working with.

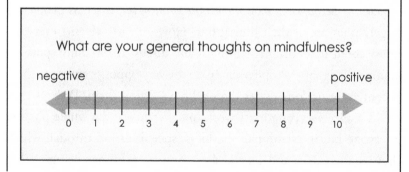

What are your general thoughts on mindfulness?

negative   positive

0   1   2   3   4   5   6   7   8   9   10

When you think of mindfulness or meditation, what kind of reactions do you have?

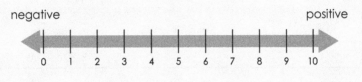

negative   positive

0   1   2   3   4   5   6   7   8   9   10

What is your reaction to becoming more mindful?

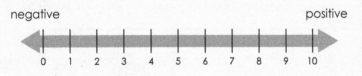

negative   positive

0   1   2   3   4   5   6   7   8   9   10

Have you heard of negative bias in thought patterns before?

Yes   or   No

Were you surprised to hear that your mind has a negative gravitational pull?

Yes   or   No

Did you know what inattentional blindness was before reading this chapter?

Yes   or   No

Jot down your reactions to this information and how it might apply to how you approach connecting with new people.

Name a time when you "just didn't see" something—either a physical object or a part of an interaction—that seemed obvious after the fact but was invisible to you in the moment.

How do you think inattentional blindness might impact your life?

What thoughts do you have re: the phenomena known as inattentional blindness?

Please take a moment to consider how your responses may inform your desire to engage in mindfulness. Please write a narrative, draw a picture, or create a song about your reactions and thoughts of gaining more control over your mind debris. Let's pull the ideas from this first part of the chapter, along with your knowledge of who you are and where you want to head on this journey. No judgment here, just information. Remember, the facts are friendly; you just need to know where you are.

MINDFUL RESISTANCE

Uncomfortable + Silence = Anxiety

If you feel excited and on board to start your mindfulness journey, yay!

However, if you've completed the action above and realize you feel hesitant or not interested, keep that realization in the front of your mind. Perhaps you have an established practice and feel as though this is all too basic for you (I'll challenge y'all in this group—there's always more to learn, places to explore, expansions to enjoy). No matter the reason, if your resistance keeps you from feeling receptive, perhaps you need to take a step back from the chapter, or continue reading, allowing yourself to hold the concepts at arm's length. There is no harm in feeling resistant. If you want to, consider why you don't want to dive in. This self-exploration and mind work can be exhausting. Take it at your pace, and be kind to yourself. The book is here for you when you want to move on.

At times you will lean into things that make you uncomfortable. Other times, you don't have the energy to push new boundaries. Remember the traffic light analogy? Pushing yourself further is when you enter the yellow zone. My goal is to spend much of my life in yellow, but sometimes I get yellow zone exhaustion— and without meaning to, I am pushed into red. That means it is time to pause.

When I need a break, I'll be more tired than I think I should be, or irritable. I begin to feel protective of my downtime. Maybe depression or anxiety will start to peek around the corner—interrupting my sleep, happiness, and giving me stress. I know when I've been pushing my own boundaries too hard for too long, and even though growth is my number one goal in life, we must all take note from the moderation page and sit down. Some say that *shavasana* (resting pose) in yoga is the most powerful pose, as it's where all the integration and rebuilding occurs. I can really get behind that thinking.

#shivasanaorbust

In general, yoga has been a big part of my adult life. It provides me an avenue for health—strength, flexibility, and mindfulness all in one! I deeply respect the ancient Eastern traditions and feel grateful that this American White girl can touch the surface of all yoga offers. With my funky hip and mental blocks on certain poses, it seems like yoga is a well that I'll never quite understand the depths of. That is a wonderful promise to me—to always have more to learn.

Sometimes what I learn is that I've reached the end of my capabilities and need to rest. Being upside down and backwards does this to me every time. I didn't even know I would hate that. But I despise back bends. In yoga you can put your legs up the wall, even on a chair, and then bend backwards with your head hanging down. Yuck. My anxiety spikes through the roof in that silent pose—I think, *I'm going to have an aneurysm right now and die. And then what will they do?* Notice these thoughts are both terrified and somehow angry. Huh. Ask me to sit silently, a little uncomfortably, and look what bubbles up. I'm respectfully friendly with my anxiety most of the time. But when there is silence combined with discomfort, our relationship becomes combative. For me, back bends are uncomfortable. I don't *like* being upside down. Often during long poses with no directions—not even a clock to let me know *how much more*—anxiety comes and sits on my chest, breathes hot air in my face. No thank you to that. Many people find anxiety in the quiet, undefined spaces of their lives—whether they are upside down or just feeling that way. Occasionally, individuals have strong reactions to mindfulness because in the end, it is quiet and undefined.

Why is it that in moments of uncomfortableness and silence, you often find anxiety? It's partially because your mind is wired to think and rework constantly. Zillions of connections in your brain are whizzing and joining, rebuilding and reconsidering, at every second. The smarter you are, the more connections your brain makes. And remember, it's built toward a negative bias—leading you down those scary paths to keep you safe. It's one of your brain's main jobs!

People are built to worry, overthink, and stress as a species; these are old struggles. For millennia, human beings have worked to slow the "monkey brain." Meditation, prayer, yoga—there are so many ancient rituals aimed at controlling your thoughts and making you feel more connected with yourself and maybe something bigger. Long before the constant digital input you receive now, wise humans knew that mind strength equals greater health and well-being. It also means taming the monkey in your brain—and sometimes, that monkey is a super scary alpha who doesn't want to be tamed. After all, stilling the mind is going against the flow. Remember, nature prefers status quo.

Perhaps some resistance you feel toward peaceful reflection is related to your fears and anxieties about what it might mean to quiet your mind. Will you be less "yourself"? Will you still be super type A and successful if you "calm down"? Will you lose your "edge"? How on earth will you make time in your busy life to do yet another thing? What's the point? What will you find in the void of your mind?

If any of these apply to you, take heart; we all feel similar reactions.

That's your mind working hard to keep you from taking control. The constant whirring makes your brain happy. That's what you've trained your brain to do your whole life, like your ancestors before you.

Your mind is like a computer you programmed to run endlessly, and then you want to take the power back. Yep, it's that real. Also, yes, I am basically making a reference to computers taking over the world as equivalent with your mind resisting executive control. I stand by it. Mindfulness is how you can alter that trajectory to one where you are sitting in the driver's seat, at least some of the time.

Ironically, calming your mind and being able to clearly and thoughtfully react to the world around you is healthy, and it seems that once you obtain the skill, your mind and body recognize the benefits of turning off autopilot, and it becomes more natural, even preferred.

MINDFULNESS MOVES US FROM AUTOMATIC PILOT

Constant stimulation ramps your mind to a breakneck speed. In return, your brain decides to employ automatic pilot. One reason silence brings anxiety is because you are numb. When you are quiet, still, open to your own sensations, it can be an overwhelming rush. The more you tame autopilot and claim your own reactions in the moment, the more easily you can switch back and forth between control/autopilot at will. Emotional success comes from the ability to control and experience the full range of emotions—and to share those feelings with others.

You must first manage autopilot.

In a car, you can sometimes drive for miles on autopilot without really being aware of what you are doing. In the same way, you aren't present moment-by-moment for much of your life. You can often zone out without knowing it. On autopilot, you are more likely to be irritable, for example.[23] Events around you and thoughts, feelings, and sensations (of which you may be only dimly aware) can trigger old and unhelpful habits of thinking that lead to a worsening mood.

By becoming more aware of your thoughts, feelings, and body sensations, from moment to moment, you give yourself the possibility of greater freedom and choice; you do not have to go into the same old mental ruts that may have caused problems in the past. The aim of mindfulness is to increase awareness so that you can respond to situations with choice rather than react automatically. You do that by becoming more aware of where your attention is, and deliberately changing the focus of your thoughts.

**A note on the actions in the remainder of this chapter:

The actions in the remainder of this chapter are a little different from the ones we have done together to this point. Instead of questions and reflections you may be able to complete in one sitting, right here and right now, some of these actions are ongoing activities that will require time to pass as part of the activity. You can decide if you'd like to do them in order, skip one and move ahead, keep several going at the same time, or take it easy and slow. Sometimes mindfulness can be triggering—because of trauma history, struggles with body image/eating, or many other reasons. Tread lightly and please choose an activity that is innocuous to you—the more boring, in fact, the better suited for this task. If something comes up that surprises you, find someone appropriate with whom to talk those reactions through.

---

23   Have you noticed how cranky children are when you remove their devices? Adults are the same. This is because your screen brings you a flood of the hormone dopamine. Dopamine feels good. Cocaine, and many other drugs, are also pathways to dopamine abundance. Your brain likes the path of least resistance, remember? Knowing the irritability is *real* and the power of your screen is biological can be helpful when you make choices about how much time you dedicate to those activities. Whatever you do, you're training your brain.

Approach these in whatever way works for you, as long as you feel growth happening, and you don't lose sight of the goal—to focus on the present moment and begin or deepen your mindfulness journey.

With all of that in mind . . .

Step Out of Autopilot

This first action is designed to bring mindfulness into your everyday life, helping you move from autopilot toward skillful control. When you make a change in your life, the first step is always to bring awareness. Do you want to change your negative self-talk, for instance? Step 1 is to always keep track, notice, and just see the frequency. This step can take weeks! This is because you are moving your mind from a place of inattentional blindness—not paying attention—toward attention. You have probably noticed in your life that once you start seeing something, you see it everywhere (remember the *availability heuristic*).

Here, you will take notice, and it can last as long as you like. Welcome to step one. Whether you're rewriting or just beginning your practice, I'm excited for your journey.

Choose one activity each day that you do often on autopilot, such as brushing your teeth, eating, attending lectures, showering, preparing for bed, walking in the park. It is probably best to stick with one activity for a week or longer rather than changing the activity regularly.

Which activity will you choose?

When the time comes for that activity, do it in a fully mindful way. Pay attention to the activity itself, what is happening right now. For example, with brushing teeth you might feel the touch of the brush, note the noise it is making, become aware of the taste of the toothpaste. When you find yourself thinking of other things, note it for a second or two and return to the sensations associated with brushing your teeth.

Mindful eating is an excellent example because the psychological and physiological benefits are equally enormous. And for training your mind, it is extraordinarily beneficial to be mindful in all aspects of your life. If you've struggled with food/eating in the past, skip this approach or discuss with your support scaffolding.

If the activity is likely to take longer than a few minutes, such as eating or walking in the park, then practice only the first few moments mindfully. Pay attention to what you see, the sounds you hear, the feeling of your clothes as you walk. What can you smell? Think of your sensations as raw data, rather than accepting the final picture your brain puts together from that information. You are getting back in touch with the data you receive. Try to focus on the sensations in the moment (sight, touch, smell, sound, taste).

Please answer the following questions:

What was your activity for this action?

What was it like to experience this activity while being mindful?

Mindfulness is a never-ending journey. There is no end point, and you often circle back to your starting place. For example, sometimes when I attempt my mindfulness practice, I find nothing in my mind but chatter and noise. Why then would I ask you to begin a practice that at times will fail? Because even in the dead ends, there is progress. Mindfulness is as much about the intention of rewiring your mind as the outcome of your practice. Here are some proven benefits of engaging in a mindfulness practice.[24]

- Improved mental health
- Increased resiliency to stress
- Universal changes to your thinking that last, alter perspective, and allow you to create space from the negative bias and move toward more control over your reactions
- Improved attention and focus
- Reversal and/or added control of inattentional blindness
- Self-compassion
- Satisfaction with life
- Higher relationship satisfaction as cortisol levels drop even after difficult discussions
- Improved physical health
- Lowered cortisol levels, stronger and more plentiful direct connections between amygdala (older part of brain) and frontal cortex
- Social justice
- Reduction in bias both toward others as well as toward your own self-defeating beliefs (sunk cost bias—which leads you to remain in situations based on how much you've already given versus whether it's a good fit)
- Increased and improved ability to be compassionate
- Impetus to protect your natural environment

---

24   Brought to you by the Greater Good Science Center at UC Berkeley—one of my favorite resources for feel-good quality information and meta-analysis.

- Conscious awareness of your surroundings
- Connection to the "ultimate dimension"—or the feeling of being connected with the world around us

It seems too good to be true—like magic—and yet, there it is. I am a believer in "It's okay for things to be good." Let's allow ourselves to believe that wonderful and simple things can be real. The amazing truth is that mindfulness improves mental and physical health, increases social justice(!), and has positive impact on climate change. It seems obvious that mindfulness might improve your mental health.

Perhaps you expected that outcome. Most of you also probably assumed physical health would be enhanced through mindfulness practice. However, it may come as a surprise that the calmer and more centered you become, the more you connect with other people and even your planet. What a fabulous side impact of your own improved well-being!

In addition to your mental health, your physical health is also improved by regular mindfulness practice. This is largely related to the lowering of autonomic nervous system response—and thus the decrease in the buildup of cortisol in your body. Cortisol is a double-sided hormone. You need it for healthy responses to keep yourself alive in dangerous situations. It aids in fetal development during pregnancy. And yet, as I discussed earlier in the book and also on a segment of *The Doctors* TV show, too much cortisol can lead to bigger-than-necessary reactions as well as increased risk of damage to your internal organs. This is one of the reasons prolonged stress responses can hurt you physically.

When you are stressed, you cannot connect meaningfully with others; your empathetic abilities are thwarted by defense mechanisms. However, through regular mindfulness practice, you increase your ability to be compassionate—perhaps by quieting the ruminating autopilot thoughts in your mind that run toward negativity. You'll also see social justice improvements through meditative practice in the reduction of bias toward others (likely that compassion piece) and yourself! You are more able to turn toward new ways of thinking and being that reflect increased self-love. And when you feel all this goodness toward yourself and other people, it translates to your surroundings as well. The connection to the "ultimate dimension" leads people to feel more engaged in the natural world and concerned about climate change and the environment in general.

WHAT *IS* MINDFULNESS?

Mindfulness = Focus on the present moment without judgment

When you attempt to connect with the world around you—knowing yourself deeply and able to quiet the mind and align with another person's experience—that's empathy. Before you're able to engage in entering another person's world, you need to manage the silence and stillness within yourself.

Without a quiet mind, you are only reacting, not creating space for human magic to occur.

Sometimes when we talk about mindfulness, people think it means sitting on the floor, legs bent inward, silence abounding for long periods of time. This isn't accurate! When I talk to patients about beginning a practice, I recommend *up to* five minutes a day. When your goals are too high, you don't reach them. It is a lot to ask someone to sit silently for five minutes. People feel more angst than joy when asked to dive into the deep end of anything. Besides the common misconception that mindfulness takes a long time, let's also clarify definitions as quick and dirty as we can.

Mindfulness can be any contemplative practice as well as a way of being and perceiving.

Some wonder at the difference between mindfulness, meditation, prayer, or other quiet contemplative practice. If you are focused and aware of your thoughts, it doesn't matter what you call it. The goal is to create more control in your mind and thus more peace.

Mindfulness creates space in your mind. It frees you from being trapped by your automatic thoughts born of the natural negativity bias, inattentional blindness, and unhelpful patterns. We therapists generally strive to make ourselves obsolete. One way we have found to be overwhelmingly successful is to give patients the gift of space between stimulus and reactions. To choose their own paths and rise above millennia of monkey-mind evolution. No one wants a monkey driving the car.

THIS IS YOUR BRAIN ON MINDFULNESS

What if you were able to take a beat when you need to, to make choices about your reactions rather than let your lizard brain guide you? This is your brain on mindfulness. Mindfulness brings you into the present moment and allows you to gain space between a stimulus and your reaction.

STIMULUS   S   P   A   C   E   REACTION

Many hardships derive from reacting instantly without the benefit of space to engage your frontal cortex so you can *decide* how you want to act in the moment. All of the mental health benefits that come from mindfulness—increased resiliency to stress, improved ability to focus, less inattentional blindness, expanded self-compassion and life satisfaction, more pleasure in relationships, and universal changes to your perspective toward the positive—are born from this S P A C E. Mindfulness moves you from instant reactions driven by the oldest parts of your mind toward increased control.

A Space of One's Own

What would you do if you had more S P A C E between stimulus and your reactions? In psychology, we call anything that happens to us stimulus (see the image above for a visual). For example, someone speaks to me (stimulus). I have a reaction (thought, feeling, or behavior). Many times, those reactions are driven by autopilot or my lizard brain. I'd like to use mindfulness to create more space between the stimulus and my reaction; wouldn't you? We start this process by growing awareness of our patterns. Let's work through an example in your life!

Please name a situation recently where you reacted in a way you would like to change. This can be something small (a low-impact situation) or huge (a longer-term/bigger impact).

You can use the model provided as a guide.

STIMULUS   S   P   A   C   E   REACTION

What would it have looked like if you had S P A C E to consider your reaction differently?

Do you normally respond with thoughts, feelings, or behaviors? It is helpful to know the order of things because awareness makes you better able to track your reactions and start to create some space. To do this, imagine the situation you described above. Now, did you think, act, or feel first? Your reactive patterns aren't universal, but they are usually dominant toward one of the three.

Write some notes and consider your pattern—draw it, write about it, observe it. Just knowing this process brings you closer to having increased control over your reactions.

One-Mindfully

"No feeling is final."
—Rainer Maria Rilke

If you create the ability to refocus your mind from anxious thoughts toward a moment of reflection that you choose, you are in control of your mind! This simple truth, that you can't think two thoughts at the same time, is why so many therapists employ mindfulness skills. You know when you hurt yourself and you grab yourself tight, it hurts less? This is because you asked your brain to hold two messages—pain and touch. The touch message dilutes the pain message. It is the same with any unwanted or loud thoughts. Of course, if you are working with a thought disorder, and have difficulty managing your thoughts without medication, this can be more difficult.[25]

I have been privileged to work with many people who have experienced trauma, as well as people who suffer with ongoing suicidality.

---

25   Mindfulness can be useful for patients with thought disturbances as well, with careful supervision and guidance.

Though some might scoff at mindfulness as "extra" or "fluffy"—both adjectives I like a lot—we know that bringing control to your thoughts is one of the most useful tools against the deepest of depressions and can help ward off reoccurring unwanted thoughts related to trauma as well. Mindfulness is powerful medicine.

It is impossible to discuss mindfulness and therapy without pointing out the work of Dr. Marsha Linehan, who created dialectical behavior therapy (DBT). DBT began to help hospitalized women managing ongoing suicidality. It has grown and is now considered a gold-star therapy for both men and women for a surprisingly wide range of concerns. The four pillars of DBT are mindfulness, emotional regulation, distress tolerance, and interpersonal effectiveness. As you can see, those are skills that will also help you grow your emotional success. One of the underpinnings of the theory, the *D* in DBT, stands for *dialectical*, and this is a concept everyone could embrace with more enthusiasm. One of the characteristics of individuals who struggle with personality disorders or experience volatile personal relationships is what we call *black-and-white thinking*. A dialectical is the idea that two (or more) things can be true at the same time. You don't have to limit yourself to oversimplified versions of people or relationships.

Think about this—what if you started replacing the word *or* with the word *and* in your mind? The results are powerful. It is a lie you tell yourself that something is this *or* that when most things are a mix! I'm strong *and* I'm vulnerable. My partner is messy *and* good at other things. You can quickly see that limiting your vision of yourself and others can lead to untrue assumptions. When you utilize mindfulness to create space between stimulus and your reactions, you can choose how to think about the situation; adding in *and* instead of *or* can often help to deescalate your thoughts and help you gain perspective. There is so much more in DBT to learn, and there are many books, seminars, and groups you can explore if this is of interest to you.

Another of the main pillars of DBT is mindfulness practice. This is because mindfulness helps patients develop the space between stimulus and reaction. When you get down to it, an urge is an urge, whether it's to react negatively to someone, bite your nails, or engage in drug use. These are all less-than-healthy coping skills that arise from urges. Mindfulness creates the space between a stimulus and a reaction (urge)—no matter what the urge is! Of course, society places all sorts of judgments and value on different urges and coping skills, but your brain doesn't. To your brain, changing a behavior follows generally the same pattern no matter what the urge may be. While some substances are more addictive than others, the behaviors and patterns around a habit are the same to your brain as any other habit, and these can all be better managed through a mindfulness practice. Mindfulness combined with the understanding that more than one thing can be true at a time are the underpinnings of DBT and have been found to be extremely helpful for many people struggling with many different things. Practicing DBT as a therapist changed my thinking so completely that I chose to entitle this chapter "One-Mindfully" as a nod to Dr. Linehan's groundbreaking work. If you aren't familiar with her work, now is a good time to learn more. Everyone can benefit from gaining control over reactions.

Work from the Outside In

You are in control of what is happening inside. Even and especially when you can't control the world around you. This comes in handy when someone tells you something that is especially triggering to your own pain and your defenses stop you from connecting. You certainly cannot be empathetic in these threatening moments. One way to use mindfulness in therapeutic ways is to consider yourself from the outside in. We know that if a person is struggling with trauma or physical pain, some mindfulness practices may *increase* cortisol and the overall stress response. For instance, focusing on the breath or full-body scans, sometimes anything with a body-oriented approach, may lead to stress. For this reason, we are thoughtful about how we introduce mindfulness practice into therapy with all patients.

At the University of Pittsburgh, Dr. Lisa Maccarelli (one of the most talented, loving, and knowledgeable therapists I've ever known) and I created a protocol for working with women college students who were in DBT group therapy with this outside => in approach to mindfulness. I use it often. The idea is that you begin outside of the body with your mindfulness practice. Unfortunately, many apps and services that bring mindfulness to the palm of your hand start with *inside => out* mindfulness, or just stay body oriented. For some people, this brings such stress to the practice that they believe mindfulness is not right for them. This isn't accurate. It's just that the classic notion of sitting quietly and focusing on the breath or inside the body is counterproductive for many people (think of me upside down in silence during yoga! Ugh!). Therefore, start with a focus on the external versus internal. You can switch it up and start getting more internally focused *if that works for you*. However, for some people mindfulness may never involve sitting with eyes closed (this can be a trigger all by itself), focusing on internal body processes as an anchor.[26] If your anchor holds you down more than keeps you steady, it isn't working. Pull the anchor and continue onward until you find a safe place to rest.

Let's explore the *outside => in* model roughly based on the work we did at Pitt.

Outside => In

I offer you a chance to practice each type of mindfulness described in this chapter. You know yourself and what feels safe for you. Pay attention to your body and mind, and stay in the green/yellow zones. If you feel as though you've traveled to red-zone land, please back up and start fresh. Mindfulness is not a competition.

---

26   An anchor in mindfulness is the way we describe something to focus on, hold on to; it is meant to help you rest without floating away. An anchor can be anything you focus on, such as your breathing, the chair, a spot on the wall. In yoga it's called a *drishti*.

Peace and all the benefits of practice can occur no matter how you approach the work. Aside from the meditation at the end of yoga, my practice is largely a contemplative one focusing on being in the moment—doing one thing at a time whenever I can. Feeling the water on my body during a shower, focusing on my walk, attempting to keep outside thoughts at bay, being fully present in as many daily moments as I can. Sometimes I can reach the magic feelings easily; other times I struggle with letting go. This is my practice. You'll have to establish or grow your own.

The following actions are starting points. You can use them however you like. As always, if you find a spot that needs work, please seek support from someone who can offer healthy loving guidance. I offer examples to practice grounding, mindfulness in the moment, focusing on an object outside yourself, classic sitting-in-stillness meditative practice, and focusing on another person. Coloring books for adults (though I'm pretty sure coloring anything will work) and other art as well as body scans are widely available and the focus of much commercial mindfulness practice. If you are comfortable with either of those, I suggest a quick search for examples and to give them a try. There are countless wonderful ways to engage in your practice more deeply. It is my hope to give you a starting point to start or rejuvenate your practice. All will bring you closer to emotional success by creating that S P A C E between stimulus and reaction, as well as connecting you more deeply with yourself and your ability to engage with another person. Good luck!

Grounding

In 2002, therapist Lisa Najavits wrote *Seeking Safety* (from emotional pain).

In it, she describes the ability to healthfully detach from pain via the mindful practice of grounding. Grounding is a seemingly simple act of literally focusing on the ground where you stand. This is our first step in the outside => in approach.

Ground Yourself

One thing I love to teach people—kids too!—is called a grounding technique. It's a positive way to "get grounded!" You can do it anywhere— sitting or standing. If you are sitting, you turn your energy to the chair. If standing, focus on the literal ground beneath you. This act of refocusing makes it impossible for your mind to keep whirring and buzzing. When you notice your mind wandering away from the ground, you gently bring your attention back. A lot of students I've worked with like to focus on the chair they're sitting on, either the bum or arm areas of the chair. Then think, Hey, this is a chair I'm sitting on. Here is my arm resting on the side of the chair, the chair is on the ground, and I am in this moment.

Grounding can help you gain much-needed perspective in the moment to regain control of your reactions. That's it! Cognitive magic! Your mind can only do one thing at once, and to focus on the here and now will bring calm and peace. It can happen anytime, anywhere. No one knows what you're doing; all they notice is your renewed calm.

If it feels scary to let go of your worries, remember that they will always wait for you—though you may not need to revisit those thoughts. Letting them go for a minute will never make the situation worse.

In the Moment

These exercises are moving from outside => in. But *in* is not the goal. Think of the way I introduce these techniques as a map of places to explore, not a task list. The closer you get to inward, the more you must be aware of possible triggers. Be prepared to take good care of yourself.

Here's another anywhere approach to mindfulness I want to share with you. Being in the moment is one of my favorite types of mindfulness practice and the one I engage in most often. I've attempted to turn my whole life into a jumbo mindfulness practice. Next time you see me at the grocery store, you'll know what I'm doing. This practice can happen anytime, anywhere, and is related to the notion of focusing on only one thing at a time, something that is increasingly difficult in the digital age, with the world in your hands. There's no time limit here; just focus on the moment, and the rest comes over time.

Quiet Moments

One-mindfully, meaning one thing at a time on your mind! This action is designed to bring mindfulness into an activity you enjoy. Often when you are stressed or too focused on meeting multiple demands, you lose the ability to engage with activities that bring you enjoyment, relaxation, or peace.

Choose an activity that you love to do—such as taking a walk, creating art, writing a poem, visiting with a friend, cooking, watching a movie, taking a shower, listening to your favorite band, playing a sport, getting a massage, drinking a glass of ice-cold water. Anything you enjoy is perfect. Write about it here.

Reflect:

When was the last time you engaged in this activity?
When you last engaged in this activity, were you fully
present and connected to the moment? If not, what
were the barriers to fully experiencing the activity? If
you were fully present, how and why were you?

Engage in the Activity:

During this week, set some time aside to engage in your
favorite activity. While participating in the activity, do it
mindfully. Be present in the moment and connect to
each of your senses. You should also be mindful of your
emotional and bodily responses throughout the
activity. Pay attention to your mind as well. Does it
wander? If so, does it go to the past? The future? When
your mind begins to wander, remember to gently bring
it back to the present moment.

Objectification

We move now toward focus from an activity to an object. This
does bring things slightly more toward your inner self. If you decide to
engage in this activity, please consider the object carefully, as a highly
emotionally charged object will likely be too distracting to be useful.
For instance, some people have reactions to the smell or memories
associated with Play-Doh, and thus we therapists always make sure
the object to focus on will be innocuous for everyone. In therapy, I've

chosen flowers, rocks—almost any inanimate object will work here, especially one that isn't triggering. Good luck and enjoy.

Focus on a Single Object

Being able to focus on a single object will help you concentrate more fully on the present moment. One of the biggest traps of being unmindful is that your attention wanders from one thing to the next or from one thought to the next. As a result, you often get lost, distracted, or frustrated. This exercise will help you focus your attention on a single object. The purpose of this action is to learn to maintain your focus.

While you practice, you will eventually become distracted by your thoughts. That's okay; this happens to everyone. Do your best not to criticize yourself. Just notice when your mind wanders and return your focus to whatever object you're observing.

Pick a small object to focus on. Choose something that can rest on a table, is safe to touch, and is emotionally neutral. You will engage in this exercise for five minutes. It may be helpful to set a timer. We use Play-Doh often to practice this type of mindfulness, but as I said, consider what works for you.

Instructions:

To begin, sit comfortably and take a few slow, deep breaths. Then, without touching the object, begin looking at it and exploring its different surfaces with your eyes.

Take your time exploring what it looks like. Then try to imagine the different qualities that the object possesses.

- What does the surface of the object look like?
- Is it shiny or dull?
- Does it look smooth or rough?
- Does it look soft or hard?
- Does it have multiple colors or just one color?
- What else is unique about the way the object looks?

Take your time observing the object. Now hold the object in your hand or reach out and touch the object. Begin noticing the different ways it feels.

- Is it smooth or rough?
- Does it have ridges or is it flat?
- Is it soft or is it hard?
- Is it bendable or is it rigid?
- What does the temperature of the object feel like?
- If you can hold it in your hand, notice how much it weighs.
- What else do you notice about the way it feels?

Continue exploring the object with both your sight and your sense of touch. Continue to breathe comfortably. When your attention begins to wander, return your focus to the object. Keep exploring the object until your alarm goes off. When we use Play-Doh, we encourage patients to engage with it! Play! Just focus on the activity and try to keep your mind in the moment.

Was this easy or difficult for you? Why?

Be Still

"Within you there is a stillness and a sanctuary to which you can retreat at any time and be yourself."

—Herman Hess

Now we move toward an internal practice. Stop if this feels uncomfortable for you and seek support. Much mindfulness/ meditation starts with this practice; however, it takes time to build to it. Give yourself grace.

Sitting in Stillness

Find a quiet place to complete this activity. Begin by getting as comfortable as possible, close your eyes, and take deep relaxing breaths. While breathing, attempt to sit as still as possible and clear your mind of any thoughts, sounds, or distractions. As you breathe, allow any thoughts you have to leave your mind so that it is left with peace, quiet, and stillness. Once your mind is clear, sit with the stillness. If any thoughts come to mind, gently acknowledge them and then clear your mind again through your breathing. If it helps, you can imagine your thoughts going to rest someplace safe, where you can visit them later. In this action, breath is the anchor—the *drishti*. Focus on it without trying to change it.

Afterwards, please answer the following questions:

> What was this activity like for you?

> What did you like?

> Did any part of this make you feel uncomfortable?

PRACTICING EMPATHY WITH MINDFULNESS

People ask me if they will be able to engage in empathy, which seems to be an internal activity, if they feel safest when practicing more "outside" types of mindfulness. *Yes!* One lesson we can all take to heart is that the other person is *outside* of you. I say this all the time in therapy. No matter who the other person is—lover, family member, life partner, best friend—*they* are not *you*. We are all separate human beings. Sometimes this reminder can help you separate from intense emotions you might feel about how someone else acts, feels, or is.

This space between yourself and others can also help you to realize that whatever information is presented to you during listening, no matter how triggering it may be, is yours to hold only long enough to find empathy—you don't have to carry it forever. It is only when you get muddied by your own reactions that you feel the other person's experience is threatening.

Our goal this entire chapter and section of the book is to improve your empathic abilities. In the next chapter we will focus on improving your listening skills. But before we get there, let's see what happens when you simply sit in silence with another person. What do you see, feel, notice? Can you find greater peace in the quiet? Remember that for many people, quiet, unstructured silence can bring all their anxiety right to the forefront of their minds.

You've worked toward being able to create some space between stimulus and reaction—and silent time looking at another person is certainly a stimulus. Before you layer on those listening skills, let's practice just being.

Quiet Connections

Let's take what you've practiced and begin to apply it to sitting with another person. In my doc program, we did this exercise more than once—and I distinctly remember the first time. Standing, we all held hands and for three minutes stared into our classmates' eyes. The six of us were very close, but, my goodness, those three minutes were long, and they bonded me to my friend in a way I'll never forget. It's amazing how little people look deeply into one another's eyes in this society.

This action can be used in any setting where the goal is to grow intimacy and connections. If you're going to share this exercise, please make sure the group members feel extremely safe with one another, the environment, and let them choose their own partners if you can. This is an intimate and moving experience. You'll need to create space to discuss beforehand and time to safely and thoroughly process after. This can be a glorious and important deepening activity for any relationship you'd like to be more intimate. Enjoy.

The Activity:

Find a safe and uninterrupted space. It can be in a loud or quiet place as long as you will not be stopped from the activity. Both people must feel safe. You can touch or not touch. Start simply with one minute each of doing nothing in the universe but looking at one another's faces. You don't have to be strict and stare into their eyes, but you can add that on if you'd like. Whatever happens is okay. Laughing, crying, nothing at all—just notice all of this, bring your attention to the present moment and the human being before you, and see what you see. This is largely what therapy is for me—plus the skills in the next chapter. Sitting with an open heart and mind in a safe space filled with love. Perhaps magic connection feelings will happen for you as they do for me sometimes. At the very least, you'll grow intimacy and connection with the other person, and who doesn't want that?

What were your reactions to the experience?

Remember, as with all actions in the book, to be authentic, set your intentions, and then process afterwards to enjoy the deepest experience.

If you spend time noticing Play-Doh or a flower and can see new things and find appreciation in those objects, imagine what magic just focusing can add to a human relationship!

CHAPTER 9

Mindful Listening

"Each voice is distinct and has something to say. Each voice deserves to be heard. But it requires the act of listening."

—Terry Tempest Williams

There's no empathy without listening. Mindful listening requires concentration of your entire physical and emotional self. You must quiet your mind, be self-aware, and hold your responses at bay to truly hear another person and enjoy intimacy and meaningful connections. Psychologists are taught these better-listening tips, and now I share them with you.

This chapter holds so many candy-making secrets. How do therapists get people to open up? I'll answer that here. Did you know that J. K. Rowling had the ending for Harry Potter in the front of her mind as she wrote the other books?

Although I wouldn't compare myself to Jo as an author, I did the same thing here. I knew what I *really* wanted to share with you and then realized it took me years to get to a place where I could engage in mindful listening. I wrote down the core things I learned in my training that helped me get here and built the book from those concepts, knowing where I wanted to end up with y'all.

The secrets in this chapter shouldn't be secrets. I wish adults taught children all the skills in the book. Then they would have so much emotional success with each other. I'm happy just knowing *you* will now benefit from these secrets of the trade. In this chapter, I share common barriers to mindful listening, how to prepare to listen (this section is especially good for those with privilege), and all the listening skills therapists learn.

It feels good to be heard. Intimacy grows when another person listens and validates your feelings. People often think of this type of deep connection as romantic. It can be, but it can also happen in any relationship. Part of the magic of therapy is this focused attention, eye contact, and validation. Eighty percent of therapy success depends on what we call *common factors*. This is the relationship—which is based on super good listening without judgment. Some people call this *active listening*. I prefer *mindful listening*. Calling it mindful listening ties together mindfulness with the process of listening to another person. Sometimes people struggle with active listening because they haven't married it to the mindfulness that's required of the skill. But now you have.

As we've said, you bring certain things to each interaction. Who you are, how you look, where you fit in each social sphere—all bears on your ability to connect. When you layer on personality type, power differentials, defense mechanisms, mood, thoughts, constant interruptions/distractions, how your day is going, and whether you are filled with mind chatter or not, and it's no wonder that mindful listening is not the norm. But it can be. It's a paradigm shift. But it's worth the effort. When you begin to engage in mindful listening, you just can't stop. You get high on being human. Love is my anti-drug.

How is listening good for you? Let's circle back around to the empathy equation. Without mindful listening, you can't enter the other person's world. Empathy helps you to connect, lowers your stress hormones (cortisol), and provides the social benefits of being close (oxytocin). Without exploration of your own worries, stresses, personality, and potential triggers/defenses, it will be hard to listen. However, after that deep dive of self-exploration, combined with familiarity with mindfulness, you're ready to deepen your listening skills.

I've taught psychology and counseling classes to undergrads, master's students, and doc students—and the basics are always the same: be 100 percent in the present moment without judgment (mindfulness). We'll add in the advanced secrets of the trade, and before you know it, you'll be eyeball deep in realness with the people in your life.

BARRIERS TO MINDFUL LISTENING

© 2016 Connie J. Sun   cartoon connie.

I waver between thinking that society is changing for the worse and feeling positive because change is a constant. Sometimes it seems people are intent on creating rather than solving problems. You may be working against yourself in numerous ways. And it all stems from blocking emotions. There are reasons to feel fearful, and yet fear tends to lead you toward greater separation. You shut down. I am asking you to open up. Allow for the things that trigger you to flow through you like a river, rather than holding on to them and reacting. As Tim McGraw says in his song "Humble and Kind," "Bitterness keeps you from flying." Bitterness is another way of saying "holding on to anger and resentment," and it doesn't just keep you from flying. Holding on to negative triggers keeps you from growing, flowing, and connecting. Remember, you've done a ton of work getting to know yourself better, and to create space for reactions to be chosen rather than automatic. Let's settle into the place where growth happens and see where you start your listening journey.

Thoughts on Listening

There is truth and openness in the kind of listening that translates to intimacy.

Let's see where you are in this process. Please think of the last time you had a difficult conversation with another person.

> What was the conversation about?

What was difficult and/or triggering about the conversation?

How did you react internally?

How did you react externally?

What would you do differently?

What would you do the same?

Are these the same growth edges you would likely have in any difficult conversation?

What would you like to do differently in the future in a difficult conversation if deeper connection is the goal?

Now you have intentions and goals to work with throughout the chapter. While reading, focus on these areas of growth, and keep them front of mind. Also, instead of being caught unaware in a difficult situation and *reacting*, remember your goal is *connecting*, and this will help give you space to use your listening skills.

Sometimes, your own inner dialogue is the biggest hurdle when you try to listen to another person. Remember, you can't engage in mindful listening without being *mindful*. Prepare yourself for connection and intimacy. Therapists are taught to work on our "unfinished business." Unfinished business is anything that we haven't worked through that interferes with our work, our ability to openly and nonjudgmentally connect with our patient. It is considered ethical practice to seek supervision and sometimes our own therapy when our own chatter comes front of mind in our work. This is how essential it is to know yourself and to continuously work toward peace and resolution to connect as deeply as you can with others. You may not be a therapist, but you want to connect.

Unfinished business gets in the way.

Without listening, there is no empathy, and no empathy means no emotional success—no connections or intimacy. We know that too many empathetic failures leads to relationship dissatisfaction and sometimes dissolution, even of the strongest bonds. In short, you must stop yourself from being in the way of connecting with others. You don't want to be your own worst enemy.

Listening is a whole-self activity. In mindful listening there is no room for rebuttal, no magic words spoken, just deep human connections. Mindful listening sometimes occurs without words, just full focus on the other. When people feel heard, they report greater satisfaction in relationships . . . and life! Being heard makes you feel safe, valued, loved, and important. The act of mindful listening leads to increased connections, and it is easy, given a few secrets of the trade. You don't have to wonder how to be a good listener; we will talk through the skills required, and anyone can grow these abilities. All it takes is focus, determination, and practice.

PREPARE TO LISTEN

Mindful listening takes concentration and determination. It also requires thoughtfulness and ongoing preparation. You can't always plan when or where you are going to engage in mindful listening—it can happen anytime, anywhere. When engaging in mindful listening, be cognizant of your surroundings. There are two things you should always consider when trying to be a good listener:

**Safety (*Physical +Emotional*)
Minimize distractions**

Basic safety and distractions must be accounted for to create space for vulnerability to occur. When I say "safety," sometimes people think I mean you must act as some kind of guard. While that's an exaggeration, if you think of someone else's comfort, and the vastness of what the word *safety* can mean, I suppose you might act as an intimacy guard.

In the next chapter we will talk extensively about the importance of creating space for connections to occur. For now, let's focus on the basics. Without feeling emotionally safe and meeting basic requirements for physical safety, intimacy won't flourish. You must feel you can be vulnerable for connections to be made.

Safety

Let's discuss safety. If you have a history of being mentally or physically violent with the person you are attempting to listen to or they have seen you act unkindly to another person, you are unlikely to be able to provide safety.

Sometimes you might not have been the perpetrator but might look like that person. This is important to keep in mind. A huge concept. I'll ask you to squeeze into the yellow zone if you must—to hear me out. It's time to circle back to our identity conversations and bring your self-awareness front of mind. In-group/out-group politics plays a role in who feels safe with whom. Let's talk about some generalities that aren't true of everyone but might get you thinking.

Emotional Safety

A person of color is going to feel less comfortable discussing race with a White person. A Black person and an Asian person might not feel safe in a race conversation either—as there are variables within each group/culture/race that must be brought front of mind. A woman may not want to discuss feelings of bias with a man. A person who identifies as trans may not feel safe talking about gender with a cis person. An employee may not want to discuss much of anything construed as intimate with someone higher on the hierarchy. A child may have a hard time speaking openly with a parent or caretaker, and certainly it can be hard with a teacher or coach!

Anytime there's a power differential, things can be/feel unsafe. When you have the power in a dynamic, you need to be aware of it. Pretending or not acknowledging the power you hold is actually gaslighting—and damaging to the relationship. If you don't attend to the reality of power in the relationship, no matter how focused on listening you are, you aren't hearing what is being screamed in the room. Therefore, before you engage in mindful listening with the goal of connecting, ask yourself if you hold the power in the relationship. Often the person with the power is ignorant of this dynamic, so how can you know?

Holding the power means you have some sort of control over the other person, you experience privilege where they have bias, or you have a say in what happens to them. Examples include teachers = grades, boss = job, person of a dominant group = privilege, parent

= control in the relationship, etc. The topic doesn't even have to be related to anything in the realm of what gives you power. If a power differential exists, it doesn't evaporate on one topic but reappear on another. It is always there.

The only true way to equalize the dynamic is to show over time that you can be trusted. In some situations, around some topics, true intimacy will never be reached because the gap is there. You have those spaces with every person in your life—the places your arrows push on others and theirs push on you (remember the bias/privilege arrows). When you try to find intimacy with others, you *must* keep this self-awareness and other awareness as well as the education we've discussed about identity and development at the front of your mind. Although you can't always close the gap, there are some things you can do to bridge it.

How to build trust when you have the power in a listening relationship:

Discuss with openness.

Never ignore the elephant in the room.

When possible, bring assurances and then back them up. Bring authenticity and truth to your words.

Don't put your needs for connection ahead of their need for safety.

Apologize and repair when you make a mistake.

Again, the first step to building trust and intimacy in relationships where you have the most power is to be aware of this dynamic. Often, when I work with people or companies, the person with the most power is unaware of this fact and its impact on their ability to connect with others.[27] Other times it seems people have learned but don't feel it in their hearts—saying the right words without sincerity. Be sure you're open and honest with who you are and how that impacts others.

No matter how inexperienced you may be at discussing power or any topic that's uncomfortable for you, the worst thing to do would be to pretend it's not there. Once you think about it, with whomever you're talking, and you realize there may be a dynamic, either as the listener or the speaker, voice what's happening in the room in whatever way you can.

I am often terribly clumsy at this, though I hope I get better with practice. There is no magic here—"Maybe it's weird to talk about this since I've never experienced XYZ. I'm here to listen, and you can decide what feels safe for you." As a therapist, there is no way I could've experienced all the things that my patients share with me. Whenever a moment arises where it seems my power is a factor (if I work at a school, for instance), I bring voice to this. Most commonly, I speak of the differences of experience we have—and that I may not fully understand. But I can be fully present and listen, and that can be healing all by itself.

Somehow, in your way, speak the unspoken. Use humor if it works for you. Comedy works because it brings awareness to things that you don't normally say aloud.

One of the things you can do when you speak to power or other important dynamics is to bring assurances of safety. Don't make

---

27   A great and extremely powerful example of this comes in racial terms in the gorgeous film *The Color of Fear* by Lee Mun Wah. I mentioned this movie earlier in the book and bring it up again because it's that good. No matter who you are, please watch this movie. There are many clips online, but I would advise you to watch the entire thing—watching clips won't get you to the same place. We all have something to learn. The movie discusses one type of power, but it can be applicable to any time in your life where you're unaware of the impact you have on others.

promises you can't keep. A great example of this part of the process is a parent telling the child they can say anything without punishment and then grounding them for being honest. If you can't keep a promise, don't make it. No piece of information you might gather in a conversation is worth eroding trust. It would be more fruitful to say, "I can't promise you won't have a consequence, but we can talk through that too."

The thing about honesty is that you must respect the other person as an autonomous creature who has a say in how intimate the relationship becomes. To grow connections, you need to move your focus away from content toward the relationship. Getting information might make you feel like you connected, but if it costs the other person too dearly, they will pull away. Let others protect themselves. They will trust and respect you as it's often reciprocal. Respect and love tend to breed like bunnies. Offer your truth, the facts of the situation, and let them decide. If you are a supervisor, you can't make promises that you won't fire anyone. And a teacher can't say everyone gets a great grade. The assurances you offer must be based in reality and be doable and true. You may not get the conversation you wanted, and that's life. Maybe you built trust instead.

Intimacy lives in trust land.

You must be authentic in this entire process. Bring truth to your words and intentions to connect—or trust will not happen. Mindful listening is like an iceberg that requires so much of your own work before you engage in the tiniest part above the water. You must be real with yourself and honest in your intentions, have awareness of yourself in relations to others, and be open in the moment. This all requires quite a lot of behind-the-scenes work, which is one of the reasons this chapter is not at the start. People often ask me how hard it can be to listen all day; it's not. It is the culmination of all my training, practice, and experience. To be a good listener, you must be aware of who you are. You must be vulnerable and authentic. If you're reading this and feeling defensive, explore those feelings. What blocking emotions are coming up for you? Why? What does it cost you to be more vulnerable, to be open to the idea that being more or less "powerful" in a situation? How can you let go any of those barriers to connection? Ups and downs in power differentials happen everywhere—in a loving ongoing relationship there is often a back and forth in "power." If you can't be aware of and speak to this, you ignore a huge part of the communication happening, and connection will falter. Remember, open versus closed. That means even the things about yourself or a relationship that make you uncomfortable.

And finally, when we talk about all of this, I hope it's easy for you to see that you're going to make mistakes. Ignoring missteps leads to a breach of trust. Get ready to apologize. Apologies have *two* parts:

(1) I'm sorry for (be specific about what you did) . . .
(2) How can I make it better?

Atoning does not equal catharsis. Often when you apologize, you want to feel better. Sometimes that's not going to happen. You can build trust in a relationship if you offer the two-part apology in a heartfelt way, then step back and have respect for the other person(s). Remember, it isn't their job to make you feel better. Wait. Deal with your own stuff. Learn the lesson without going back to the person you needed to apologize to and making them do the work for you. This can be so hard. But remember, it isn't another person's job to teach you how to not offend. Educate yourself; that's no one else's responsibility. Do some reading, think back on the moment, ask other people, and sit in your discomfort until and if the person you want to connect with feels safe enough to reengage with you.

If that happens, please, sit quietly and listen. Quiet here is good. Your own ego is generally not helpful in building intimacy. Here is especially a place to hollow out and let in another person's experience. This mantra can help if you have the power in a listening relationship: "It's not about me." Repeat. Be open. Keep learning. Magic waits on the other side.

Physical Safety

Physical safety is a basic human need. Without a feeling of safety for oneself and loved ones, it is impossible to engage in relationship building. If physical safety is an issue, this must be managed immediately, whether it is obvious (an abusive relationship, a refugee) or less so (hospital patients with upcoming procedures). Many pediatric hospitals have child-life specialists and/or social workers for all ages, who work to ensure safety. For someone who has experienced trauma (and it is all around you, whether you know it or not), many things can be triggering—such as sitting with a back to the door, being alone in a room with someone with a closed door, etc.

Build awareness around what helps others feel safe and provide that space as best as you can. Make it a priority. Is there adequate lighting? Are people spread out and alone? What are backup safety plans? For instance, at many places I have worked, we have panic buttons in our desks in case of an emergency. This is a backup plan that helps the listeners feel safe to do the work. Your plan doesn't have to be that dramatic because it depends on the level of threat, but please, consider safety. A great way to enact this is to ask what would make people feel safe. I hope at this point in our time together, you're not assuming anymore. Apply the Platinum Rule.

Finally, let's imagine that it's you as the listener who doesn't feel safe emotionally or physically in the dyad/group. You must be aware of this and, if possible, bring attention to the dynamic, take care of yourself, and consider the cost of creating intimacy/connection versus whatever it will cost you to engage in the work. Only you can know that cost/benefit analysis, and I hope you will be respected for protecting yourself. Sometimes, you can leverage the areas in which you feel confident in order to grow the intimacy you seek, while on other occasions it may take more time and effort for you both. Good luck on this journey, and remember to stay in the yellow zone—not 100 percent comfortable but also not unacceptable.

Minimize Distractions

While you consider emotional and physical safety, you must also work to minimize distractions to get as connected as you can. Every parent can tell you how hard it is to have a conversation with another grown-up when you're constantly interrupted. You lose your train of thought, start over several times, and although most of the content might get shared, it's hard to enjoy that conversational high you can have from mindful listening and being heard. In the loss of focus, the connection is less. Sometimes, that is all you can accomplish. Other times, you have the control to minimize distractions and maximize mindful listening.

There are several things to consider when attempting to minimize distractions: privacy, comfort, and eliminating outside interference.

The first thing you should consider when you're talking deeply with another person or group is whether you have privacy. It is easier to speak openly when you feel safe. This includes between people, as described above, as well as the assurance that what you discuss will remain within the circle. Of course, you can't always make this so, but isn't it lovely when there is space and time dedicated to connecting? When you can make this happen, it opens the door for greater connections. People often talk in coffee shops, on walks, around other people—if what is discussed feels private, that's what counts. To ensure everyone feels the privacy of the moment, you can always ask, "Does this feel like a good place to talk?" Asking is a sure way to find answers. And if you're asked, please answer honestly. False responses to preference questions never lead the relationship to connections. Take the chance, be honest, say what you want.

Being comfortable is underrated. I talk to new therapists all the time about making sure bodily needs are met. You can't focus on the moment if you have to use the restroom or are hungry or tired. You can't always control your state in the moment when listening starts, but taking care of your physical needs is important. It's okay to say to someone, "I need to use the restroom; can you please hold that thought?"

People have a magic inner device that lets them know when the other person is distracted. Unfortunately, it doesn't tell them *why*. So, your need to pee can be misconstrued in several unfortunate ways that leads to loss of connection. This might sound simple, but it matters. Are you physically comfortable? Discomfort will interrupt the moment as your body repeatedly sends the reminders to the front of your mind. Clear up whatever you can so the only thing front of mind is the person in front of you. Go pee. Reengage. Find connection. This could've been the name for the book; it really covers all the topics.

Let's switch gears to technology for a moment. When we talk about eliminating outside interference, I hope you think of your phone. Put it away. Unless you've got an emergency, turn it to silent and facedown—or better, stick in your pocket. We are all addicted, and it blocks our ability to connect with other humans. When you bring your devices into the space, I'd like you to imagine the air all around you getting filled with the random things you are looking at, responding to, thinking about. You are not 100 percent present in the moment, and everyone knows it. Please practice respect for others. When conversations are happening, put it away. You can say, "I'll need to check it in thirty minutes" or something similar to ensure you can be calm and centered in the moment without experiencing total device-free meltdown. Smart watches are just as bad if not worse. They literally tap you on the wrist to let you know the world is calling. There are so many ways to control this to create space in your life from a constant barrage of outside information. Make a favorites list that includes any numbers that you *must* receive messages or calls from. Then put the devices on "do not disturb" or "focus" settings while you engage in your conversation or mindful moment, etc. Whatever works. But please, minimize outside interference. The subtext of being on the phone or looking at your watch is "You are boring me," or worse, "Something/someone else is more important." It's so frustrating when you're talking with someone and they keep staring at a device or trying to respond on their watch. If you're the culprit, just realize you are creating a disconnect with the other person.[28] Let's all reengage the basics—eye contact and being fully present. If you take nothing else from the entire book, you'll enjoy greater intimacy with these two practices.

WHAT IS MINDFUL LISTENING?

I would like you to take a moment, close your eyes, and consider how it feels to be heard. There is magic in communication—a true communion where something powerful and important passes between you. Mindful listening is part of the sacred connections humans make. It can be verbal, nonverbal, or a combination of both. You know when it has occurred because both listener and speaker are changed by the experience. When everything else falls away, you have a singular focus on the other, you stop thinking/reacting, and you quiet your body and mind. You create a new space for intimacy to occur. You are built to both listen and to use your voice.

This skill and the joy that comes with being a part of this transformation is available to everyone.

Three aspects of mindful listening:

1. **Goal of connecting**

2. **Focus on the moment (consider space, self)**

3. **Quiet self (judgment, fixer brain, chatter, self-awareness)**

---

28   Snubbing someone for a device is called *phubbing* by some, and research shows it is ruining your relationship. I feel like this word hasn't caught on, so I include it here as shorthand for that behavior, and maybe the word will take off and the behavior will diminish? Maybe.

Mindful listening is when you seemingly set yourself aside with a goal of connecting. You focus on the moment 100 percent, and you quiet your own ego, thoughts, and reactions.

Goal of Connecting

When you focus your mind, you don't even see the world around you. Remember inattentional blindness; it works to your advantage here. If you choose to dedicate yourself to something, you have a much higher rate of success than if you aren't sure, hesitate, or don't bring your intentions front of mind. When you start a process with a goal in mind, you are more likely to make it happen.

Step one: when you want to listen, get yourself ready to listen. For me, that means setting down whatever I have in my hands and turning toward the person. This shows on many levels that I am present and my goal is to connect. Anytime I have a reaction outside of that goal, I remember my goal of connecting and refocus. Regrouping is normal and happens to everyone—constantly.

When patients recount a recent unsatisfactory interchange, I like to ask what their goal was during the conversation. It is a question you don't normally ask yourself, and it requires practice to have in-the-moment clarity. If you approach each conversation with the intent to connect, guide, show love, whatever it may be, your behaviors will be better matched to help you reach that goal! It's like the trick when you want to draw a straight line; you don't look at where your pencil *is*, you look at where you want it to *go*, and voilá! You get straight lines. When you bring an intention to the front of your mind, your brain seems to color everything that happens afterward with that goal. The more you practice this intention setting, the better you get at tuning in to prepare yourself. The switch here is shifting from listening in order to enjoy, look smart, or even "win" a discussion toward listening for the sake of connection. You don't even need to know exactly what connecting looks like. You only need to know that's where you're headed, and this intention will guide you. What a "secret" that everyone should know.

Focus on the Moment 100 Percent

Once you have a clear goal of connecting with the person/people you are talking with, you can focus on the moment with your whole self. This requires consideration of the space you are in as well as control over your own distractions. We discussed above how to prepare for listening by minimizing distractions; this continues as you engage in listening. Remember to consider the space as well as your own distractions and find a way to focus on the moment 100 percent.

Quiet Yourself

Sometimes you can't focus on the moment because your self-talk is so *loud* that you can't begin to connect with someone else. Of course, this happens sometimes to most people—you get tongue-tied or nervous—but when it happens often and precludes you from making space to practice mindful listening, it's time to explore why that is happening. You can talk with honest loving friends, family, or a therapist.[29] There are three components to quieting yourself: don't judge, don't try to fix, and figure out defenses.

No Judgment

We've talked about judgment a lot. Am I asking you to accept everyone and everything without evaluating whether it matches your values, interests, etc.? No. At the same time, if your goal is to connect with another person or people, judgment has no place. As we've discussed, you must have unconditional positive regard. If you are being told something intimate you didn't know before, judgment can be smelled 100 meters away. You are wired to know when someone isn't connecting with you, and then you shut down. Unless your goal

---

29   If you consistently have trouble connecting with others, this is one of the best times for group therapy! In group therapy you can figure out what might hold you back in a safe space to help your growth as a human being. I can't say enough about group. It's magic!

in mindful listening is to shut the other person down, and possibly damage the relationship, then zip the judgment up.

Compassion does not equal judgment. Remember, judgment is always tied to a blocking emotion such as fear or shame. When you judge, it is generally either something you don't like about yourself, something that scares you, or something that makes you feel bad. If you score high on judgment, I ask you to figure out ways to quiet that part of yourself when it's time to listen and connect. When I have a difficult time finding empathy as a therapist, I switch my goal to *find something to love.* I begin to seek out anything that I can attach positive regard to . . . sometimes simply landing on a person's humanness. Then, once I've found a foothold for my compassion, I am ready to refocus my goal on connection.

When you find compassion, you are suddenly in-group with the other person. You are both human beings. At this most basic level, you can't engage in othering, and then you are one step closer to connection. Remember, moral disengagement happens when you allow yourself to think another person is less human than you are. It seems so terrible; the simplest and most powerful thing you can offer another person is an opportunity to transform through connection, yet people often close that door.

The Fixer

A lot has been said on the notion of problem-solving in conversations. There has even been a fair amount of gendering as part of the rhetoric, which I find hilarious—the notion of men as fixers and women as listeners. Both skills are essential, and everybody can join in (not to mention the whole binary gender concept). I don't care who you are; you must be able to both fix and hear. For this chapter, we are focused on listening. The entire rest of the book, and especially the next chapter, can be about what you do after you hear—the fixing part, if it comes to that. Let's consider that when you jump to fixing, you aren't listening anymore. Instead of listening, you've affixed a cape to your lapel, and you are ready to save the day. You fix because you love, can't tolerate another person's pain, feel shame at their words, aren't listening, got bored, or a zillion other reasons.

Ironically, "fixing" often doesn't fix and instead creates frustration, invalidation, and blocks connections. One of the tenants of feminist psychological practice is that each patient has the answers within themselves and knows what is best for them, based on their own life experiences, goals, etc. The idea is that when we think we know what's best for someone else, especially when there is a power dynamic in the relationship where we are the one "on top," instead of pushing our agenda on the patient, we guide them towards their own solution. Sometimes our totally brilliant wishes/dreams/hopes for their path match, and other times they don't. But underneath there's a fundamental trust that the patient knows what is best for themselves, and it is our goal to help them get there, not create a path *we* think is best.

While it can be frustrating to seek answers and instead be given guidance to explore oneself, in the end you learn more when you figure out a problem on your own, with love and guidance, rather than using a road map created by someone else. I apply this thinking to most interactions, including with my children. It can be *so hard* not to just tell them my way of thinking or handling a situation, but that doesn't encourage growth or respect their capability as an autonomous person, does it? Actually, taking over and managing the situation in *my* way fulfills more of my needs than theirs. One size does not fit all, for almost anything. Your way may have worked for you, and you can offer it as information, but people are so vastly different from one another. What if people gave one another the space and respect to find their own ways more often? Of course, sometimes you need to lay the path, give the answers, etc. But here's another perspective to consider.

Let's remember your focus in mindful listening is to connect. Fixing something for someone else isn't necessarily going to help. In fact, as therapists know, telling someone just what to do may lead to satisfaction in the moment ("Ah, I have an answer!") but eventually can lead to lack of trust in the relationship ("That didn't work"). This is because the only person who really knows what you should do is yourself. Yes, of course parents need to make choices for children—there are times you must wield your power. Even and especially in those situations with a power differential, listening builds trust and connections. What you do after the talking, with love and care, is separate. Please, put away your toolbelt because simply being there is exactly what the doctor ordered.

TRIGGERS

One reason you might have trouble listening is because your own triggers get in the way. Something that is said gets between the other person and yourself, causing your defenses to go up. This is part of the reason you've done so much work in the book to find out where your defenses lie. You can be ready for those triggers! See those defenses coming and ask them to sit down for a moment while you focus on connecting. When you have a reaction that pulls you away from the speaker and toward yourself, notice it. Learn from it. Keep it for later consideration, and then return to the task of the moment. Don't worry; your triggers will be there waiting for you to examine later. They generally don't evaporate on their own. If you leave them alone for a few moments, I doubt they'll run away, and good for you if they do.

PSYCHOLOGICAL SECRETS =>
BETTER LISTENER

Therapists learn how to listen, and you can too. If you start with the basics outlined above—an eagerness to focus on the moment, a goal of connecting, and the ability to quiet yourself—the rest is bonus. Let's add some icing to your listening cake.

You are wired to listen and repeat. Remember mirror neurons?

They are busy little cells. Here are some skills to help hone those abilities you already have.

Nonverbal

- Eye contact
- Body language
- Facial expressions

Verbal
- Ask questions
- Open-ended questions
- (Avoid curiosity—stick to the focus *they* have)
- Restatement/Mirror statement
- Double-sided statement (super advanced)
- Summarize
- Offer empathy/Reflect feelings (Know your own feelings)

When you listen, you have verbal and nonverbal responses. Sometimes only nonverbal. These must all be attended to. Nonverbal includes all your body language, including facial expressions, body positioning, and type of eye contact. Verbal is the asking questions, encouraging, validating, and restating. Let's practice.

Rules of Engagement

The remainder of this chapter offers an opportunity for you to practice all the skills that will help you be a mindful listener. We will assume you're prepared—meaning you have a goal of connecting, you're 100 percent focused, and you're ready to quiet yourself. For the actions in this chapter, I suggest a buddy. Someone you trust, who you can continue these activities with as you progress. Of course, that's not necessary. You don't need to be in the room with the other person. Though my old-school brain likes the idea, you can be anywhere the distractions are small and you can see as much of the other person as possible. It's harder to let those mirror neurons fire if you can't see hands, whether their legs are crossed or not, etc.

Get centered and . . . you're ready!

When you engage in the verbal listening activities, the speaker can discuss whatever they want to. It helps if it is something they care about but not too intensely—think ongoing dislike of job versus marital challenges. Let's start with things you can cope with as you're practicing skills. Try to be as natural as possible in this conversation. Remember that if you make a misstep as the listener, and you will, just sit quietly for a second; even in silence, things will right themselves and you can try again. Enjoy.

Directions:

Here are the directions for all the actions for the remainder of this chapter.

Remember, circle back around and reference both the rules of engagement and these directions as you complete each action regarding mindful listening.

You'll need a buddy. You must both feel safe and comfortable, as though you can speak freely (it doesn't have to be a private space, but this does help). Remember, set the goal of connecting, focusing 100 percent, and quieting yourself. Remember to keep with your nonverbals, and now you can practice adding on questions. You've got this.

Spend the next three minutes having a conversation. Speaker, remember the advice offered earlier; and, listener, try the specific skill for this section. After the three minutes, process how it went (limit processing to three minutes as well). Switch if you'd like and repeat.

Next, spend the next five minutes having a conversation. Spend no more than five minutes processing. Switch if you'd like and repeat. See if anything was different the second time.

From here, you can try ten minutes, fifteen, etc., until you get to thirty—then try fifty if you like. Processing time should not be longer than five minutes after each person, no matter how long the listening time goes. You can practice this at school, work, or with loved ones. If you do this in a bigger setting, be sure to add time for the entire group to process the action when you come back together. You can allow more time to process depending on the size of the group. Don't let processing be longer than the total time of the action (for the three-minute sessions, that would be twelve minutes: 3 minutes listening + 3 minutes processing = 6 minutes x 2).

Silence Is Golden

This action is a little different from the rest in the chapter as there is no speaking. Therefore, please remember the "Rules of Engagement," listed above but you can refer to the directions herein for this action.

Let's focus on body language. You will spend three minutes noticing nonverbal communication. As a bonus, you'll also gradually get more comfortable with silence. Silence is part of listening. You don't need to fill up space because of your own anxiety. That's not quieting the self. When you speak to control your own emotions, you generally aren't listening anymore; you're just reacting mindlessly.

Prepare for the action: Remember to create the goal of connecting, focus on the moment, and quiet the self. Find a comfortable sitting or standing position about two feet away from each other. Set a timer for three minutes. That's it. Look at one another, notice what comes up for you, and let your mirror neurons do their work. Let one person be the listener for three minutes and then switch. Keep this front of mind to discuss:

- Eye contact
- Body language
- Facial expressions

Reactions?

Now, set a timer for five minutes, and this time mirror everything they do. You can make this dramatic, silly, serious, or whatever happens. It's all practice, and it all counts. Take turns.

Reactions?

Verbal Listening Skills

Listening is a skill. There are psychological secrets therapists use to get you to keep talking. Creating space for the other person to talk is an important part of being a good listener. Journalists, lawyers, stylists—everyone who listens to others as a big part of their job knows some of these tricks, and now you will too. Briefly, these secrets include skillful questioning, restating, summarizing, and effective validation.

- Ask questions
- Open-ended questions
- Restatement/Mirror statement
- Double-sided statement
- Summarize
- Offer empathy/Reflect feelings

Take time to practice each of these skills. You'll begin to utilize them in your interactions with others all the time. The work we've done together brings you to this moment—you are prepared to create space to take in whatever the other person shares, and to offer back empathy. That's a big deal!

Verbal: Asking Questions

Being a good listener is about creating space for others to share. Part of the magic of listening, what helps guide you to new insights, is great questions. Again, mindful listening is not about satisfying curiosity. If a story is told and you are curiously asking questions about nitty-gritty details but the speaker has gone off in another direction, you're no longer listening. We teach therapists to be able to answer the question "Why are you doing what you're doing?" at any given moment in therapy. If you want to be an effective listener, I suggest you adopt this thought. Listening isn't about getting all the details; it's about following the path the speaker lays out and walking along that trail with them. To get there, there are two types of questions: open and closed ended.

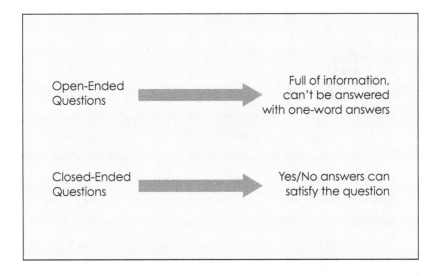

There is a time for closed-ended questions—when information-gathering about specific facts, for instance. Everyone asks them, especially when they aren't focusing 100 percent. These questions are easier, and they are the kind of questions you normally ask. Open-ended questions get much more data, though, and lead the person speaking to offer more information—and sometimes to find their own answers.

Let's compare:

Closed: Do you smoke?

Open: How much do you smoke?

See the difference? Think of the responses to the open-ended question. If the person doesn't smoke at all, they will simply say that, or start talking about how they used to smoke, etc. The closed question will likely get a yes/no response, and then you have to follow up with more questions. Closed-end questions are often dead ends. But when you give people space to talk (open-ended questions), they generally do.

Open-Ended Questions

Many people find it more difficult than they assume to ask open-ended questions. Here is your turn to practice! Please make the "Rules of Engagement" and "Directions" page from earlier in the chapter handy. Next, using the timing and outline for a practice session, please follow the directions with a focus on asking open-ended questions. Remember, an easy way to avoid closed-ended questions is to avoid anything that can be answered with a simple "yes" or "no." When you've completed the mini-sessions and processing, please take a moment to note your reactions to this practice here. By the way, you'll ask some closed-ended questions probably, and that's okay. Just keep going. You can always build an open-ended question onto a yes or no answer. And if you get stuck, just regroup.

Reactions?

Mirror, Mirror . . .

Once you get the hang of riding along to wherever the person speaking takes you, you're ready to begin mirroring them. When I first learned about mirroring, I didn't believe it could be true. I remember thinking that it would be obvious to the other person that I was basically just saying back to them *what they just said*. But, sometimes, you just want to be heard, and hearing your own words spoken aloud by another person can both be validating and lead to deeper insight. You'll see.

There are a few different types of what we call *reflecting*. The first is restatement or mirror statement. This is when you simply repeat basically what the person just said.

Speaker: "I'm so angry. I don't understand why she does this all the time."

Listener: "You're so angry."

Yep. That's it. You'll be amazed what can happen when you're "in it" with someone and you say back a version of what they just said. This can also be a little more complex, and that's the second type of mirroring statements. We call these *double-sided reflections*. This is a wonderful way of offering validation!

First, you reflect what they've said. Second, you also state that they've been heard. Here's how it can look:

Speaker: "I'm so angry. I don't understand why she does this all the time."

Listener: "You're so angry, and you'd like to get a break from this cycle."

See what I did there? I reflected just like above, then added a twist that took what they said and showed that I get it! I love double-sided reflections! They are where the empathy magic really starts to shine! You are feeling the empathy, naming the feeling, and letting the other person know you got it! That's the empathy equation at work! Double-sided reflections are advanced, so take your time when learning, and be kind to yourself. Remember, you must be authentic, or it won't work. Believe what you say, and your compassion and care for the other person will come through. That's really what we're aiming for.

Restatement/Mirror Statements

This might feel forced at first, but I promise you, people are surprised by how wonderfully they feel when someone mirrors their words. This practice helps to deepen the conversation.

Please make the "Rules of Engagement" and "Directions" page handy. Next, using the timing and outline for a practice session, please follow the directions with a focus on restatement/mirror statements. When you've completed the mini-sessions and processing, please take a moment to note your reactions to this practice here.

Reactions?

Summarize

Summarizing allows you to get all the benefits of reflection, plus it helps make sure what the listener *heard* is what the speaker was trying to convey. Often, when you summarize, you are right on, but sometimes you are wrong. For instance, either the listener doesn't get it quite right or when the speaker hears their words back, it needs adjustment. This is a fabulous exercise to get to the heart of what is being discussed and allow the person talking to sink deeper into what they want to share. Here's an example:

Speaker: "I'm so angry. I don't understand why she does this all the time. I've been waiting for her to respond for seventy-two hours, and I'm frustrated. She knows this brings up my anxiety, and she does it anyway. It's like she doesn't care about me. That thought scares me, and then I'm left feeling horrible and anxious."

Listener: "You're angry, hurt, and worried—you want her to respond and let you know that you're loved, and you'd feel better."

Mirroring and double reflections are like mini-summaries of the last few things that were said. Therefore, summarizing should be a little easier for you now if you've practiced all the skills to this point. If you get anxious, take a breath. I've found I need to be fully present and in flow for summaries to work. And when they do, they are so powerful. Wouldn't you like to be heard on this level?

Summarize

Think of the last time you summarized back to someone what they just said. I don't do this unless I'm at work, being a therapist. And yet I know it's a simple and wonderful way to show the other person that I hear them. The obvious secret is that you can't summarize when you aren't really listening. You have to give your whole self over to the process, and in summarizing, you are both validating the speaker and also showing your 100 percent attention. Wonderful!

To do this action, pull up the "Rules of Engagement" and "Directions" page. Next, using the timing and outline for a practice session, please follow the directions with a focus on summarizing. When you've completed the mini-sessions and processing, please take a moment to note your reactions to this practice.

Reactions?

Offer Empathy/Reflect Feelings
(Know Your Own Feelings)

The goal of mindful listening is to engage in empathy. Remember the empathy equation?

Empathy = Enter the Other Person's World +
No Judgment + Understand Feelings +
Communicate Understanding

So much of empathy comes from being able to engage in mindful listening. Here, we have fully entered "understand feelings +

communicate understanding" land.

If you are going to offer empathy and reflect feelings, you *must* know your own feelings and be comfortable with the full range of human emotions. Much has been said up to this point about knowing yourself, limitations, and triggers. Reflecting feelings requires you to know the feeling the person describes, and then to talk about it with them—to hold their experience comfortably enough to engage in the mindful listening that will bring you closer. Everything we've done together has led to this skill. You can do it.

Here's what this looks like:

Speaker: "I'm so angry. I don't understand why she does this all the time."

Listener: "I can feel your anger. I feel angry too!" or "It's confusing! That would make me angry too!" or "It makes total sense that you're angry; most people would be!"

I speak (and write) with a lot of exclamation marks—maybe you don't. You'll have to do what is real for you. Also, please don't say anything you don't believe. We are building connections—be yourself, or it won't work.

Validate = Offering Empathy/ Reflecting Feelings

How does offering empathy/reflection of feelings look different in practice than summarizing? When you summarize, you broadly offer a quick and dirty version of everything the speaker said. Here you'll move from that important skill to a more focused approach when you focus on empathy and reflection of feelings. In this action, rather than summarizing, you will go deeper into the emotion of what the other person says, even if they don't use emotion words at all. You'll get a feeling about what their emotions are, and this is the time to practice reflecting those reactions.

Remember, it helps to be able to identify emotions in others when we are fully aware of our own Rainbow of Emotions. We are building on that knowledge now in order to deepen connections.

To do this, as you've been doing, bring the "Rules of Engagement" and "Directions" front and center. Even though you've done a few actions using these guidelines, please reread them again and make them fresh. This is all practice for you, and we want you to "practice the way you play," meaning let's do it right. Next, please follow the directions with a focus on empathy/reflecting feelings. When you've completed the mini-sessions and processing, please take a moment to note your reactions to this practice.

Reactions?

Putting It All Together

This is it. Bringing together of all your mindful listening skills, which build on self-awareness, empathy, all the education you've garnered from the book so far. This action is a chance for you to deliberately practice all the skills in the chapter explicitly—questions, reflections, and empathy. Please don't get too caught up in your head; flow is important. I created this action to carve out space for practice, though the more you work these skills into your life, the more second nature they will become. Sometimes, because I'm a therapist, when I'm practicing mindful listening in my everyday life someone will ask me if I'm analyzing or therapizing them. I always answer that I'm not; I'm just listening. People look at me funny because it's so outside the norm to be fully listened to. Now they can look at you funny too. Welcome to the mindful listeners club, friend.

Put It All Together

You know what to do at this point. Start with three minutes and use whichever mindful listening skills feel appropriate in the moment. Look back to "Rules of Engagement" and "Directions" for guidance. Sometimes it helps to keep this list beside you as a reminder, video the session to watch later, and note what skills you used. Try to approach it as naturally as possible. Enjoy!

Nonverbal

- Eye contact
- Body language
- Facial expressions

Verbal

- Ask questions
- Open-ended questions
- (Avoid curiosity—stick to the focus they have)
- Restatement/Mirror statement
- Double-sided statement (super advanced)

- Summarize
- Offer empathy/ Reflect feelings (Know your own feelings)
- What else do you notice about the way it feels?

When you have completed the mini-sessions and basic processing, be sure to discuss what came naturally, what felt harder, how it felt to each of you, what you'd do differently next time.

Please consider what skills you can see yourself using in everyday life.

Many times, after engaging in listening practice like the journey you just took, graduate students will say how much they use these skills in everyday life, and how it has improved their communication with others. That is emotional success. And just like that, you're skilled at mindful listening. Congratulations.

CHAPTER 10

Radiate

hope you want to share your emotional success. Being more connected is contagious. I want you to be confident and kind in your approach to supporting others to find deeper connections. This chapter will show you how to help people of all ages safely lower their defenses and feel comfortable engaging in meaningful conversations—as well as how to grow and maintain your newfound emotional success.

"We all know this work demands of us something radical and deep which is to completely change the paradigm of our believing, thinking, and acting . . . to change lifetimes of conditioning."

—Marianne Hughes

Imagine yourself as a plug with many different connectors radiating from the center. Throughout this whole book you've been growing those new ways of seamlessly pairing up with others. And now, you might be looking for ways to use these new parts of yourself—to radiate your empathy, understanding, and desire for connections into the world.

Once you get good at connecting, you'll want to do it all the time. Sometimes it will be easy—you'll find ways to keep growing your self-awareness, educating yourself, deepening your empathetic abilities. And then you'll want to talk about it with important people in your life. The last secret this book will offer you is how to create spaces where deep connections can be made.

"Love and work—work and love. That's all there is. Love and work are the cornerstones of humanness, but they're universal too."

—Freud

When we think of radiating, let's consider love and work. I chose these two areas because they hold almost everything in our lives. The last two chapters explore psychological secrets to help you find emotional success in these two primary categories.

This chapter is an overview to help you radiate emotional success. We will discuss what change looks and feels like, how to ready the space, how to bring children into the fray, and next steps for you to consider. In other words, how to radiate connections everywhere you go.

RADIATE SAFETY: BUILD THE FRAME

We've talked so much in this book about safety—helping ourselves and others feel confident and comfortable enough in our surroundings to be able to engage in this essential work.

We've spent the bulk of our time together exploring, sharing language, and preparing for courageous interactions to deepen intimacy and better understand others. Keeping all of this in mind and holding the importance of safety (both yours and theirs), timing, and your goals at the heart of it all, now we consider how to create spaces for these interactions with others. I'm going to share with you some of the ways I prepare people to move from being strangers to sharing intimate reactions in a short period of time so that you can do this in your own life. You don't have to run therapy or training groups to use these skills. They can help grow intimacy and deeper connections in all the places in your life—at home, work, or at a party! You'll see. In fact, just like a party where you set the table, prep the food, and turn up the music, we do something called "create the frame" in therapy to allow intimacy to bloom.

Create the Frame

In therapy, we consider all the things I've just mentioned—who we are, who the patient is, what the atmosphere of the space is, emotional and physical safety—and then we build on it.

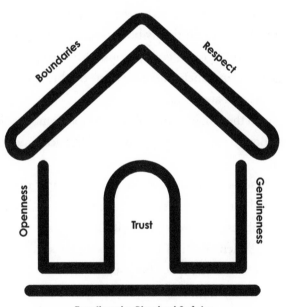

As you can see, without safety, there is no foundation to build a house. Head back to chapter 9 for a recap if you're unsure what this entails, where we discuss the idea of "safety" at length. Now you build the house. I'll assume you've accounted for safety at this point. To make sure you've met this requirement, you can ask yourself and others involved,

- What does safety look like for me? How do I know I am safe?
- How could I voice my reaction if I lose faith in the safety of the moment?

Once everyone can answer those questions, and you can ensure everyone's safety is maintained, you're ready to create the frame for your house. First, the walls—openness and genuineness. You must engage with your true self if you are going to find connections with others. Remember: true self = genuine + open.

When you step outside your authentic self, you create boundaries that make it hard to connect with others. You must also be open. I'll ask you to remember to finish any business that keeps you from being open so you can allow greater connections. Other people can feel when you aren't genuine and open, and they won't be able to enter the house of awesomeness you are building.

Next, put on the roof to keep y'all dry. The roof is made of boundaries and respect. Boundaries include protecting the space/time/focus of the conversation.

Respect is self-explanatory. We've talked about it throughout the book and called it many things—most namely unconditional positive regard. Without respect, everything will fly right out the ceiling, and that's just sad. When you find yourself losing respect, take a mindful step back and create some space for yourself to redevelop perspective.

No one is going to go into your intimacy house without the trust door. Everyone walks through it, and it is a gorgeous door. Trust is built by keeping the frame steady and honoring your promises over time. If you can't provide a trusting environment, connections will not be made or maintained. Everything we've covered together in the entire book is encapsulated in the process of creating the frame. You've done all the work, and now you can practice. You'll need to bring your "house" to love and work; let's make sure it's steady.

One thing you can do if you plan to use this in a formal way is to openly discuss the process of creating the frame. Ask if it feels like that has been achieved or not. This way you'll know if you're starting from a solid place. In less formal situations, you can keep the frame in your mind and practice building and rebuilding to ensure the best environment for intimacy to bloom.

RADIATE THE RIGHT CONNECTOR: MEET PEOPLE WHERE THEY ARE

Now you've got a cozy little connection and intimacy cottage—but no one wants to come to your housewarming party. Huh. Why might that be? First, check your assumptions. Make sure you've done all the work you think you have. You may have built a straw house (which no one feels comfortable in) when you think you're lighting your "welcome home" candles in a brick house. The best way to figure this out is to *ask*. Find a safe and productive (if it's a workplace, preferably truly *anonymous*) way to see if you need to go back and do some additional prep. I've seen many workshops, conversations, etc., where one person thinks they've done all the work and are ready to engage, sometimes overly ready to engage, and the others don't feel safe—perhaps not even safe enough to voice their safety concerns.

Look at your situation and attempt to evaluate power differentials, etc., that may make it difficult for others to join your super-duper "let's get connected" party. If it's a relationship, a conversation will do. At work, sometimes an outside objective person can come in to help (this is part of my work as a consulting psychologist, for instance). There are lots of ways of approaching the situation when connections are required but stuttering.

Let's assume you've done it! You created the space, did the growth for yourself, you're ready to make space for renewed and deeper connections, and still, no one comes to your party. Maybe you've even invited a guest DJ to run the show . . . and still no one. You've read every word in the book, evaluated who you are, what privileges you have, attempted to create safety based on all the things, grown your empathy, and still no takers on your connection journey. This could be because you aren't meeting people where they are. In this case, I offer you a joke:

How many psychologists does it take to change a lightbulb? One. But the lightbulb has to want to change.

Yep. No matter how awesome your offer of connection is, if the people you want to connect with don't want to connect with you, you aren't going to get very far. While I beg you to always keep in mind whatever you might be doing to make connecting difficult, I also offer the idea that people change only when they want to. And connecting in a new and deeper way requires change on your part, so due to the transitive property, it will for others too.

Theorems

**People only change when they want to.
Whether another person engages in lasting change
(or not) has little to do with anyone else.**

This is sometimes an unpopular opinion—and yet it's true. Lasting change must be intrinsic. You can get someone to stop with an ultimatum (sometimes), though time and again you'll see ultimatums lead to sneaking/underground behavior because the desire to change *must come from within*. In the end, people are all autonomous creatures who can't be controlled. If you're trying to find intimacy according to the insight in this book, you may find that at times you're not working from the same model as the other person(s). If the other person or group of people doesn't want to engage in connecting like you do . . . it won't work. You must always check yourself first, then make sure you're on the same page.

As I've mentioned, in therapy we call that "meeting people where they are." We know there are stages of change, and that people have internal drivers for change that don't seem to have external switches. Here are the basics of the stages of change, a drawing by Ignacio Pecheco, which can help you understand yourself a whole lot better too.

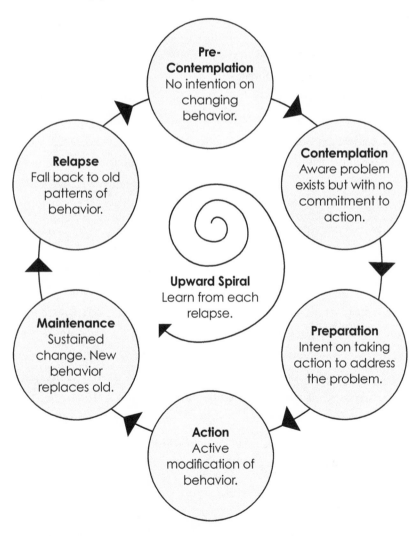

I offer you the cycle of change. As you can see, Prochaska and DiClemente work within a "relapse" model based on unhealthy coping skills; however, it works for any change. Also, to give you a construct to help you understand how complex change can be, I would like to suggest an alternative to hoping for big, giant changes in others: what I call *nano changes*. Nano changes seem to happen much faster than *big* changes. If no one is coming to your "let's get connected" party, consider, in addition to *always* looking inward, if what you're asking is too far a leap from where they might be to start with.

Would a tiny, small, mini, nano conversation be a place to start the deeper engagement? Anyone can make these nano changes and see where they take them. In this arena, I'm speaking of taking in a little more information than you normally might. Or considering an idea that is new or different. Small things.

Let's set realistic expectations. I certainly don't want you to try to drag others along, causing space where connections could be. Always look inward and accept nano changes toward greater intimacy. Consider where people might be and meet them where they are. You can't drag someone to connection town. Except yourself. And only when you're ready.

RADIATE GROWTH: CONNECTING WITH KIDS

Deep connections can help keep kids safe. Teens and preteens need to explore, but wouldn't it be great if you were along for the ride instead of always trying to catch up? You can be. It will require you to ride the wave, grow trust, and understand a little about their world. Whether you're a parent, teacher, caregiver, etc., these ideas can help you connect with the kids in your life, and every child needs at least one adult they can turn to unconditionally. This cannot be overstated (more on attachment in chapter 11). Use these ideas to help you stay or become that person for a child. I talk about parenting and caregiving interchangeably in this section. Translate the message for your relationship needs with kids; different types of adult/child interactions have varying boundaries, depth, etc. However, the messages for connecting with kids applies no matter your role. If you are around growing humans, you have an opportunity to give care and grow their emotional success by modeling your own.

Thoughtful time and space to help kids transition into adulthood is so important. We know that 33 percent more children committed suicide in the last ten years than the decade before that—*33 percent*. That's avoidable! There are a few reasons for this dramatic rise in suicidality. And I'd like you to read and consider the young people in your life.

Preteens and Adolescents Have Half Brains

Preteens and adolescents are advanced in many ways (technologically, academically, worldly) beyond where people were a generation ago, but evolution hasn't caught up. This leads to two main realities:

Lack of Control

The thinking/planning/higher functions of the frontal lobe are not fully developed to stop the less thoughtful parts of their brain from taking charge. Impulsivity can be fun! It can also be dangerous.

Lack of Perspective

Metacognition is when you think about what you're thinking—it also helps to be able to get perspective on oneself and the situation at hand. Adolescents do not have the life experience or mental capacity to engage in this practice like adults do. In fact, this is wisdom—and everyone could use more of it. For instance, the increasing suicide rate described above includes a disproportionate number of teens who identity as LGBTQ+. The It Gets Better project created by Dan Savage exists to help show kids who identify as LGBTQ that what they may be experiencing won't last forever; the bad times they may have now won't be their whole life. This is true for all teens and why those numbers are growing. If they endure hardship, it is difficult for young people to know that what is happening now won't always happen. They don't have enough experience to see that things change. Organizations like the It Gets Better project help to give them that awareness. Everyone can help by sharing their own stories of difficulty, to give credence to these struggles. Minimizing or treating mental or physical health worries as a "not a big deal" or a "cry for help" won't help. Empathy and specific support scaffolding must be employed by the adults who spend time with children, teens, and emerging adults.

Adolescent Development Is Based on Peer Acceptance

At no other time in life are humans more wired to lean toward in-group acceptance. Adults may scoff at what psychologists call *fishbowl syndrome*, but teens aren't wrong; everyone *is* looking at them. They *are* being judged, often most cruelly by themselves.

The first ten years of life, you mirror your family. The second decade, you mirror your friends. The third decade is when you figure out who you are. The fourth and beyond, you strive toward self-actualization while you juggle all the balls. This is normative human development. Adolescence is a phase—an appropriate, important, essential one— to learn who you are in relation to others. Being separate from your peers can lead to failure in this phase, what we call *developmental asynchronicity*—and it matters.

Children and Teens Lack Basic Autonomy

Living at home creates many boundaries that can make people feel trapped and as though they will never have the life they imagine. This is particularly salient for kids who have identities that don't match the family's ideas.

They Never Get Downtime

The internet has opened new ways to connect. This has led to kids getting exposed to trauma they wouldn't have known. It has also led to ongoing bullying that never stops and can block kids from feeling whole or safe. This feeling can lead to hopelessness, and that is a dangerous place to be.

Understanding the realities of life for kids can help you realize that they come from a more complex place than you did. Many people are aware of bullying, and much attention has been brought to this area. In modern culture, people no longer shrug and expect kids to just "figure it out." As an adult, you realize that being out-group is socially isolating and can lead to emotional trauma. Think back to our discussion of in-group/out-group; it is at the core of human experience to be included. Exclusion can hurt you at an emotional and cellular level. When we talk about kids' experiences in the world, I ask you to hold an open heart and mind to their experiences as real, foundational, and deeply important to both their current and future emotional success.

Talk about It

It's time to talk to your kids. About sex,[30] identity, love, bullying, fear, the future, everything! A mutually caring connection with a trusted adult can sometimes stop a kid from risky behaviors. They are still trying out different identities, and it can be a scary time, but this is also a time to ride the waves and potentially get even closer. You do this by building trust . . . just like with anyone else.

---

30 Please talk to your kids about sex. If you don't open that door despite how uncomfortable it may be, gaps will get filled in by their friends, porn, and potential partners. No one wants this. You get them prepared for everything else; make sure they have knowledge about this aspect of their lives/development as well. That way when they do explore with partners/porn/whatever, they have a base schema as well as an avenue for communication!

PARENTAL ATTITUDES AND BEHAVIORS THAT GENERATE TRUST

Attending and listening
Empathy
Structure
Genuineness and self-disclosure
Respect
Caring confrontation
Attention to nonverbals

What does this look like? Respect for space is a big piece of this. People talk a lot when parenting or teaching adolescents about privacy, often asking themselves, *What is safe? How much privacy is okay?* This is a huge question, and my answer is a typical therapist one: it depends. Have you created the frame throughout your relationship? Can the kids in your life come to you with anything (or do they have a trusted adult they can talk to)? Have they given you reason not to trust their judgment? Remember, the goal is respect and increased autonomy when people making. Keep that front of mind, and utilize respect, appropriate boundaries, and caring confrontation when necessary.

Obviously, I could (and may) write an entire book about how to connect with your kids; for now, the big takeaways are that they don't get enough respect or autonomy. My goodness, as a teacher, therapist, and parent I can say that giving space is so hard. Is it enough? Too much? It's a balancing act, and everyone gets it wrong . . . a lot.

> ### Theorem
>
> ***There isn't some goal you're working toward that you will meet and then be able to wear a button that says "good parent"—or "great relationship." It is a fluid, constantly moving, never-ending ebb and flow of what the moment requires (and how tired you are).***

But you know what's magic? People know when you're trying—when you're open, vulnerable, and ready to connect—and if you can do this, you'll see the relationship open between you and the child you love. Parents do a lot of protecting, and for the first ten years this is appropriate. As a child moves into the second decade of life, though, a balance between welcoming the teen into the adult world and maintaining that adult stance is the real game. For younger children, you can be honest while also excluding things that may not yet be appropriate. As kids age, though, holding back reality can lead to a feeling of disingenuous communication. Obviously, boundaries are appropriate, but so is honesty. This piece is up to your family culture, and you'll have to see what works. Vulnerability and openness generally help intimacy, and connections grow—so try it out, and see how it feels.

What's Normal?

Let's talk about what's "normative" development. Caregivers often ask me what is normal. Here's a super quick reference. For more, there is a field of study, developmental psychology, that you can read more about; this is one of my favorite topics and encompasses many more psychological secrets.

What Is Normal

- Testing the atmosphere
- Periods of silence and awkwardness
- Tentative exploration with some risk-taking
- Trust is an ongoing and central issue

When you move toward new phases of life, the rules seem to change. Many times, kids are nervous that they will be judged or get in trouble if they are honest with the adults in their lives. Kids are nervous about what they can bring up, how it will go, and where the boundaries are. For these reasons, it's up to the caregivers to set these boundaries in clear and loving ways.

In my house, my children know that they can ask anything, and we will answer as honestly as we can. They also are told (I hope it sinks in, but you never know) that they don't get in trouble for honesty. We try to support their adventures and are open to guiding or listening when they need either. If you want deeper connections and intimacy with children, you need to be prepared to have conversations that you may never have had before. I like to remind parents that there is no right answer except honesty, vulnerability, and respect.

Concerns Lots of Caregivers Have

- How much to disclose
- Being judged
- Acceptance
- Expectations
- Safety
- Appearing stupid
- Communicating

These are the main concerns I hear from caregivers about open dialogues with kids, especially about big topics. Do any of these apply to you? The best way to alleviate any tension or defenses around these areas is to openly discuss this with the child. Remember . . . intimacy is born of vulnerability. It's the same with your kids. A strong front may be good to shield your kids at times, but when it is actually working to protect *you*, it becomes a barrier between you and your kid. There are no right answers here except to be true to yourself and open with your child. If you work with children, obviously there are boundaries in place for the depth of the relationship, what can be appropriately revealed, etc. And just like any power differential, open talk about how to navigate that in your relationship with loving kindness is key.

Sometimes, you feel like you do everything right, and still the connection is lost. This is normal too. At these times, provide love, support, space, and more space—make yourself available emotionally and physically for conversations to occur. When they start, let them happen. I have found that car rides can be a great time for conversations. Like all mindful listening, remember to let the other person take charge of the conversation, and provide the feedback you've practiced. There may be no greater relationship on earth to practice those skills than with the kids in your life.

What do you do when there's already a rift? Lean in. Try to repair it.

Kids, even young ones, have real concerns and difficulties in their lives. Giving them space and time to talk and acting as a mindful listener to them will create a foundation for the future. With a difficult time, being available, firm but kind, and always loving will help repair. If there is a behavior that upsets the child, consider changing it. Sometimes adults deny the validity of a child's opinion of their behavior as a defense mechanism. Instead, I encourage you to consider the words of others as information to help you grow. Apologize when you need to. Show vulnerability and allow space when it's appropriate. See a therapist. Work together. Things can be fixed if you both want them to be healed.

HEALTHY IDENTITY DEVELOPMENT

Let's circle around to bullying. We know that a positive self-identity can protect kids from some of the impact of bullying, and from becoming a bully! You can avoid both scenarios when you create a positive self-identity as a foundation for empathy and understanding others. In addition to the general focus on mindful listening and creating an open and loving relationship with your children, let's take a moment to discuss how you could apply the thinking and learning you've accomplished in this book to your family. Now that we've discussed the basics of connecting with your kids more deeply, let's spend a minute talking specifically about how you can discuss identity in your families to build up that aspect of self. This practice will also give you a starting place to build the types of conversations that can lead to greater openness around all topics.

How can you focus on identity development in your home or work with kids? The following chart is a "how-to" on growing identity development in your family (or in your interactions with children/teens). Take some time to read it through. Consider how identity impacts who you are, how you operate, and how to help your children engage in this reflective process. As you can see, it is a micro-journey based on the ideas in this book.

**HOW TO GROW IDENTITY DEVELOPMENT IN
CHILDREN AND TEENS**

EDUCATION/CAN YOU ANSWER?

Who are you culturally? Ethnically? How do
others see you?

What privileges and power are you aware of? What oppressive/disadvantages are you aware of?

Can your children answer these questions?

THINGS YOU CAN DO

How often does your family engage in activities within/outside of your cultural center?
Do you expose your children to the variation of human existence (e.g. books, movies, festivals, travel)?

SELF-AWARENESS

Acquire tools to speak with children about identity and how it relates to their life.

Consider where you are in the cultures of your work and home life.

Open yourself to your strengths and areas of growth related to your own diversity, levels of empathy, and desire for authentic connection with others.

Learn what your style of approaching diverse people and ideas may be, and how to improve your productivity through greater ability to deeply connect.

EMPATHY

Explain what empathy looks like and how to practice this skill.

MODELING

Show children how to be empathetic by teaching them the empathy equation and talking about it openly in your daily lives.

I included this graphic to help you begin to work through identity development in your family—summarizing all the things we've done up to now to help you create a strong family identity and to help your children form their own identities. It can also be used any place children/teens are—just alter it to suit those needs. So much of identity development happens at school; it's a lovely place to help kids learn more about themselves.

Identity development is the work of a lifetime, and it will happen with or without your input. This is an area for positive connection and growth that can help protect the child in your life from influences that may not be healthy. Kids will experiment, of course, and sometimes in directions you don't like or that make you scared. At the same time, a solid foundation of self can be thoughtfully integrated into family or school life, and this will serve as a base to return to when the relationship inevitably experiences discord. Also, practicing your connection and mindful listening skills to grow your family or school identity together can be a wonderful starting place for many courageous conversations with kids. No matter how you are around or how you work with kids, these ideas can help you find deeper connections and thus build that foundation of trust and vulnerability to help them have a base to return to when they need a break. Enjoy!

CHAPTER 11

Emotional Success in Love

The next two chapters pull from the rest of the book—propelling you into emotional success in love and work. In both, I use the terms *love* and *work* to describe whatever they mean to you. Think about it: they are both huge concepts and mean different things to everyone. We will take time to define what they each mean and clarify how all the psychological secrets you've learned throughout can be applied with laser focus to the love and work in your life. Then I will launch you out into the world to radiate emotional success.

This chapter has a focus on love. There's nothing I love more than love. I mean, the subtitle of the book is *It's All About Love*. Love has been the heart of everything, and I hope you feel it. I thought about writing a chapter each on relationships, family, and friendship, but then I realized: just like "work" encompasses all the productive things you do, "love" holds the components of your emotional life. In this chapter, I offer the psychological secrets of attachment theory to know yourself better, love languages to communicate those needs, and a formula for ensuring you get your needs met. Together, these psychological secrets will give you greater emotional success in love.

Let's bring these ideas to the front of your mind so we can work on them.

Let's think about love. What is it? Love is unique to each person. There are scientific explanations for the feelings of comfort, arousal, closeness, protectiveness, and warmth you feel when close to people and things you love. But everyone identifies it differently. One of the difficulties I often see in therapy, and I've mentioned this elsewhere, is that you assume your experiences are the same as others'. If you hear nothing else I say, please hear this: *they don't know unless you tell them* (remember psychic syndrome from chapter 7?). To put this reality into action, I'd ask you to stop assuming your inner world is somehow universal. This will save you much heartache and misunderstandings. Communication is the key to happiness. Clear, loving, and open rivers of information between loved ones is the quickest way to build intimacy. People often mess this up by creating inner narratives that aren't true, and then not checking for accuracy. I would not have a therapy job if everyone knew themselves a little better and realized no one else is a mirror for their inner worlds.

You can know others deeply. At the same time, the sheer complexity of perception mixed with all the input you sort through, colored by who you are, cannot overlay perfectly onto anyone else. The definition of love varies from person to person. And, of course, the experience is different. No one sees things exactly the same, even love. Isn't that great?

What Is Love?

Let's explore what love is to you. When you have a clearer picture, it will be central in your mind. This will help to explore the ideas in the rest of the chapter. Love is ephemeral; it helps to have concrete ideas to work with. Answer as honestly as you can. Share your responses with loved ones. Ask them to work on this as well. More information about one another leads to greater intimacy.

Please answer the following questions. Love talk brings many strong emotions to the forefront. Much of therapy is centered on these topics. If you delve in and feel the need, please build support scaffolding.

What is love? For this question you can draw a picture, sing, dance. I suggest free association, but you do you.

Please describe love in ten words.

How does love feel to you?

Does it feel comfortable to discuss love?

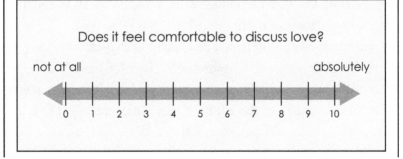

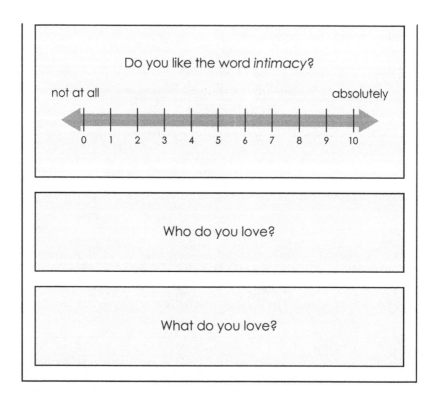

YOU ARE WIRED FOR LOVE

When we talk about love, we should start at the beginning. You learned how love feels when you were a baby. Of course, you've built on those ideas. How much awareness do you have of those early impressions? Do you know how your attachment style and love languages impact your relationships?

Human babies are the least useful infants of all mammals. You plop out with a giant head and what seems like a boneless body. Your floppy limbs flail, and you can't do much to serve yourself. It seems that your most basic functions are flawed. Even your senses are dull at first. You can't really taste or sort out what you hear. Your eyes can only focus six to eight inches away.

And yet, under this seemingly helpless façade lies a powerful tool. Through evolution our species figured out the most important key to survival: love. That squishy lack of innate abilities checks the "take care of it" box in the adult human brain. For instance, what is often about six to eight inches from your face as a newborn? Traditionally speaking, the face of a mom when she's nursing. There's more. Human baby brains are programmed to *love* human faces. They can't sort through much, but we know they prefer to look at faces. If you give them a choice between almost anything and a face, they will consistently stare at the face. Eye contact leads to oxytocin release (as does breastfeeding),[31] and oxytocin makes you feel bonded. When you're a useless round blob, it's helpful to have the adult human feel love for you.

Humans Need to Be Liked

For humans, survival goes beyond physical safety. You must ingratiate yourself to your pack for the best chance to thrive. The glue that holds everyone together is love. Love happens when you act certain ways. First, generally speaking, you like people near you. Believe it or not, it is sometimes that simple. This is called the *proximity principle*. Have you noticed you start to like someone just from spending time with them? This may be related to kin evolution. It's true what your parents said: you become like the people you spend time with. Obviously, parents, caregivers, etc., spend a lot of time with newborns and children. All that time and effort strengthens the love bond that began with physical closeness and blubberyness.

Humans are vain. They like to be liked. In fact, when someone prefers you, you are more likely to have feelings for them than for someone who doesn't show interest. It's not a mistake that when someone you weren't interested in begins to show you a lot of attention, you begin to feel more attracted to them. It is attractive to be attractive. We call this *reciprocal liking*. It's the reason marketing is powerful. If

---

31   Do you need to breastfeed to encourage oxytocin release? No! It's a pre-wired reaction, but you get oxytocin from any loving touch. Also, anyone feeding a baby can be six to eight inches from their little face, staring away into their eyes and making everyone feel warm and fuzzy.

other people are doing it, and I know I'll be liked when I do it, sign me up! Babies are intrinsically aware of these powerful principles. They understand psychological secrets without reading the book.

Babies look in your eyes, need you, want you, activate your caretaking, and then, to really put you over the love edge, they mimic you. The ultimate compliment or curse, depending on your mood. There has been much debate through the history of philosophy and psychology regarding whether babies are what John Locke called *blank slates* (a.k.a. *tabula rasa*). We know now that genetics, epigenetics, space, time, the butterfly's wings, and massive readiness to copy what you see—all of this plays a part. You can think of it this way: when someone asks you, "Nature or nurture?" you say, "Yes." All these pieces of the giant puzzle create each person's experience.

You start out with your DNA, temperament, health, circumstances, and caregivers of varying degrees of capability/availability. One thing everyone has in common as babies, and throughout their lives, is the urge to connect as a survival mechanism. Remember mirror neurons? As a baby, you kick off the process of connecting with others through attachment. Then, you carry these lessons through your life, repeating your attachment style and finding ways to give and receive love based on these early lessons. I called this the *music-of-love dance* earlier in the book. Now we explore in-depth what that means.

ATTACHED

Attachment is a warm and fuzzy topic, and one that makes me happy. It describes the process of bonding and growth between people. Who doesn't appreciate a clear and concise theory to sum up one of the most complicated notions? In the beginning of psychiatry and then psychology as a distinct field, and throughout much of time, men were the scholars, and it didn't fit the mold for them to be interested in children or families. (Aside from Piaget, whom I mentioned earlier, there was a dearth of information about kids at all, and certainly nothing about parenting besides Dr. Spock.) Suddenly, though, in the late 1950s, the field of psychology was burgeoning, and study pertaining to children, love, and families began to bloom.

Attachment theory is one such area. John Bowlby and Mary Ainsworth developed a way to understand how you attach to others beginning in infancy— and how this impacts your loving relationships throughout life. That is not an understatement. Although you can change much about yourself, your initial attachment style impacts you forever. Especially if you aren't aware of your attachment style or what it means. My goal is to share these psychological secrets with you to help you see what you may have learned, and how it impacts you today.

Let's talk about what attachment is, and how it impacts your life. There are four types of attachment: secure, ambivalent, avoidant, and disorganized. Think back to your childhood or, if you're a caretaker, to the relationship you have with the children in your life. Using a real example will help you frame and understand each part of attachment on a deeper level.

Secure Attachment is when you feel sad when you detach from someone you love but can soothe yourself. You are excited when they return and don't feel as happy until they're with you, but you can still have a good time.

Ambivalent Attachment occurs when the primary attachment figure isn't consistent. In this case, it's hard to feel calm because the relationship is sometimes close and other times distant.

Avoidant Attachment occurs when emotional sharing is minimum. As a way of dealing with the lack of affection, you disassociate and become avoidant to the relationship.

Disorganized Attachment often happens when children do not feel any attachment to caregiver and thus react by acting out or engaging in any activity that will draw attention.

Attachment Styles

Let's take a moment to explore your attachment style. Everyone has more than one style, with a primary and then secondary style. It is helpful to see the way you connect with loved ones and how that plays into the dynamics of your life. If you notice something that triggers you, please seek therapy or a trusted friend.

When we talk about early needs and desires—as well as primal responses to caretakers—responses can be surprisingly deep. Again, employ support scaffolding as needed.

What do you feel is your primary attachment style?

> What other attachment styles do you have?

> How do these styles relate to the relationships in your life today?

Remember the "music of love" conversation we had in chapter 7? Let's build on that, as promised. For this metaphor, think of love as music and attachment as the way you dance. You learn what the music sounds like when you feel love, and the dance is your relationship with caregivers. Then, throughout your life, whenever you hear the music of love, you begin your dance. You choose partners who match your dance as best as possible. Sometimes you dance alone. Whatever dance you learn early, even if it isn't the best dance for you or is downright bad or dangerous, you prefer to mirror the early dance. When you know what your dance is and can choose how to dance, and with whom, by better understanding why you dance like you do, the entire party can be a lot more fun!

Attachment begins with met or unmet needs. When you are tiny and you have a need, does it get met? At that point in life, your needs are basic: *I'm hungry. Do I get fed? I am lonely. Do I get held?* At this early stage, you don't yet have a self; you are simply the reflection of the caretaker. If the caretaker consistently meets your needs, you begin to build trust—trust that your needs will be met; trust in yourself as a being. As the trust grows, you build your ego/sense of self from that home base. Think of the children you know; they orbit the primary caregiver in ever growing circles. Most toddlers explore, then check in, as if they are asking, "Are you still here?" I used to watch this process and say to my girls, "Yep, still here, not going anywhere. Let's just skip this phase and move to some trust." They kept circling around anyway. I guess you can't talk your way out of a developmental stage.

Psychologists call this transfer of trust from the primary caregiver to yourself *object relations theory*. Think of it this way: you have a secure attachment to a caregiver. They meet your needs and provide a place to build your own identity. They are a good object. A rock to build your ego onto. Because they are good, you are good. The reverse is unfortunately true as well. Object relations theory explains why children have "lovies." A lovie is how some people refer to a blanket, stuffed animal, shirt, etc., that small children have and get very upset when separated from. The lovie is what we call a *transitional object*—it can stand in for the primary caretaker when they are unavailable. When children don't have a lovie, transitions without caregivers can be harder. Additionally, if the lovie is lost, the grief is real (please do everyone a favor and buy five of those things and put them on rotation). The lovie makes the child feel as though the object, their rock, is present with them. Easy magic.

You can see how starting life with a healthy ego can lead to later emotional success in love. If this didn't happen for you, this is what much therapy strives to do. Nancy Chodorow wrote a gorgeous book called *The Reproduction of Mothering*,[32] and it illustrates how the therapist can act as the primary caregiver in some emotional ways, launching a patient into a new and healthier attachment style, with a stronger ego.

It might seem like a healthy attachment is the only way to have healthy relationships and emotional success in love. This isn't so. Being aware of your style and how it plays into your relationships is what leads to emotional success.

---

32   Much language in the field of attachment and object relations is feminine based, using terms such as *mother*. We know now that it obviously does not need to be a female caregiver. In fact, it doesn't have to be a parent at all. Any loving, consistent caregiver can become the primary attachment figure, the good object, and thus create a secure attachment for a child.

FAILURE IS ESSENTIAL

Perhaps you feel pressure after reading this to provide a perfectly secure attachment for your children or other loved ones. This is not necessary. As Donald Winnicot so beautifully stated, "All you have to do is be the *good* enough mother."[33] The idea is that when you know you can find a safe place to be yourself and feel bonded, you learn you will be safe even when your primary attachment figure fails you. You will be okay. Psychologists believe that failure is necessary to a healthy relationship. Failing is inevitable.

As I set aside time in my life from being 100 percent available to my children to write this book, they balk at my mental and physical unavailability. They sense my preoccupation. Guilt reigns supreme. And yet, like any other missteps or empathetic failures I make, I know that how I manage the gap is where our dance gets good. When you fail—as a lover, friend, parent, caregiver, spouse, worker, human being—what you do afterwards is also what matters.

Being honest about your shortcomings is huge. Everyone must work toward vulnerability. It is hard to say, "I'm sorry," to admit when you fail. The idea that you must be right all the time will harm you and anyone you're trying to be close to. Intimacy grows in vulnerability, sadness, and how you handle your mistakes.

---

33   Again, we need to historically situate the term *mother*. Think of it as *primary caretaker* as that's what it means.

How to move through missteps

- With as much love and openness as you can, validate the feelings of your loved one and apologize for your behaviors, not their feelings.
- Ask what you can do to make it better.
- Do not seek absolution. It is not their job to make you feel better. That is your job.
- Sit with their feelings.
- Offer space.

When you work through these steps each time you fail, trust builds. The people close to you begin to realize they can fail too, and that you both will be okay.

Theorem

Everyone will fail. It's what you do next that matters.

Of course, you can try to avoid failure, learn more, do your best. But remember, even the best dancers step on other dancers' toes sometimes. Just as you must let your loved ones fail to grow and learn, you must believe you can come through missteps stronger together. There is so much more here to learn and practice together. Individual, couples, and family therapy are based in helping you move through attachment, failure, and to work on your dancing. If this bit of the chapter has piqued your interest and you want to work more, seek therapy!

There are also many books that will lead you into new ways of being in love. A few of my favorites to consider love of yourself and others are also classics. They are easy reads with big topics that might alter your paradigm. I know they each shifted mine. I return to these books repeatedly and offer them to patients and friends. I think of these three as neo-philosophies on love and loving. These include the following:

- *The New People Making* by Virginia Satir
- *Gift from the Sea* by Anne Morrow Lindbergh
- *The Art of Loving* by psychoanalyst Erich Fromm

Dig deeper, find therapy, unlearn patterns that don't serve you well. Now that you are more aware of your attachment style, it will help you to see how you operate in relationships—what you need and what you give. Let's talk next about how to communicate these complex ideas.

HOW TO GET YOUR NEEDS MET

Sometimes when I'm screaming, "*They don't know if you don't tell them!*" from the rooftops, people ask me a simple question.

How do I tell them?

There are so many reasons you don't know how to answer this question. Perhaps open dialogue wasn't part of your family dynamic, you prefer to avoid the vulnerability, your ego feels too exposed when you venture to intimacy town, you aren't sure what to say, you've been treated badly in the past if you opened up, or you just need practice. Let's consider your thoughts on deep communication before we move on.

Talk It Out

Let's consider your thoughts on open dialogue in love. Remember, love is whatever with whomever, as you defined it earlier in the chapter. This exercise can be very helpful when completed by whomever you would like to communicate with, and then you can use it to communicate!! Meta!! Please answer the following questions. Good luck, y'all.

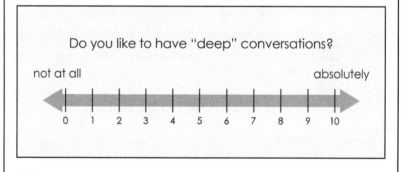

Do you like to have "deep" conversations?

not at all   absolutely

0   1   2   3   4   5   6   7   8   9   10

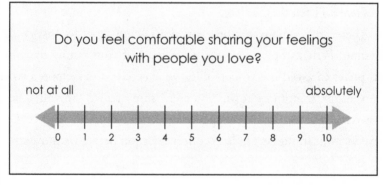

Do you feel comfortable sharing your feelings
with people you love?

not at all   absolutely

0   1   2   3   4   5   6   7   8   9   10

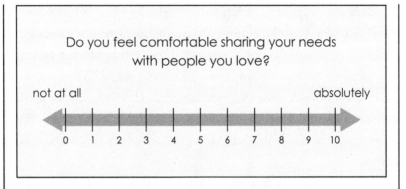

Do you feel comfortable sharing your needs
with people you love?

not at all   absolutely

0   1   2   3   4   5   6   7   8   9   10

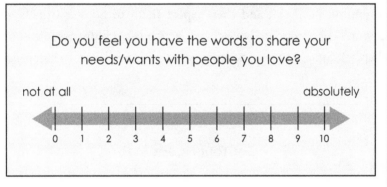

Do you feel you have the words to share your
needs/wants with people you love?

not at all   absolutely

0   1   2   3   4   5   6   7   8   9   10

Please think of the last time you needed or wanted
something in a love relationship. Describe that situation here.

What did you do?

Were your needs met?

What would you do differently?

Because everyone is different, from the love music you hear and the dance you do to how you perceive each situation, disagreements and misunderstandings are a certainty. These missteps occur especially when you are unaware of your own needs and wants. When you don't really know or can't voice what you need in a clear way to your partner, you often go to defense mechanism town—think "passive aggressive." Unfortunately, needs don't usually get met when you employ your defenses.

Needs do get met, however, when you know what they are, clearly communicate them, and then expect them to be met (this is also how to set appropriate boundaries, which we will discuss in the next chapter). Since you need to know what your needs are, let's start here.

Get Your Needs Met

1. Know Your Needs

2. Clearly Communicate

3. Expect Them to Be Met

Know Your Needs

Part of growing your emotional success in love is to get your needs met. As I just stated, the first step to need fulfillment is to know your needs. Sometimes you can feel and articulate what you need. Many other times, you need a few tools to help you clarify, for yourself, what need isn't being fulfilled. Let's use a popular psychological theory to help you begin to know your needs.

In the 1990s, Dr. Gary Chapman, a pastor, noticed that many of his parishioners were expressing similar difficulties in their marriages. Based on his pastoral counseling practice, he wrote a book to help people clarify what they need and how to ask for it. These became known as the *five love languages*. While Dr. Chapman is not a psychologist (his doctorate is in adult education), his ideas are often featured in therapy circles. Love languages offers a simple approach to help you start to know what you need, and that's a great thing. It doesn't explain why you need what you need—that's what we've been exploring throughout the book, and what therapy and deep conversations with loved ones can do. I include these ideas as a jumping-off point. Start here, with this helpful chart by author Julie Nguyen, and go deeper if you'd like.

	How to Communicate	Actions to Take
Words of Affirmation	Encourage, affirm, appreciate, empathize. Listen actively.	Send an unexpected note, text, or card. Genuinely encourage, and often.
Physical Touch	Non verbal—use body language and touch to express love.	Hug, kiss, hold hands, show physical affection often. Make intimacy a thoughtful priority.
Receiving Gifts	Thoughtfulness, make your spouse a priority, speak purposefully.	Give thoughtful gifts and gestures. Small things matter in a big way. Express gratitude when receiving a gift.
Quality Time	Uninterrupted and focused conversations. One-on-one time is critical.	Create special moments together, take walks and do small things with your partner. Weekend getaways are huge.
Acts of Service	Use action phrases like "I'll help . . ." They want to know you're with them, partnered with them.	Do chores together or make them breakfast in bed. Go out of your way to help alleviate their daily workload.

Love Languages

Please take a moment to review the love languages chart above. You can also head to Dr. Chapman's website to take a quiz, delve deeper, and find out more about the idea of what love languages are and how the theory might help you describe your needs to your loved ones in a clear way. Here, we use this theory as a tool to help formulate your needs. Once you have looked over the chart, please answer the questions below.

Think of the last time you felt angry at a loved one. Briefly describe here.

Can you identify what need wasn't met for you?

Describe how you tried to get the need met and whether your attempt was successful or not.

Looking at the chart above, please list which love languages feel most like you.

I offer this simple, popular psychology theory because it is often a helpful way for people to start talking about their needs. Sometimes, when you have a framework and language, you can go deeper from there. You can use the idea of love languages as a tool to help you develop a shared understanding with someone you love, work with, care about. This may take some of the heat off an argument when what you really need to do is share an unfulfilled need, but instead an unproductive argument has erupted.

Clearly Communicate

It does no good to be clear about your needs if you can't share them with a loved one. Yay for clarity, but boo because most people aren't clairvoyant (remember psychic syndrome). Step two of getting your needs met is to clearly communicate. These steps may sound obvious to you, but in the heat of the moment, you often don't know what to do and are left feeling confused and deflated. When you break things into simple steps, though, it allows you a road map you can remember when cortisol is high. These straightforward paths lead to increased satisfaction, trust, and thus emotional success.

How can you communicate clearly? You need to trust the relationship and start small. You may get into patterns where you talk backwards, engage in magical thinking, or just avoid discussions altogether. These behaviors will not lead you to a place you want to go. At best your relationships will be boring and at worst ungenuine and unsatisfying. It can be scary to say the things that lie under the surface! Like every other topic in this book, the underlying belief is that only through authenticity can you find emotional success. Besides, all that side-stepping takes energy. Perhaps it is time to ask yourself what you are avoiding.

Maybe you are preserving something that doesn't serve you anymore. When you can't be yourself, ask for what you need, seek to grow, what are you doing? If you want to grow and change, sometimes you must take risks. Clear communication of needs can be risky. The risk is worth it.

One of the great things about clear communication is that it is contagious. Once you start, you can't stop. It will leak into every area of your life. This might sound terrifying to you. You've come this far, through so many deep topics; if you want to exist on the surface, be my guest. But I know you can dive a little further. Glenn Singleton of Pacific Educational Group uses the phrase *courageous conversations* in his work related to race and culture. I love that phrase! No matter what the topic, it requires courage to be vulnerable and open.

To communicate means to send and/or receive information. If our message gets stuck due to our inability to share it, there has not been communication. Whatever your definition of love is, communication is a central feature. Love is a living entity, and it can stall without change. Growth and change between two people primarily happens through communication. We have spent much time delving into who you are and what it means to others. Of course, we communicate all of this consciously and unconsciously. Let's focus here on direct verbal communication. You are a good listener now; you can also learn to be a good speaker.

Communicate

Please answer the questions below. Consider your responses. All people can be clearer. If you practice this exercise in your daily life, it will become a habit, a new way of communicating. If you get stuck, employ your support scaffolding. Friends already know where you get stuck, and they may be able to help you grow.

Please think back to your defense mechanisms. List them. How do they impact how you communicate?

What feelings do you have about communicating in an authentic and clear way with your loved ones?

State a current unmet need.

How could you ask for that need to be met?

Reread your statement. Is it clear? Does it offer actions your loved one can do? If not, please clarify.

Name a need you know a loved one/coworker/friend has.

Have you worked to meet this need?

What tools do you need to help you meet this need?

When you identify your needs and clarify how to ask for them (in ways your loved ones can meet), you are more likely to experience relationship satisfaction. You must also work to meet others' needs in the same way. It's that simple. And scary. Sometimes people say no, and you must figure out what that information means.

Expect Them to Be Met

The final piece of finding emotional success in love is to expect your needs to be met. Sometimes, you get to a place where you've stopped asking because you have never been in a situation where your needs were met. Look back to your attachment style here; it has much to do with your expectations. If you primarily have a secure attachment style, you likely already expect your needs to be met because starting very early in life, your needs *were* met. Remember, systems love status quo. Once you get used to something, it is what you expect, whether you like it, it's good for you, and you want it, or not.

This is a delicate area because we are talking about unmet needs throughout life. What could be more tender? If you haven't explored this area in your heart and mind, please establish support scaffolding before you delve into these waters. For everyone else, please prepare to have emotions, including grief, about what you may find under the surface. Take care, and "just keep swimming."

What to Expect

Do you expect your needs to be met? Please answer the following questions so we can see where your starting point is, and what you think you deserve based on your attachment style. Please do both as best you can.

Do you deserve to have your needs met?

not at all   absolutely

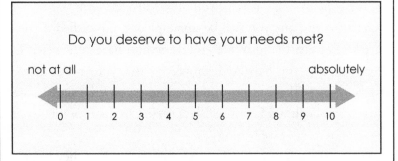

Do other people deserve to have their needs met?

not at all   absolutely

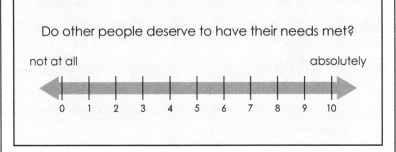

Think back to primary attachment styles. What is your primary attachment style?

How do you think your primary attachment style impacts your beliefs around getting needs met?

You deserve to have your needs met.

There are so many reasons you might struggle with this idea. No matter who you are, you will be unhappy and unsatisfied if you do not take to heart the idea that you deserve to have your needs met. Of course, first you have to acknowledge that your needs may not have been met. This can be traumatic and require the support we've discussed throughout. It isn't selfish or "extra" to have your needs met. It's essential to your well-being.

Most people know the difference between things they want and need, but in case you don't, I'll give you a little clue. If you dream about something, long for it, can't stop seeing it everywhere, and notice that other people have it, it may be closer to a need than a want. Honestly, life is short, and I'm not sure it matters which it is. If you long for something, and it keeps popping up, you can either choose to try to suppress it or speak to your loved ones and see if you can satisfy your craving, whatever it is you desire.[34]

For a concrete example, look no further than the obvious. Sex. I don't know if you've read Dan Savage, but if you haven't, and you're the kind of person who likes to read the personal ads in the back of a newspaper, look up *Savage Love*. You're welcome. Dan Savage is a brilliant human being and sex columnist I mentioned in chapter 10 when I discussed the It Gets Better project.

Additionally, he coined the term *GGG*—which stands for *good* (in bed), *giving* (of equal time and pleasure), and *game* (to try new things). You can see the parallels with wants/needs here, right?

A few psychologists led by Dr. Amy Muise conducted a study to see if being GGG was beneficial to both partners. Turns out, when you meet other people's needs, you enjoy sex and your relationship more in the moment *and* over time! So, if getting your own needs met isn't high on your priority list, maybe get your needs met so your loved ones can feel good too.

---

34   If you have a history of obsession, addiction, compulsions, or perseverating, consider if what you want is healthy or "feeding that demon." This is true for everyone. A great way to discern if something fits is often to get feedback from your support scaffolding.

If you don't get what you want/need, those desires will leak out. When you suppress, things go upside down in a hurry. The key is to know what you want, ask for it, expect to get it. And be willing to sit with the outcomes. I hope you get buckets of oxytocin, whatever that means for you and the people/things you love.

CHAPTER 12

Emotional Success at Work

"When we strive to become better than we are, everything around us becomes better too."

—Paulo Coelho

What an exciting time it is for the world of work! Many jobs are shifting to remote options, and the consideration of corporate culture (once just the purview of industrial/organizational psychologists and human resources teams) has become center stage. In other words, for many, work is being redefined. We can apply all of the book to the world of work, and in fact, I wrote the book with an eye to corporate culture throughout.

No matter whether you are in the office or working through Zoom meetings most of the time, workplace and company culture is undergoing an overhaul. Many of the topics covered in the book are coming to the surface, and discussions of identity/balance/quality of life as well as the importance of physical and mental health have resulted from the pandemic. To me, this is a glorious gift! As a culture, humans are reevaluating the nature of what it means to work, and how much of themselves and their time they are willing to give to productivity.

As you read this chapter, please consider how you can incorporate emotional success into your work life for yourself as an individual as well as how you may bring these ideas into your workplace. Emotional success is essential at work.

Of all the things we discuss in this book, there are few things that pull together the ideas of privilege, power, diversity, meaning, and purpose like work. This is the reason it's the final chapter. Work is what you spend the most hours focused on, and where you find much of your definition of self. Let's be clear—here, work means "what you do with your time." The outdated and oversimplified version of work as the place you go to make money simply doesn't encompass enough of human experience. Here, work is what you do to contribute: to yourself, your family, community, bank account—or all four.

This could be school, parenting, a job, career, art, athletics, or pursuing a dream. Everyone works. It may be traditional or not—but it exists for you and is part of your identity. Your work changes over time. Sometimes you hold on to what *was* or what you hope *will be*. You may be retired, but you do something with your time. What is it? How do you fill your day? What is the work of your life, right now? I am interested in the present moment because it is what you have right now. It's time to see how emotional success looks for you in this part of your life. Let's start with a basic question.

What Is *Your* Work?

Please answer this question. Take a moment and write about what you do. What is your work? Do you make bowls of tomatoes? Help people with their health? Write poetry? Put sleepy children to bed? All of these? When I did this exercise, I couldn't believe what filled up the page. Turns out, I have a lot of work. I then took the list and made categories because that's what I do. You could do that too. Or think about it while you're driving. Or draw a picture. Manipulate the idea of "work" in your mind, please. What is it? What does it mean to you? We will delve deeper into your specifics in the next action.

What is your work?

THE PSYCHOLOGY OF WORK

In Pittsburgh there is a retired World War II submarine in the river. It is docked by the Carnegie Science Center. In middle school we took a tour. I learned that day what claustrophobia feels like, and it was only a thirty-minute tour. Can you imagine what it must have been like for the men who lived there? How smelly it would be? So hot and with no privacy, not even in your bed. Apparently, one man would jump out of the bed for his shift to begin, and another would crawl in. Have you wondered how men were selected for these assignments?

The answer is closer than you think. Any personality quiz you've ever taken comes from the same place: psychologists. During World War II the Department of Veterans Affairs realized that psychologists were a great help at divvying up soldiers into roles based on their personality types. After the war, an abundance of underemployed men suddenly needed gainful employment. The VA stepped in and asked the same psychologists who had helped to choose appropriate duties to sort through options and help soldiers become working civilians. When you know who can survive on a submarine, helping people find meaningful work is likely a welcome change of pace.

There is a ton of research in the area of career satisfaction. Many companies utilize what are now called industrial/organizational psychologists to effectively pair candidates with positions, help clients find meaningful work, and steer best practices in the world of work. Perhaps because of its origins working with soldiers who had job choices to make, the field has a reputation as having a privileged focus. For example, it can cost thousands of dollars for a client or company to have a full career/interest assessment conducted and to help someone sort through how to find their calling. If you take a step back, I hope you can see that the very notion of having a choice about where to work or what might make you most satisfied is a privilege few people in the world experience.

For decades, the academic way of understanding work centered around a narrow window, and a narrower population. A basic equation: work equals a very specific list of possibilities; workers match those choices. Many psychologists began to see the gap between the research and what people experience in real life.

Let's consider what work means to you, and where it might fit into your life.

What Is Work?

Consider what work looks like in your life. When you start tackling a giant topic, sometimes it helps to start with the basic five questions—who, what, when, where, and why. Let's consider these aspects of what work is to you. I've offered some prompts to get you thinking, but you can ignore these for your own thoughts if you'd like to free associate. Please bring your thoughts about work front of mind, and to clarify what it means to you.

Who?

Who do you work with? Who are you at work? Who do you want to be? Who are the heroes—or the villains—in your work life? Who are the people you work with, both coworkers and those you may serve?

What?

What does your work look like? What do you do? What do you accomplish? What are your goals? What are your feelings about your work?

Where?

Where do you work? Do you travel? Where are the people you work with? Where do you want to be? Where did you work before? Where does your work primarily occur?

Why?

Why do you work? Why do you like or don't like your work? What is your why (a favorite therapy question)?

How?

How do you work? How do you meet your goals? How do you feel/react when you aren't able to finish your work? How do you feel about work? How are successes/failures managed at your work? How do you set your goals?

It wasn't until the early 2000s that Dr. David Blustein and colleagues began to address the outdated notions of career. These theorists paint a broad picture of what it means to work. They seek to answer the five questions you've asked yourself above. The answers are broad and show a depth of meaning and purpose in work as varied as humanity. And at the heart of it all is the idea of decent work as a human right.

This is called the *psychology of working framework*. This moved the idea of career from a side note to identity central. This makes sense as your work does define aspects of your identity, and the ability to do meaningful work is deeply important to having a sense of purpose in life. This is so central to identity in many cultures that when you meet someone, you ask, "What do you do?" Let's pause here.

What Do You Do?

Please take a few moments to consider the following questions:

> What do you say when someone asks,
> "What do you do?"

> How do you feel when someone asks you
> what you "do"?

> Is this question different from "What is your work?"

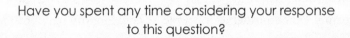

Have you spent any time considering your response
to this question?

Does this question relate to your identity?

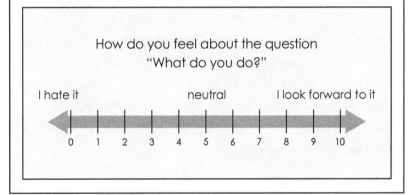

How do you feel about the question
"What do you do?"

I hate it   neutral   I look forward to it

0   1   2   3   4   5   6   7   8   9   10

If you are lucky enough to love and feel proud of your work, traditional career theory is for you. However, for most people, work is a mix of necessity and some degree of (dis)satisfaction. Your answers in the last two actions matter. It is an act of resistance to displace your work self as primary in this society. Think of the people you know who place other aspects of their identity higher than work. They are often outcasts. It has been this way throughout time because work is one of the ways systems keep people where they are "meant" to be. Of course, it is the American Dream to rise up by one's bootstraps from nothing . . . but the fantasy is often stacked against anyone without means and White maleness. Your identity can often answer the question "What do you do" as loudly as "Who are you?"

Let's discuss identity politics for a moment. Have you heard the phrase "The personal is political"? Perhaps you've never been political. When you see the call "Equal pay for equal work," it may feel confusing. Let's consider an example of how identity plays into work to illustrate how the personal and political are wound together. Women make less money than men. Black and Latino women make less than White women. As of the writing of this book, trans individuals *just* got protection to keep a job regardless of their identity status.

Work is sustenance, fulfillment, identity, purpose, and meaning. When you think of work, I'd like you to think of the fullness of what work means for you and everyone else. This is a psychological secret that can bring greater awareness to this aspect of your identity. In 2018 David Blustein, Maureen Kenny, Annamaria Di Fabio, and Jean Guichard published an article called "Expanding the Impact of the Psychology of Working: Engaging Psychology in the Struggle for Decent Work and Human Rights," tying together the ideas we've been discussing. Here is an excerpt from that article that summarizes the importance of meaningful work:

> The Psychology of Work Framework (PWF) has sought to highlight and examine the role of human rights in the workplace, the impact of work in the fulfillment of essential human needs (i.e., needs for survival, social connection, and self-determination), and the relation of work-related issues within broader psychological, social, and economic contexts. The PWF is framed around the following assumptions: (1) work functions as a major context for individual well- being and the welfare of communities; (2) work shares psychological space with many other salient life domains with mutual and recursive impact; (3) access to work is constrained by powerful social, economic, and political forces; (4) working includes both efforts in the marketplace and in caregiving contexts; and (5) psychological and systemic interventions need to include all of those who work and who want to work.

It is a dense paragraph. I feel thrilled when I read phrases that hold the depth of what work means, like "human rights in the workplace," "fulfillment of essential human needs," "psychological space," and so many more. Let's focus on needs for survival, social connection, and self-determination. When you think of your own relationship with work, how do these three themes interplay with your experience?

> *You work for survival, social connection, and self-determination.*

Survival

Does survival fit into your notion of work? Would you have a different relationship with work if it did/didn't?

Social Connections

Social connections at work often make up the foundation of your relationships. Besides school, work is where you meet most people. The health of your work connections is directly related to how happy/satisfied you are. There are countless studies about the importance of a healthy work environment to promote well-being. Think of your own life. When you have trusted friends who share in your work, it is more enjoyable, meaningful, and fulfilling. It is also more productive. When I teach companies about diversity, inclusion, and bias, they are often surprised to know that employees do better when the workforce is diverse and welcoming. It makes perfect sense—when a variety of viewpoints can shine, the work is better, the people are happier. Of course, the opposite is true as well. An unhealthy work environment stifles new ideas and limits everyone.

Self-Determination

Self-determination refers to your ability to control your destiny. Can working hard lead you where you want to go? Does a pathway seem clear toward your goal? If you put in the time, can you benefit? Human beings like to know they're going somewhere. You thrive when you feel like your time and efforts are productive and lead toward a goal. Self-determination is so huge; it can help you answer all three existential questions at the same time!

- Who am I?
- Why am I here?
- What am I doing?

When you have purpose, can reach your goals, and know how to get there, you can answer all three of these questions! I often think of the ability to engage in self-determination as what many people refer to as a "calling." The unicorn of job qualities. I know why I do the work, where I'm heading, and what I'm doing.

Does your work help you answer these questions? When you can't answer these existential questions, life can feel uncertain.

SYSTEMS THEORY AT WORK

Work can give you meaning, purpose, a social life, means to survive, and a home base to situate your identity. It can also deteriorate these fundamentals. What a huge thing. Remember systems theory? Work and school are two of the primary ways systems impact your life directly. When you change institutions, you change society. I wish for you the ability to see your work, how you feel about it, and how it impacts your ability to live an authentic life. When work fails you, you cannot find emotional success.

Access to decent work can change your life. Work can lift you up or make your life more difficult. When work is meaningful, safe, and provides financial support, you thrive. At other times stress, bias, harassment, being undervalued, or lack of safety can lead to anything from dissatisfaction to death. The importance of work in your life cannot be understated. For yourself and your coworkers, you need to see the weight of work and the fact that the same place can be salvation for one person and abusive for another *at the same time*. To help people understand the different experiences coworkers at the same job can have, I offer this questionnaire. I let participants decide if they want to share anonymously or not. Either way, there is often rich discussion due to the variation of responses. You can use this where you work (or live) to understand your own situation, or to compare with others.

What Is Work Like for You?

Please answer the questions below, using the continuums. Please be sure to jot down your reactions to each question. If you complete the action and see there is a lack of safety or other issue comes to the forefront, please employ your support scaffolding. Work is a huge part of life, and it impacts your mental health in positive and negative ways. Share to compare or use it as a self- assessment tool to know how you feel about your work, today. Obviously, if you have remote work, some of these questions do not apply or have to do with other areas of your life.

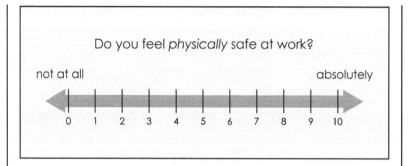

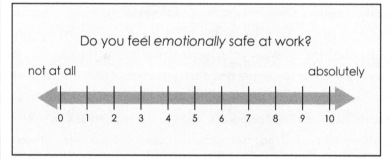

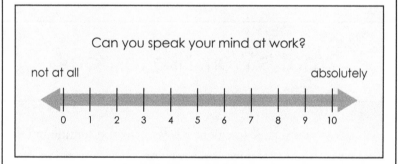

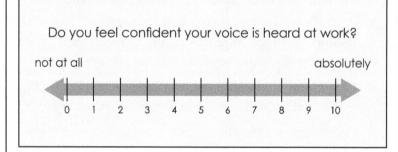

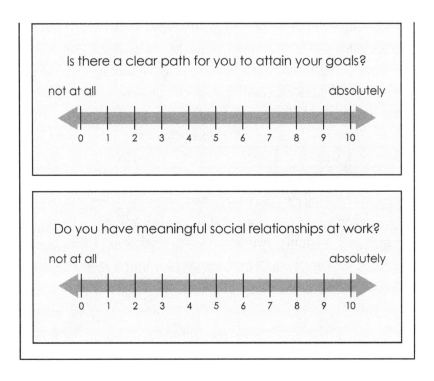

EMOTIONAL SUCCESS AT WORK
FOR EVERYONE

Whether or not your needs are met at work, everyone can improve their situation.

You can also be more aware of the people around you and open to the possibility that you all experience things differently. We have a saying in psychology: no two children are raised in the same house. Meaning even though you may sit one cubicle over from another person, it doesn't equate to the same experience. This is especially true with the increased possibility of remote work. When you assume your journey is universal, you run into gigantic misunderstandings. If you open your mind to see there are as many realities as human beings, your curiosity (rather than assumptions) will benefit everyone.

Some work situations are not safe, emotionally and/or physically. I am not your therapist, so I can freely offer advice—get out. If you can find any other way to meet your needs, take it. Emotional and physical safety are paramount. People are obviously becoming aware of the importance of choosing a healthy work culture as we've seen with "the Great Resignation." There are laws and other protections in place to ensure safety of body and mind at work/school and outside the home. If your work is inside the home or remote and you have limited choices or resources, please reach out to friends or services in your area to seek support. If nothing else, discussing what you see and how you feel can help alleviate some of the pain and stress. This will not improve the situation as it is but may help you work through it in a different way.

There are two psychological secrets to improve your emotional success at work:

- Know your worth
- See the systems

When you know your worth and see the systems at play, you can navigate into more emotional success. What does "Know your worth" mean? It is a huge statement that encompasses your work abilities and your intrinsic worth as a human being. Even though it may feel so at times, you are not a cog in a wheel. You provide something unique.

Perhaps you already feel this way. Many people do not. We know that men tend to feel they can do a job when they meet only 20 percent of the criteria, while women will not apply until they reach 100 percent. It's a confidence gap that translates into women asking for less, reaching less high. Of course, there are also a million reasons why this occurs, many we've discussed in this book. There are of course singularities: men who don't assume they are capable and women who do. Regardless, the metric shows a pattern, and I'd like you to consider if it applies for you. When you know your worth, you tend to ask for more. High expectations lead to high outcomes. Make realistic goals at different intervals. I like the five-five-five rules here—five weeks, five months, five years, with matching dreams for each time frame. No matter what your work looks like, you get further toward your dreams when you set goals and make plans to reach them.

Know Your Worth

Please take a moment to answer the following questions. These are important questions to examine the way you view yourself related to "work." Remember, work here is whatever you do that is productive in your life, however you defined it earlier in the chapter. Again, these are deep and meaningful topics—support scaffolding is always a good idea.

What are you worth?

Do you feel that you have intrinsic value at work?

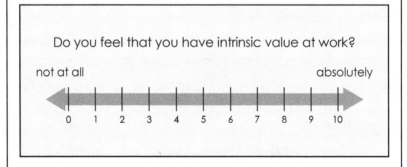

not at all   absolutely

0   1   2   3   4   5   6   7   8   9   10

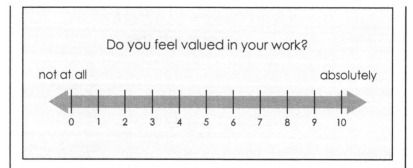

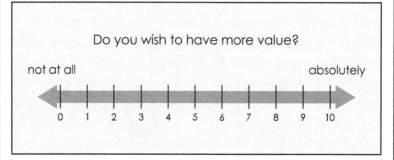

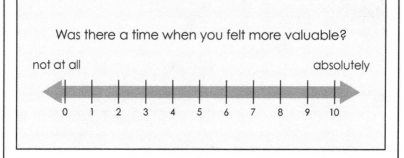

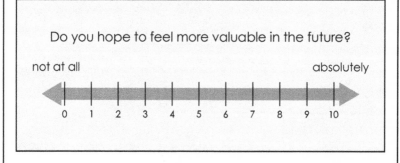

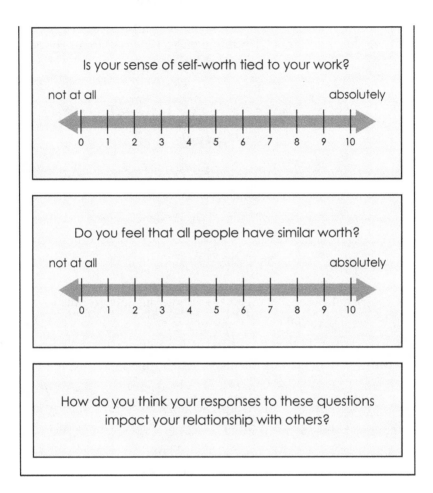

Is your sense of self-worth tied to your work?

Do you feel that all people have similar worth?

How do you think your responses to these questions impact your relationship with others?

Goal setting also leads to increased satisfaction, productivity, and a sense of accomplishment. You can set goals no matter where you start. Know your worth.

Take the time to rethink where you want to be and plan accordingly. Remember, big changes happen with a zillion tiny steps.

The funny thing about knowing your worth is that when you feel whole, valued, and heard, you tend to value others more too. Of course it's like this. Judgmental people judge themselves the hardest, and so on. When someone feels valued, they are more likely to value others. When you know your inherent and specific worth, you will see it in those around you. When you feel small, your world is small. Your universe shrinks or grows depending on your perception of yourself. Grow your worth, and you amplify others as well.

EMOTIONAL SUCCESS IN A REMOTE WORLD

"Remember to enjoy freedom of being able to work from anywhere and the flexibility to adapt your work to your life rather than the other way around."

— Alex Muench

Recently, I closed the physical location of my therapy office. I was sad. It was a beautiful office and a dream to have my own practice. However, I can't do therapy with a mask nor guarantee the safety of my patients in and out of the office. When things returned more to "normal," I chose to remain 100 percent telehealth. Like so many people, I've somehow ended up spending more time staring at a computer. I was included in an article in *PopSugar* that included ways to deal with telework exhaustion. Have you noticed being on the computer all day is extra tiring? People are getting used to it, but it remains an entirely new way to work for many. Remote work has benefits and costs—and will require a different skill set than the way it used to be.

There are a few ways to build your emotional success in a remote work world. You can use the skills and realizations we've worked on throughout the book just as you would in real life. The psychological secrets that may help the most here are how to set appropriate boundaries, change our expectations, and be aware of our surroundings. Let's work through these.

Three Steps to Healthy Boundaries

When work and home are all mixed up . . . you can get mixed up. For those who can remember, cell phones and email were pretty exciting at first. The initial excitement was followed by a period of horrific realization that you could be reached *anytime*. There was no more "I wasn't home." Work intensified as availability increased. This continues today, twenty-plus years later. Now you are in your home, and work has set up primary residence right beside you. What everyone needs are some healthy boundaries.[35] Boundaries help you all the time. Sometimes you sense you need boundaries but aren't sure how to engage in them. This is a magic time for the world of work—where definitions and ways of thinking that remained steady for generations are suddenly up in the air. Culture is shifting, and life is suddenly placed higher on the priority list than productivity. Use this moment to define your boundaries and seek your balance.

Three Steps to Beautiful Boundaries

1. Know what you want

2. Clearly communicate your wishes

3. Hold the line

---

35   These boundary tools can help in any area of your life. I encourage you to employ them with vigor.

Know What You Want

First, you must know what you want. This sounds easy but it's not. When you feel overwhelmed, it is essential to take a step back and assess what you need. Then, be able to translate that into some action you ask of another person. For example, your boss wants you to be available all the time. That is overwhelming. You want to know when you're working and when you're not. You decide what you want is to have set work hours. Now you know what you want. Of course, this isn't possible at every job, but it's a great and effective example.

Clearly Communicate

After you know what you want, you need to clearly communicate your wishes. Everyone struggles with this. When you get emotional, you can have a hard time being clear. If you want to set a boundary, you must be clear. In this example, you would state that you would like to have defined working hours, from 8 a.m. to 5 p.m., Monday through Friday. Make sure what you offer is what you really want. Don't forget, renegotiating opens options for both parties. Be as clear as possible. Try not to cloud the communication with much else besides the ask.

Hold the Line

The last piece of boundary setting can be the most difficult. Hold the line. Be firm. Remember, systems love status quo, and there will often be pushback if you try to make a major shift. If you've been available anytime someone reached out, they will continue to push those boundaries. I encourage patients to decide how they will manage boundary violations before they occur. What will you do? Ignore? Remind clearly and simply and then ignore? If you find yourself giving way or engaging in argument, circle back to the start and retry. I promise, once you hold the line for a short period of time, a new boundary will be set. Voilá! Magic!

Beautiful Boundaries

Think of a boundary you would like to create. Work through the questions below, and then when you're ready, put it into practice.

What is the situation where you'd like to make a new boundary?

What do you want?

How can you clearly define what you want so it is clear to the other person?

What will you do when the boundary is broken?

Good luck!

CHANGE OUR EXPECTATIONS

This Great Pause and following Great Resignation is a time for new thoughts. You must maintain an open stance and accept things differently than you have before. Everyone will benefit from a change of expectations.

This reminds me of my first week back to work after I gave birth. I was sitting on my supervisor's couch, crying. I was upset because she mentioned making a pie. I lost myself. I couldn't imagine a time when I would have it together enough to make a pie. Ever again. I started to lament, wondering when the "old Kelly" was coming back. Now, my supervisor is a woman to respect, who I love very much. She looked me right in the eye and said, "Kelly, she is never coming back." Almost ten years later, I reel when remembering this interchange. As I've said many times, denial is quicksand. It keeps you stuck. The more you fight, the stuck-er you are. I'm here to tell you, *this is the new normal*. What was once doctrine is now open for discussion. How exciting!

When you think of remote work or communicating extensively online, the first thing you need to do is clear your assumptions. I've noticed when someone is new to telehealth, they think it will be less. Less real. Less good. Less meaningful. Both patients and therapists have shared these reactions. Perhaps I'm primed for telecommunications because I've taught online for many years. Is teaching online the same as in person? Nope. But you can do cool and different things in both settings that don't work quite the same in the other. Yep. Pluses and minuses for both. I love telehealth. It gives patients/clients who live far away a chance to engage in therapy or coaching. It offers flexibility.

When I considered closing my physical office, I asked my patients what they thought. One hundred percent wanted to stay telehealth. They stated that it is more convenient and feels the same. It feels the same! This shouldn't be shocking, and yet it is. Think back to our discussion of empathy. I showed you a painting from nearly a century ago, and you felt for the other humans. You feel strong and powerful emotions when you watch movies. It seems that emotional energy doesn't have physical boundaries. For example, reiki is an ancient healing energy practice that can happen remotely.

Would I love to be in a room with all the people I speak with? Yes.

Do I also see the benefit of being able to be close to people I otherwise couldn't see? Yes.

Both things are true. During this unsettling and uncertain time, I have seen people bend or become more rigid. Remember, when the wind comes, you can either bend with the breeze or risk breaking.

You can panic or plan. It is up to you. Accept what is and find ways to create the life you want, given the new circumstance. Eventually, I started to make pies again. I use grocery store crust now. Some things just need to go; what can I say? Alter your expectations and create your life in the circumstances as they are, not as you wish them to be. There is growth and possibility in this new world.

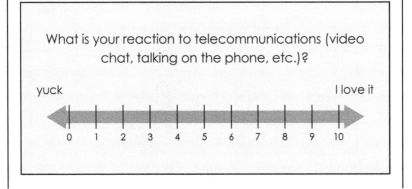

Remote World

Please take a moment to answer these questions. There are continuums to assess your quick responses, be sure to also write longer reactions. Please complete both.

What is your reaction to telecommunications (video chat, talking on the phone, etc.)?

yuck   I love it

0   1   2   3   4   5   6   7   8   9   10

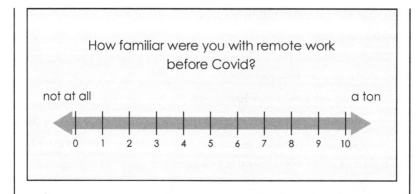

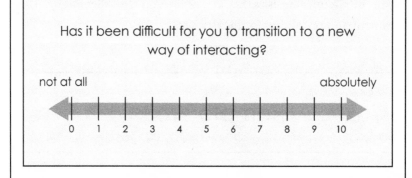

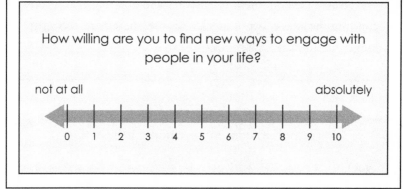

No one knows exactly what direction work is heading in—it seems safe to say things will be altered. It feels thrilling to know that people have an opportunity to rewrite the way society thinks of work, and what people are willing to accept as far as the psychological health of their workplaces. While there is so much you can't control, you can shape your own reactions, expectations, and requirements. You must find ways to alter your expectations, to embrace as much as you can, to be innovative, creative, and ready for the challenges ahead.

Be Aware of Your Surroundings

You can prepare for your work in the same ways you prepare to engage in meaningful listening. Think of safety, space, and be prepared for the work ahead of you. Additionally, it helps if you treat work like work.

This may not be a popular opinion, but it is one backed in science: get dressed for work. I know, I sound so Gen X. When I started writing this book, I didn't think that was a psychological secret I would share. However, here we are. Psychologists know that when you make your bed, and otherwise get ready for the day, you prepare yourself for the tasks ahead. While many work remotely, and may for the foreseeable future, you can still maintain your routines. Routines help your days have structure and meaning. Structure and meaning can keep your mental health intact. When you get dressed for the day, you are therefore protecting your mental well-being. To be clear, it doesn't matter what you wear. Just the idea of "getting ready" is what matters. Put on your work pj's; the idea is more about mental preparation for something ahead.

First, if you can steer clear of your sleep space at all, please do it. Good sleep hygiene is important, and having your office in your bedroom is decidedly not helpful. It's too hard to wind down when your work area is winking at you from the corner. Not to mention the lack of clear boundaries. At the very least, when you finish working, turn it all off and eliminate any light/noises you can from devices. If there is a way to create a nook, area, space, corner where you *work* that is separate from your life in any way, even if it means you never use your dining room again, do it. You can thank me later. Nothing says boundaries like separate spaces.

Obviously, it would be great if you could also limit interruptions, remain focused, and have a dedicated space to work. But that isn't possible for many people. I've seen the inclusion of intrusions such as children, family members, neighbor noises, pets, birds, lawn mowers, airplanes, and fire alarms in people's lives have altered expectations. And I love it. Cultures shift, and here's to your work world being a more balanced, equitable, courageous, creative, and productive one. Here's to the new normal, and your emotional success at work—and in love.

CONCLUSION

Last Words

"What we do is more important than what we say or what we say we believe."

—bell hooks

However you're arriving at this paragraph, I'd like to believe your mind and heart are more open than they were before you read all the words that came before. Some of you have worked through the entire book, while others read a chapter or skimmed.

Before you go, I will leave you with one last secret: the basic pattern for change. It isn't the deepest thing that's happened in therapy land, but it is clear, and it works. The pattern is simply to make a clear intention, practice the new way, accept setbacks, and repeat. Every new behavior you've learned in the book can be applied to your life using this basic template. Behaviors, thoughts, and feelings are connected. Before you know it, behaviors will pull the other two along to the new place you'd like to be. When you get stuck and you want to change your path, remember this basic pattern and give yourself time, usually a minimum of three weeks (an average amount of time to make a lasting change), to engage in the process. Before you know it, the new you will show up, and it will be time to take on a different challenge.

BASIC PATTERN FOR CHANGE

Make a clear intention for a small change
you'd like to create.
Practice the new way.
Accept setbacks.
Repeat, repeat, repeat.
New pattern/way of interacting emerges.

You can apply this pattern for change to all the things in this book to help you connect better with others—or any new way of being you'd like to try. Human beings are fluid creatures who thrive on learning. You can stay in your same town, house, or chair all your life and still have a wildly active and engaging inner world. You came here to find greater emotional success, embrace the changes that will happen, and allow yourself to flourish into a new version of yourself.

In Conclusion

Self-awareness, education, and empathy have been explored and applied to work and love.

What do you think of when you hear the word *radiate*? Let's focus on the sun—radiating warmth and life to everything on earth. I particularly like the idea of you as sunshine, radiating the ability and desire to connect more deeply with others.

The magic thing about the sun's warmth is that when it touches something, the energy is transferred. Like a blanket dried in the warm sun, with the psychological secrets you've gained here you are ready to radiate warmth through increased self-awareness, education, and empathy. Now you're like an awesome, powerful human extension cord—ready to share and grow with others.

Xo

For now, Doctor Kelly

ACKNOWLEDGMENTS

To the woman who inspired me to love reading, Mrs. Perry. Mrs. Ferret, because you introduced me to the Chronicles of Narnia, *Anne of Green Gables*, and *My Side of the Mountain*—gifts that can never be measured. To Dr. Collin Wansor, who taught me to write.

The women at Chatham parts I and II, who shaped my worldview and showed me how to see the matrix. Dr. Patricia Demase and Dr. Beth Roark—for making me a student. For my Chatham sisters, we were so lucky to have the magic all to ourselves; it was precious, and we knew it. Emily, Shanon, Cari, Kirsten, Ann, Meredith, Laura, Jane Ann, and Fantauzzo. You danced your faces off with me for years. To Stephanie for growing in friendship with me and giving me a gift of depth, history, and fun as we enter this middle part of our lives.

At Pitt I learned I loved graduate school and being a therapist. To Dr. Carl Johnson, who is the first person to suggest a doctoral program to me and teach me how it all worked. For Dr. Mark E. King, for bringing something poetic to graduate school.

In Boston there were mentors and soul mates. Dr. M. Brinton Lykes for lighting the activism inside me, widening my horizons, and putting up with me when I lost my way that second year. Dr. Guerda Nicholas—for showing me so much of what I didn't know and welcoming me into the research team before I was ready. Dr. Jim Mahalik, for guiding me kindly on my path toward gender research.

To Dr. David Blustein, your kindness and love made the psychology of work an exciting concept.

The friends I made during my years in Boston are right here beside me today. Brinton's Babes, Carla and Kerri. To my school and life partner, Meagan Dupuis—who has a very big and important job and yet is still able to have so much fun. And my bestie and butt-to-butt sleeper, one of the most loving, intense workers and smartest, big-boss ladies, who always can teach me a thing or two, Dr. Angela DeSilva Mousseau: I love you.

Back to Chatham and the faculty who molded me into the psychologist I am today . . . from yelling down the hall at me to sending me on new practicums, asking a lot, and supporting us in a way that was only possible for the very first cohort—I thank you. It was a lovely time, and I think of you all so often. Dr. Mary Beth Mannarino, for your velvet fist and more love than I deserved. To Dr. Britney Brinkman, for carrying me through. Dr. Anthony Iasacco, for your endless professionalism and steady hand. To Dr. Joshua Bernstein, for stepping right on the line, and for Sheila, for not killing me when I lost those keys. To Dr. Deanna Hamilton, for the depth, kindness, scholarly model, and brilliance you shared with all of us. For Dr. Mary Jo Loughran, who I now consider family. And to my cohort and cohort B . . . we did it together. Somehow, our messy, inappropriate group carried ourselves into professionalism, and out we all came. Lisa, Danielle, Christina, Christa, Geoff, Brittany, Ryan, and Nick. Lord, did we all have fun. All the fun.

I've been so lucky to have clinical mentors and champions who dove deep and pushed me to funky, magic therapy places. Everyone at Carnegie Mellon University Counseling and Psychological Services—I'll never be able to describe to anyone how much my time at CaPS refined my therapy. I was so, so lucky to be in the bubble. To Dr. Michelle Keiffer, for walking down that path with me. What a classic, gorgeous, jaunty scarf-wearing group of academic-therapy-loving magical folks. Thank you for letting me in when students weren't the norm.

To Dr. Kym Simmons for your all-enveloping love during the biggest transition of my life. Without you, I don't think I could've done it. To Dr. Lisa Maccarelli for guiding me into independence during my post-doc; you are one of the best teachers I've ever had. Dr. Dana Rofey, thank you for introducing me to hospital work and trusting me to be independent. I grew so much during my time with you. It was an honor to be supervised by you.

For Lulu Orr, who shared me with her incredible family. Lulu, Prentiss, Lee, Uncle Terry, and Charlie, you've been with me through it all, and we are family now. To Lisa Millspaugh Schroeder, who has been one of my most steadfast mentors throughout my life. I am so proud of what you've done, and I couldn't know anyone better. Thank you for trusting me with your beautiful babies. To Liz, Ned, Emmie, and my very own godson, Henry—you're pure love. Lydia, Tom, and Jack, I love you very much, and I'm wishing all the things for you that you want in your heart. I am so lucky I got wedged into your life.

To my cousins, for your fun and love. My aunts and uncles and grandmothers now gone . . . you always saw me and built me up inside. I felt deeply loved. To Mimi and Great-Grandma Anne, I can feel you both, and I'm grateful. It will never seem quite real that you're gone. For Thomas, for making it possible for me to have the time to write the book. To Level Agency and Young Presidents Organization (especially the spouse forum) for teaching me so much about owning a business and having friends who could understand.

To my friends back home in Pittsburgh—Jess Smith, Sophia Van Gorder, and Dr. Christina Wallace—you're missed every day. To the Bontrager-Kostiews, we are family, and there's nothing to be done about it. You make me laugh, and you have given me space to cry. I'll see you at Stormalong Bay.

In Charleston, all you gorgeous smart ladies keep me smiling, happy, and dancing. To Darcy, Danielle, Jen D., Bernadette, Katie, Lisa, Jess, and Kelly, I can't imagine my life here without you. To Dr. Jenna Abetz for your listening ear. To Colleen—for preserving some peace during a wild part of life. For my Mermaid Manor neighbors, for looking out for me before I even moved in. Tui, Ryan, Lisa, and Nick—you made the transition to single life feel safe and fun. I am so grateful to be sandwiched between y'all. And to Linda Nichols for being my very first friend in Charleston.

To all the colleagues who've pushed and guided me. The jobs I hated that propelled me back to school. To my agent, Barbara Ellis, who took the book and helped me make it real. Your steady hand has been deeply important to me. To Koehler Books, for making it happen, and to Hannah and Lauren, for making it better. Thank you to Connie Sun, Ignacio Pacheco, James R. Detert, and countless others I've worked hard to name who allowed me to share their work in this book, bringing complicated concepts to life with their creativity.

For my parents, Rob and Jackie Rabenstein. Dad, I've modeled myself after you in two very different ways. Your love of Mom as an example of how to love fully and wholly. And your ambition, which inspired me and just hasn't stopped. You are good and kind, and I'm so lucky you're my dad. Mom, you're my stalwart companion and best friend. You're the person I call when there's something to say. You support me and have always seen me as better than I am. Your passion, dedication, and professionalism have always inspired me. I could never have gotten a better mom, and now the girls have you too.

To the girls, for making me a mom and teaching me things about life I didn't know existed. Ella, you are strong, kind, smart, funny, loving, creative, and disciplined. Annie, you are larger than life with your voice, your commands, your dreams, your presence. I love your smart, sensitive, thoughtful brain. I cannot wait to see where you two go. I hope I'll remain a confidante. I love you and hearing you speak.

To Glen. All my life I was looking for you. You've made everything better. You are the butter to my bread and the breath to my life. "I love you" doesn't cover it. I am so excited for all of the fun and love we are going to have together.

To all the patients and students I've loved—thank you for sharing yourselves with me. What an extreme privilege to share my life with you. I think of you and carry you around with me. If I touched your heart, know that you touched mine too.

To you, dear magical reader, I thought of you every day while I wrote. I think of you now. I hope you find the transformation and connection you seek. I send much love.

NOTES

_____

_____

_____

_____

_____

_____

_____

_____

_____

_____

_____

_____

_____

_____

_____

_____

_____

_____

_____

_____

_____

_____

_____

_____

_____

_____

_____

_____

_____

_____

_____

_____

_____

_____

CPSIA information can be obtained
at www.ICGtesting.com
Printed in the USA
JSHW032137060922
30074JS00002B/11

9 781646 637607